The Ephrata Commune

The Ephrata Commune

AN EARLY AMERICAN COUNTERCULTURE

E. G. ALDERFER

UNIVERSITY OF PITTSBURGH PRESS

Published by the University of Pittsburgh Press, Pittsburgh, Pa., 15260

Copyright © 1985, University of Pittsburgh Press

Feffer and Simons, Inc., London

Manufactured in the United States of America

Library of Congress Cataloging in Publication Data

Alderfer, E. Gordon (Everett Gordon), 1915–
    The Ephrata commune.

    Bibliography: p. 247
    Includes index.
    1. Ephrata Community—History.   I. Title.
F159.E6A43   1985   271'.8   85-1044
ISBN 0-8229-3813-8
ISBN 0-8229-5801-5 (pbk.)

The letter A on the title page and the Z on p. 206 are from the ABC Book of Letter Styles for Fracktur-Schriften, Ephrata, 1750. The decorative initials that open each chapter are from the stylebook prepared in the writing room of the Ephrata Sisterhood. Both were graciously provided by the Pennsylvania Historical and Museum Commission, Harrisburg, Pa.

To the memory of
Henry Allebach Alderfer
(1874–1960)
and Harold Freed Alderfer
(1903–1983)
with timeless gratitude

Contents

Preface

VEN today, two and a half centuries after its formation, the religious commune of Ephrata is little known and understood. To the many who visit its carefully reconstructed remains in Lancaster County, Pennsylvania, Ephrata may seem strange and remote, merely a provincial oddity. It richly deserves a better fate — hence the basic motivation for writing this book.

Ephrata's accomplishments are remarkable. It created the first original corpus of music produced in America, and its German writers of mystical poetry possibly outnumbered all the English poets in the colonies. Ephrata also developed the most complete printing and publishing establishment in early America, producing many of its own writings as well as the works of others. As a whole, the literature of Ephrata may be considered the most substantial expression of mysticism in this country's history. Ephrata's scribes produced some of the finest illuminated manuscripts of colonial times; today these works are closely guarded treasures. The inspiration for all this creativity was Ephrata's founder, Conrad Beissel, a profound but little understood mystic.

Part of the reason for Ephrata's present obscurity is the fact that its language was German, and a difficult Swabian form at that. Another part of the problem of assessing Ephrata is our remoteness from its mystical character, which was laden with arcane symbolism and more medieval than modern. Hence, the obstacles to understanding the character of Ephrata are substantial.

To cope with these obstacles, it has been necessary, in my first two chapters, to reach far back in time for the historical origins of Ephrata and its charismatic leader. Without that background, its historical significance as what I have called a "counterculture" would remain provincial and shallow at best.

Throughout the Ephrata chronicle itself I have deliberately *ix* emphasized the relationships of its inner life and drama to events, ideas, and movements in the world around it—in short, placed it in the broader stream of history. Hence, I have adhered carefully to the chronology of the Ephrata story so that each phase of its internal development can be seen as a counterpoint to events around it.

The decision to conclude the work with a final chapter exploring the relevance of the Ephrata story to later movements and experiments up to our own times was more difficult and, I must admit, fraught with some peril. Several readers of the manuscript objected, convinced that the Ephrata story should stand by itself. Yet, or so it seems to me, omitting the finale would leave the Ephrata experience vacuum-packed in its own time capsule. What it represented in the eighteenth century has too many correspondences to counterculture movements of our own era to ignore. In that sense, "the Ephrata motif" is still very much alive, even though the memory of Ephrata itself has faded.

Moreover, the text of the book (as distinct from its documentation) has been written for the general reader and should therefore relate in some perceptible manner to movements and ideas present in the modern world he or she lives in. This reader may ignore the notes and bibliography, the special province of the scholar. Nevertheless, seven years of steady research on the subject convinced me that extensive documentation was imperative, if only because the literature on Ephrata and its milieu is generally inadequate in that respect or leads one astray with irreconcilable variants and sometimes with chronological confusion. The present work offers a considerably wider range of source documentation than any prior writings on Ephrata and its Pennsylvania German milieu.

As the notes and bibliography will attest, the literature relating to Ephrata is surprisingly abundant. Although much of it is narrow gauged, the principal sources are rich in detail and are cited frequently with, I hope, a sense of gratitude, even when I differ with them. The primary source on Ephrata's history is, of course, the *Chronicon Ephratense,* the commune's own "official" account of itself; but later writings of William Fahnestock, Oswald Seidensticker, and especially Julius Friedrich Sachse, and, more recently, of Walter C. Klein and James E. Ernst, among others, add important dimensions to the story regardless of my own and future research that may alter or modify their findings. For that matter, Ephrata research is still

evolving, as is evident, for example, in the more specialized
studies of Betty Jean Martin (on Ephrata music) and Klaus Wust
(on Ephrata extensions to the western frontier) that have appeared during the last decade. Many valuable writings about
Ephrata are, unfortunately, difficult to obtain except in a few
major libraries; the principal works are either out of print
or, in some cases, reprinted in overpriced editions for limited
circulation.

In addition to the *Chronicon,* primary sources produced by
the Ephrathites themselves — the mystical poetry and prose, the
few extant letters, the richly illuminated music manuscripts —
are the best evidences of the commune's inner life and spirit.
For that reason I have referred to them often, less analytically
than they deserve, perhaps, but as a mirror of the life of the
community. Very little of that literature has been translated
or assessed in depth, and that may be the next frontier for
Ephrata scholarship.

For guidance and access to many of these primary materials, I am especially indebted to Barbara Deibler, Curator of
the Rare Books Division of the Pennsylvania State Library; to
James Mooney, Director, and Linda Stanley, a researcher in
the Manuscript Department, of the Historical Society of Pennsylvania; and to the Rare Books and Music divisions of the
Library of Congress. The annotated bibliography of Ephrata
prepared by Eugene Doll and Anneliese Funke (1944) has been
an indispensable tool in the search of both primary and sec-
ondary materials, and the valuable collection of accounts by
firsthand observers and contemporaries of Ephrata, edited by
Eugene Doll and Felix Reichmann, saved a lot of search time.

Readers of my manuscript in various stages of its preparation were unusually generous with their time, and their many
suggestions, queries, and criticisms were invaluable. The final
draft owes a great deal to the scholarly recommendations of
Don Yoder, Professor of Folklore, Folklife, and Religious
Studies at the University of Pennsylvania. Christoph E.
Schweitzer, Professor of Germanic Langauges at the University of North Carolina and an expert on Ephrata studies, also
read an early draft with much care, helped me avoid some pit-
falls, and contributed valuable suggestions at various points.
John L. Kraft, until recently the Pennsylvania Historical and
Museum Commission's administrator of the Ephrata Cloisters

and now administrator of the Pennsylvania Farm Museum, provided both encouragement and important suggestions regarding the text. His successor at Ephrata, Nadine Steinmetz, was generous with her time and assistance in helping me survey the photographic archives at the Cloisters. Harold Myers, Associate Historian of the Commission in Harrisburg, provided similar help and guidance relating to archival and illustrative materials maintained at Commission headquarters. At an early stage of manuscript preparation, Robert Bray Wingate, retired chief of Rare Books, Pennsylvania State Library, and now a consulting specialist on rare book collections, offered valuable guidance. Barbara Deibler, present librarian of the State Library's rare books division, was especially helpful in tracing various Ephrata sources and making available numerous imprints of the Ephrata press for on-site study. Vernon Nelson, Chief Archivist of the notable Archives of the Moravian Church in Bethlehem, Pennsylvania, read and advised me on chapter 7 relating to the Ephrata role in Count Zinzendorf's troubled "Pennsylvania Synods." Finally, I owe thanks to my son W. Henry Alderfer and his wife Lauren, both students of the mystical life, who read the manuscript with great care in far-off Ecuador; their queries and comments led to numerous useful changes in the text.

My own affinity with the Ephrata phenomenon is partly attributable to my Mennonite heritage. Mennonites trace their origins to the Anabaptist "left-wing" of the early Reformation, a tradition to which Ephrata owed much of its religious inspiration; in fact, many of its members were originally Mennonites. But my real introduction to the study of religious communes began with an assignment from my father when I was still completing my studies at the University of Pennsylvania and beginning an editorial career, thanks to his small publishing firm in Harrisburg, Pennsylvania. By agreement with the author, the assignment called on me to edit and condense a massive manuscript comprising the memoirs of John S. Duss, the last director of the once-powerful Harmony Society, a communal enterprise of the nineteenth century with striking similarities to Ephrata in the eighteenth. My numerous visits with Mr. Duss, then a sometimes testy old man but full of zest and a brilliant raconteur, whetted an enduring interest in communal history. In 1943 Mr. Duss's *Harmonists* was published.

After 1943 my career pointed in other directions, here and

abroad, but as time allowed I continued studying the early times
of Pennsylvania. These studies took shape in a little volume about Johannes Kelpius, leader of a mystical pre-Ephrata commune on the Wissahickon, published by Harper in 1941; collaboration on a study and selection of William Penn's writings, issued by Macmillan in 1957; two county histories, and various articles, including my first piece on Beissel's Ephrata (1955).

In 1970 a longstanding mentor and friend, the late S. K. Stevens, then Director of the Pennsylvania Historical and Museum Commission, arranged for me to work for the commission on four short-term writing assignments. One of these related to Ephrata Cloisters, another to the final home of the Harmonists, now known as Old Economy near Pittsburgh, both of which were rehabilitated by the commission and are now administered by it. It is a pleasure to express my gratitude to the commission now after an interval of some years, for these assignments, especially the one relating to Ephrata, helped prepare me for the present work.

Further research into Ephrata was deferred for another seven years until I sold my Washington typesetting and editorial firm, when I determined on a completely fresh start on my own resources. I soon realized that what I had previously learned of Ephrata was merely the exposed surface of a large iceberg. I cannot pretend that I have taken the full and definitive measurement of it; much of its bulk remains submerged in deep waters. My efforts took far longer than first anticipated, and since they were unsupported by any external agency or institution, I shall ever be grateful to the constant encouragement and support of my wife, Henrietta.

It is hoped that the nonspecialist reader will find in the present work some excitement in discovering a neglected aspect of our national history. Perhaps, too, the scholar of the Ephrata phenomenon, of the Pennsylvania German milieu, and of the communal tradition past and present can use this work as a launching pad for further inquiry. If these two hopes are justified, so is the work itself.

The Ephrata Commune

Prelude

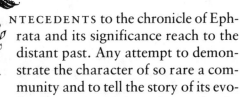NTECEDENTS to the chronicle of Ephrata and its significance reach to the distant past. Any attempt to demonstrate the character of so rare a community and to tell the story of its evolution on the early American frontier without reference to the spiritual antecedents from which it emerged would lack both depth and perspective. To provide at least a bare scaffolding on which to build a better understanding of Ephrata is, therefore, the aim of this first chapter.

The Ephrata chronicle itself lies between this and the final chapter. For the most part, it takes place in the eighteenth century, an age of so-called enlightenment, of rationalism, scientific inquiry, technical and social change, leading not only to political revolution but also to changes in the way in which people perceived their connection to the life around them. We in the twentieth century can still appreciate that quantum change in the perceptions of the Western world, for our own world is its offspring.

But Ephrata was different. Its frame of reference was mystical rather than rational, spiritual rather than scientific; it deliberately avoided entrapment in "the ways of the world" and the tensions of political and social change around it. It was an island to itself, a "counterculture" example that demonstrated a way of life in the image of its Christian antecedents before the new age of rationalism and revolution. Its aspiration and vision were, above all, God-centered, and hence its lifestyle evolved in forms unfamiliar to the world around it.

Yet, for a generation in the middle of its century, Ephrata

did have an impact on the minds of seekers and observers. To some of them its name suggested a utopian potential, a "pre-vision" of what *could* take place on a new frontier untroubled by Old World power struggles. Historical forces made that vision impossible, however, and indeed its potential was never real. By the end of the century, Ephrata, still clinging to a faint semblance of its old life, was virtually forgotten. Even its memory was not revived for nearly another century. Curiously, though, some characteristics of Ephrata's religious and communal counterculture reappear again in our day in reaction to "norms" that seem to have lost meaning—a phenomenon explored in the final chapter of this work.

The physical remnants of Ephrata's spiritual center, known as the Ephrata Cloisters, are located hard by the later town, also called Ephrata, about fifteen miles north of the city of Lancaster, Pennsylvania. The surviving buildings have been accurately rehabilitated as part of a state-administered historic site. The unique architecture of the principal buildings had neither precedent nor sequel in America. Many thousands of tourists visit the cloisters each year. But the life that was housed there, its meaning and soul, vanished many generations ago, and the modern visitor is more likely to be taken with the antique strangeness of the place than with its remarkable accomplishments and its proper place in history.

There is no denying Ephrata's strangeness. Part of this is attributable to the feeling it gives us of being in a different world, a world remote from modern times, suggestively gothic and medieval in spirit, in which the self is denied and humbled by intentional poverty. Ephrata is also a Germanic world of an older, European form, not only in its language and literature, its arts and music, but also in its psyche and thought processes. And what little understanding we may have had of that world was essentially eliminated by two world wars, when "German" in any form was suspect. Although Ephrata was an integral part of the Pennsylvania German milieu in the eighteenth century, its qualities were quite different from what came to be called Pennsylvania Dutch in the century following—the *gemütlich,* prosperously peasant, and pastoral lifestyle of later times.

If one penetrates behind the surface history and physical remnants of Ephrata, what is most strange and alien to us is its mysticism. It is richly evident in the remaining architectural harmonies and the lush *Fraktur* (a broken or "fractured" style

of ornate lettering and illumination) of the many illuminated
music manuscripts. Ephrata's choral scores and hymn-poetry,
constituting the first original *corpus* of music created in the
New World, are suffused with mystical sounds and themes.
The "angelic" music, an eerie combination of medieval and
baroque qualities, is strange to our ears and cannot be performed today as originally intended. One writer called the Ephrata music "a foretaste of heaven."[1]

Ephrata created a surprisingly large body of mystical literature. The earliest works were printed in Philadelphia by the
young Benjamin Franklin, who had little sympathy for German clients, did not know the language, and was not yet an
accomplished craftsman. However, most of it was produced
at Ephrata, which had the most complete publishing unit in
the colonies. Much of this literature remains unstudied in any
real depth, and two experts, Guy Hollyday and Christoph
Schweitzer, have noted that "precisely the literary aspects of
Ephrata have received least attention so far."[2] Perhaps with
good reason. Its dialect is troublesome, and its language is
loaded with esoteric and arcane imagery remote from contemporary understanding.

Ephrata's mysticism, and the communal structure that hus-
banded it, lead far back into history, to ancient Greece and
the Near East and to the very origins of Christianity. One is
reminded of the social "harmonics" of Pythagorus and of the
ideal community of Plato's *Republic*. The succeeding Roman
world, infatuated with empire, erased the Greek ideal of the
semicommunal small city-state *(polis)*. However, movements
quite foreign to the Roman concepts of society and its spiritual base were at the same time appearing in remote sectors
of the Near East. As early as the second century B.C., the Jewish mystical cult of the Essenes escaped the worldly weight of
Rome in the deserts of the Dead Sea country and adopted an
ascetic, communal lifestyle.[3]

Of more enduring importance was the rise and spread of
Gnosticism, a farflung, unorganized, mystical movement that
accompanied "primitive" Christianity (it flourished most widely
in the years A.D. 80–200). It evolved a worldview and a symbolism based on the "hidden wisdom," the mystical revelation
beyond the ken of common folk, a wisdom that came to be
personalized in the term *Sophia*, the Divine Wisdom, a term

and aspiration deep in the heart of Ephrata sixteen centuries later. The Greek word *gnosis,* through generally signifying "knowledge," here has a deeper, more specialized meaning, which Elaine Pagels aptly translates as "insight"—meaning the attainment of a personal, spiritual, intuitive wisdom and serenity. It is comparable to what the early Quakers meant by the Inner Light, "God and Christ within us," and what a contemporary religious movement calls "Self Realization." The early bishops of the imperial church, who were growing in power and property and accommodating to the secular world, soon labeled Gnosticism a heresy. The writings of the Gnostics were destroyed or hidden away, and their "gospels," based on still older works originating at the very beginnings of Christianity but differing significantly from the orthodox canon represented in our New Testament, were repudiated. Not until the middle of our own century has a major portion of this literature reappeared.[4]

Ephrata itself, though an inheritor of many strains of mysticism, was a latter-day haven of essentially gnostic ideas and terminology—conceptions and symbols that had penetrated most of the unorthodox religious movements in Christendom since the end of the second century.

The central element in both the social and spiritual idealism of Ephrata, along with its gnostic orientation, was the vision of the spiritual power and community cohesion of the first Christians as recorded in the Acts of the Apostles, chapter iv: "And the multitude of them that believed were of one heart and of one soul: neither said any of them that ought of the things which he possessed was his own; but they had all things common. . . . Neither was there any among them that lacked: for as many as were possessors of lands or houses sold them, and brought the prices of the things that were sold, and laid them down at the apostles' feet: and distribution was made unto every man according as he had need." This was the taproot that nourished Christian countercultures through the succeeding ages. We have lost sight of its original power, intensity, and joyousness (in spite of Roman persecution and the redirection of later orthodoxy). The *agapē* rite, the love-feast celebration practiced by the first Christians and revived in the Radical Reformation, has been largely forgotten, and the old Greek term itself, signifying a union of human and divine love embracing all time and all life, is not translatable.

It was natural that this new kind of human experience took
a communal form. The *agapē* motif demanded an intensely collective communion in which ego and materialistic instincts had no place. It transcended the institutions of property and family, the egoism of the sex drive, even fealty to state and empire. Though willing to "render unto Caesar the things that are Caesar's," early Christianity rejected the state and all that its predatory power stood for, replacing it with a society of brotherhood. We do not know how long the brotherhood-community of goods persisted. "Appetitive" instincts no doubt took their toll. But as late as the second century, the satirist Lucian of Samosata, the most authentic pagan writer on Christendom, noted that "they despise all worldly goods alike, regarding them merely as common property."[5]

When at last church and state were wedded under the imperium of Constantine in the fourth century, the Christian community changed into an imperial structure quite unlike its original. Heretofore, as Tertullian, one of the fathers of the early church, contended, a Christian considered it impossible to serve both the Kingdom of Christ and the state: "For us," he said, "nothing is more foreign than the commonwealth. We recognize but one universal commonwealth, the world."[6] Such thoughts were soon considered heretical. The hierarchs of the new imperial church, moreover, became embroiled in disputation. As Edward Gibbon phrased it, "the principle of discord was alive in their bosom, and they were more solicitous to explore the nature, than to practice the laws, of their founder." The Swiss historian Jacob Burckhardt deftly referred to the church in that age as "rapidly disintegrating in victory."[7]

What was disintegrating most seriously was the "hidden wisdom" of the apostolic era, the gnosis, the revelatory power reserved for the committed, secreted in the Gospels but not of this world and far out of the ken of empire.[8] Many sought escape from the imperial net in remote communal enclaves. Finally the church institutionalized this drift away from the world by putting its stamp of approval on a communal monastic system under its direct authority. But more radical Christians, appalled by secular and corruptive tendencies in church officialdom, formed independent communions or simple cluster-movements of their own consonant with the primitive apostolic spirit. The result was a widespread "heretical" counterculture that persisted, in the face of extreme repression, up to the Reformation and beyond. Some of the principal pre-Reformation movements are outlined in table 1 in the Appendix.

The hidden residue of revelatory mysticism burst forth again in the Germanic world of the fourteenth century. Its principal inspiration was Meister Eckhart, the first of the great speculative mystics of the West. His followers, Johann Tauler of Strassburg and Heinrich Suso of Constance, along with the society of *Gottesfreunde* (Friends of God), spread the revival of mysticism through the Rhine corridor; it then blossomed in the work of Jan van Ruysbroeck and Gerhard Groote (founder of the Brothers of the Common Life) in the Netherlands. In the next century Thomas à Kempis wrote the classic work of the new spirit, the *Imitatio Christi,* a work still widely read in various languages.

A second flowering of Germanic mysticism that occurred in the seventeenth century was crowned by the profoundest mystic of them all, Jakob Boehme, of whose influence we shall hear more as the Ephrata story unfolds. It was from this Germanic *Urgrund* of mysticism that the peculiar mind-set and imagery of Ephrata evolved.

If we find it difficult today to appreciate the mysticism of Ephrata, we find it easier to understand the communal structure that developed from it, for the antiestablishment syndrome of the 1960s spawned hundreds of small communes, though of a quite different order and style. It must be remembered that Ephrata's communalism — a means of attaining spiritual unity and *agapē* in the image of the first Christian communities — is quite foreign to the hyperindividualism and egocentrism of our own day.

Ephrata was closer in time to the centuries when much of Europe accepted the communal structure as a natural form for municipal development. Communes began to spread throughout Europe as early as the ninth century; village communities reorganized as independent, semisocialistic units to free themselves from the dominance of secular barons and episcopal feudatories of the church. Their growth was phenomenal, and though in time they came to be dominated by a narrow mercantile bourgeoisie, the idea of the commune as *imperium in imperio* (an independent "state" within the State) persisted for many centuries. Ephrata perceived its own relationship to the world around it in just such terms.[9]

As a commune, Ephrata did not take shape in a vacuum,

for it was preceded by three other Protestant communes in the New World (discussed in chapter 3) and was conscious of a wide variety of older European prototypes. Moreover, the counterculture of which it was a part extended well beyond the strictly communal groups. Pennsylvania became its most natural home, for William Penn deliberately recruited European dissenters for it. The province was soon flooded with a variety of German-speaking sectarians who had rebelled against the oppression of the state-church establishments of Europe and formed their own communions. Mennonites came by the shipful, followed by Dunkers, Amish, Schwenkfelders, Moravians—all discussed later as an intrinsic part of the Ephrata milieu—and a host of unallied Separatists who regarded formal creeds with suspicion. For the most part, these groups shared a common ground with Ephrata—Christian pacifism, rejection of the oath of fealty to government, restriction of baptism to adults fully aware of its meaning, the ideal of mutual aid within a closely knit society, a pastoralism with a deep respect for stewardship of the land, separation from "the world." By the second quarter of the eighteenth century, they probably equaled, perhaps even surpassed, the English-speaking population of the province.

As a whole, the Germanic sectarians trace their spiritual inheritance to the so-called left wing of the Reformation. They were part of a widespread impulse to return Christendom to the purity of its apostolic origins. Thirteen years before Luther posted his theses on the door of the castle church at Wittenberg, Erasmus, the most learned man of Europe, had pled for such a return, and by the early sixteenth century religious reform was epidemic.[10] In large measure its original inspiration was pre-Constantine Christianity.

That inspiration faded all too soon into divisiveness and contention, both theological and political. The mainstream Protestants (Lutheran, Reformed, Calvinist) shared the same political presupposition of the Middle Ages, viewing church and state as inseparable components of one universal Christian society, encompassing all, even infants (hence perpetuating infant baptism, which was virtually unknown to the ancient church).

The Radical Reformers, however, most notably the Anabaptists, tried to approximate more closely the character and practice of the primitive church; they perceived the relationship of the individual to both the faith and the state in quite different terms, much like Tertullian: "For us nothing is more foreign than the commonwealth," that is, worldly government.

Like many (perhaps most) early Christians, Anabaptists and their sectarian progeny were therefore nonresistant pacifists, refusing association with the power of the state as inimical to the peace of Christ. The majority refused any participation in government. Christian nonresistance has a subtly different shade of meaning from what we think of as pacifism today. Many modern pacifists can identify with the nation-state, even though critical of its engines of war. But the Christian non-resister thinks of himself and his brothers as existing apart from and above the state. We shall see this principle at work in the Ephrata story. To the Ephrathite, even the Quakers (a peace sect owing much to the Anabaptist tradition) took a wrong turn in assuming sovereignty in early Pennsylvania, for in doing so they would lose their souls, their commitment to the Christlife, which may exist *in* this world but cannot be *of* it.

Hence too the Anabaptist sectarians rejected the institution of the oath. The oath was the basis for all legal testimony, and Western man could hardly conceive of a relationship between an individual and the sovereign state without it. Its rejection was a daringly revolutionary position, for it challenged the very source of worldly power. The Anabaptist believed that a regenerate man's word should be his bond, since his whole being was enwrapped in the Logos, the living Word. "Swear not at all," Jesus had admonished. Moreover, many Germans who came to Pennsylvania, not only sectarians, were suspicious of oath taking and instead practiced the tradition of the *Handgelübde,* agreement by handshake only.

But if he rejected participation in government, resisted armed service, refused the oath of fealty, how then could an Anabaptist conceive of a social cohesion at all? In the first place, "separation from the world" implied thinking of society in spiritual rather than geopolitical terms. In the place of sovereignty he opted for brotherhood, the intensive community of faith and spirit. His kind of community was typically small, local, voluntary, intensely welded together, as were the first Christian communities. The "other" world, the world of the established order, was not to be trusted.

Anabaptists had good reason for thinking so. Their movement originated early in the 1520s with a group known as the Swiss Brethren, but as early as 1528 Emperor Charles V decreed that they were to be exterminated by fire and sword. The decree was no doubt prompted by the alliance of some of the more fanatical Anabaptists under Thomas Münzer, "the Zwickau prophet," with the oppressed peasantry in the massive upheaval known as the Peasants' War that flashed through the Germanies in 1524–1525. The revolt was ferociously suppressed, the very name of Anabaptist was proscribed, and the great majority of peace-loving Anabaptists suffered with the revolutionaries; many were banished, imprisoned, tortured, or put to death. They were driven from towns and universities into remote corners of Europe, but the movement survived in secret conventicles and community cells. The impulse for a radical return to apostolic Christianity persisted under different guises through another century and a half of extreme oppression by both Reformation and Catholic establishments.[11]

It was thus inevitable that the dissenting movement launched by Anabaptism took on a closely-knit community (if not specifically communal) coloration. All of its succeeding sects bear that characteristic. Their forced diaspora through Europe and subsequently to early America demanded that kind of internal cohesion. The Hutterian Brethren, for example, after establishing a communal system in 1528, migrated from their Tyrol homeland to Moravia, Hungary, Transylvania, the Ukraine, and finally in our own century to Canada and the United States, where they still practice the community of goods.[12]

As a general rule, the succeeding sectarians, widely dispersed into "families" of the committed, quite naturally addressed each other as Brother and Sister. The communal core of Ephrata, however, went one step further: it displaced the natural family altogether; members dropped their family names and adopted new given names to eliminate blood-tie loyalties in favor of spiritual cohesion. The marriage state itself was eliminated because it perpetuated not only a divisive concern for property and the materialistic instincts of acquisitiveness, but also the "fatal flaws" of sexuality. The acquisitive instinct, whether for mate or property, was scrubbed clean in the highly charged act of rebaptism (i.e., Anabaptism), preferably by trine total immersion as practiced by the ancients.

It is important to remember that the Ephrata communal system developed not in Europe but on the frontier of Pennsylvania, one of the very few areas known to European dissenters where toleration was officially assured. William Penn, himself a radical Christian and missionizing Quaker, had developed a "Frame of Government" for Pennsylvania (1682), "a holy experiment," as he termed his province, that was far in advance of other colonial charters.[13] He had deliberately sought out the dissenters of Europe, especially in the Rhine corridor, and invited them to his colony.[14] The tide of dissenters continued rolling in until at last the French and Indian War broke the pacifist Quaker hegemony on the rocks of English and French colonial ambition and private land hunger.

Curiously, Ephrata did not result from any preplanned group migration. It simply "happened" because of a single personality seeking not communion so much as solitude, a lone mystic and seeker from the Rhine country whose ideas were nurtured in the European religious underground. Ephrata evolved from Conrad Beissel's peculiar *magia,* a charismatic magnetism effortlessly drawing others to him, a power he himself did not seem able to control. But though often an enigma to his followers, perhaps even tempted by messianic delusions, he was the commune's centripetal spiritual force. He did not pretend to manage its daily practical affairs, but there was a heavy demand for his guidance, and he was remarkably productive in preaching and writing and music.

His and Ephrata's story (for they are of one piece, even after his death) has all the components of an epic saga—the mobilization of historically significant antecedents, the pain of rejection from the homeland, migration to a world frontier, the magical charisma of its "hero," the unplanned "happening" of communal formation, a dramatic crisis of will and ideas, followed by a golden age of unique creativeness in its own terms. That, in turn, is followed by a desiccation of the spirit of the place and a tragic disjointing of its unity by forces and events over which it had no control, climaxed by a sorrowful denouement in the crushing pressures exerted on it by the American Revolution. Yet even in its latter days, Ephrata searched for renewal on frontiers farther west, leaving a pale afterglow in the succeeding age.

After some generations of neglect, the chronicle of Ephrata brought forth a substantial literature (ample evidence of which may be found in the bibliography), but much of it not only shortchanges us in documentation but also reveals a chronological ineptness, isolating Ephrata events and activities from their proper time frame and the broader milieu in which they occurred. The epic quality of the story is thereby obscured and the end product provincialized. Ephrata is a good deal more than a provincial curiosity. Our "mainstream" historiography has largely ignored it, and our creative writers have virtually passed it by, in spite of the drama in the saga itself. Only one major writer of our time (and he a German)—Thomas Mann in his novel *Doctor Faustus*—has used elements of the Ephrata story as a subsidiary theme; more will be said about this in the concluding chapter.

In his study of Western civilization, Oswald Spengler predicted that out of the mounting evidences of decline a "second religiousness" would blossom.[15] Strange evidences of this phenomenon may already be observed. When and as they come into focus, the Ephrata prototype will be awaiting rediscovery.

The Making of a Mystic

CONRAD BEISSEL'S YOUTH,

WANDERJAHRE, AND EXILE IN THE

RHINELAND, 1691–1720

NOWLEDGE of the early life of the founder of Ephrata is largely limited to what is reported in the *Chronicon Ephratense,* the official chronicle of the community, but this appeared almost a century after Conrad Beissel's birth. By then the days of his youth were remote in both time and place, and the chroniclers, though they came from the same part of the world only a decade or so after him, must have relied on faded memories and old hearsay. By then too the aura of sainthood had settled firmly over the memory of Beissel, and grosser elements of his life may have been deliberately omitted from the chronicle, though it is often surprisingly candid.[1]

Relatively recent researches in baptismal records reveal that Conrad was born in the year 1691, not, as previously supposed, in 1690.[2] His date of birth is generally given as the first day of March (O.S.). Although he was always known as Johann Conrad Beissel, the baptismal record lists him as Georg Konrad Beisel. He was born in the strategically located town of Eberbach on the Neckar River, then within the Electoral Palatinate, now a part of the German state of Baden-Württemberg. It is still an attractive region, and the historic old town itself is romantically situated at the foot of the Katzenbuckel, where the river, flowing northward from its sources in the Black Forest and the Swabian Alps, turns westward on its picturesque way to the Rhine. Eberbach was founded in 1227 when Henry VII, king of the Romans (as the king of the Germanies was

then called), obtained from the bishop of Worms the ancient
castle there (now in ruins). The seats of power of the Counts
Palatine, powerful electors of the Holy Roman Empire, were
located downriver at Heidelberg and Mannheim. Heidelberg
was distinguished for its imposing castle and its great university, founded in 1385. Mannheim, located where the Neckar
joins the Rhine, was repopulated at the beginning of the seventeenth century, by Protestant refugees from Holland.

Throughout the seventeenth century the Rhine corridor, ex-
tending from the high lakes of Switzerland to the North Sea,
was a cauldron of contention. In the first half of the century,
the Thirty Years' War (1618–1648) reduced the German population by about one-third, from an estimated 20,000,000 souls
to some 13,500,000.[3] The Neckar Valley was ravaged by the
Catholic armies of Spain in 1620, and again during the plun-
dering French intervention beginning in 1635. The Peace of
Westphalia temporarily ended the carnage, but though it
marked the end of the wars of the Reformation, it inaugurated
a new epoch of power politics, when secular interests and naked
force predominated. The worst was still to come.

The France of Louis XIV was now reaching the apogee of
its power and territorial ambition. In the French-Dutch war
of 1672–1678, the French mounted a full-scale invasion along
the Rhine and into Holland. William of Orange was driven
to halt the French tide by cutting Holland's dikes, but this did
not stop Louis's depredations in the Rhine Valley. He laid claim
to all of Alsace, and his troops occupied Strassburg (renamed
Strasbourg) and Luxembourg. Leopold, the Holy Roman emperor, was at last driven to organize the League of Augsburg
in 1686 to confront Louis with the combined resources of the
empire and other European states. But in 1688 Louis invaded
the Palatinate, and the next year, not long before Conrad Beissel's birth, French armies sacked and burned both Heidelberg
and Mannheim. Pillage and a scorched earth policy devastated
the whole area. Even years later Voltaire was appalled: "It was
the heart of winter. . . . Men, women, old people, and children departed in haste. Some went wandering about the countryside; others sought refuge in neighboring territory, while
the soldiery . . . burnt and sacked the country. . . . For the
second time this beautiful country was ravaged by Louis XIV."[4]

Louis's ambition now overreached itself. To support his
war he had bled the French people white by taxation and con-

scription. Resources of the nation were used up, trade dwindled, manufacturing ceased, the economy verged on collapse, and by 1694 famine spread through France. All Europe was horrified by the mindless carnage of the Palatinate. In 1697 the Peace of Ryswick brought an end to it, leaving incredible misery in its wake.

That was the world of Conrad Beissel's childhood. The fabric of life in the Neckar Valley had been torn asunder; madness and drunkenness spread like cancers, and thousands of homeless wandered about aimlessly. Poverty came on the heels of war, and no security was in sight. Conrad's father, Matthias Beissel, a member of the local bakers' guild, seems to have become an alcoholic during the depredations. Whether from that or other causes, he died in abject poverty a couple of months before Conrad was born. Anna, the child's mother, remembered in the *Chronicon* as "a pious and devout woman," tried to hold together a large family with the help of Conrad's older brothers. And then, when Conrad was only eight or nine years old, his mother died, worn out by impossible odds. Conrad grew up, therefore, in ignorance of the consolations of family life—a fact that undoubtedly contributed to his later search for spiritual solitude and his rejection of the natural family as an institution.

Conrad was passed around among older brothers and sisters, all of them very poor, and he suffered severely from undernourishment. That evidently accounted for his unusually small stature. He was too small and weak to play with other boys of his age, so his mind was turned inward when he was very young. Tradition says that he made a remarkable record in the parish school, as long as he was able to attend, and he developed unusual powers of concentration. Even as a boy he learned many things without any instruction, according to the *Chronicon*.

Young Conrad was eventually apprenticed to a good-natured baker in Eberbach. Their relationship must have been happier than in most such cases. For one thing, the master was a good fiddler and taught Conrad to play the violin. Evidently, the lad grew inordinately fond of music, which deeply influenced his later life in quite a different way. Now, however, the master and the apprentice began to play at weddings and other festivities, and Conrad was much taken with the gayer world that opened up to him. His social graces developed,

and for a few short years fiddling, country dances, and flirtations provided the only real lightheartedness he was ever to
experience. He found out that he was an attractive showman,
and he must have discovered there was some unusual quality
in his personality that drew others to him, particularly women.

Then came a sudden change. While still an apprentice, Conrad came under the influence of the Pietist movement spreading through the region, and for a while he gave up the festive
life and its temptations. He began attending the secretive Pietist conventicles, where he befriended George Stieffel, who
came to America with him some years later. In the months
that followed his first attachment to Pietism, Conrad vacillated
between piety and gaiety; there are hints that he sometimes
was tempted from grace by flirtations. But no matter how often
he was tempted, his life had been permanently changed.

In some degree the seeds of the Pietist movement may be
traced to the liberating influence of Ulrich Zwingli in sixteenth-
century Switzerland and the Reformed church that emerged
from it, and to the rise of Puritanism in seventeenth-century
England and Scotland and the Cromwellian revolution.[5] But
it was an Alsatian Lutheran, Philipp Jakob Spener, who gave
focus and force to the new movement on the Continent. The
principal monument of Pietism was his book *Pia desideria,* the
English title of which is *Earnest Desires for a Reform of the
True Evangelical Church,* published in 1675.[6] By that time Lutheranism had lost much of its original ardor, and its spiritual
thrust had become blunted by doctrinalism, dogmatic formularies, and a loss of participation by the laity. In short, as in
some of the German Reformed churches, Lutheranism had lost
its "common touch."

Spener foresaw that the only way to renew the participation of the laity in order to restore the spiritual life of Protestantism was to form small, semi-independent lay groups un-
burdened by clerical rules and attitudes — in effect, *ecclesiolae
in ecclesia,* little devout, spiritual groups within the church,
which came to be called conventicles. He established one in
his own home, but church and state soon outlawed conventicles, so that most of them had to become secret, at least from
the authorities, much like the primitive Christian communions
under Rome. Both Lutheran and Reformed establishments were
offended by Pietism, but the movement spread rapidly.

Pietism insisted that Christian belief be matched by Christian practice energized by a fresh study of the Bible and the early church. It urged the replacement of dry theological rhetoric with an emphasis on enlivening inner devotion and renewing the Christian ethic in daily life. It pleaded for sympathy and kindness, rather than establishment harshness, in dealing with the heterodox. It viewed the function of priesthood in universal terms, transcending church hierarchies and involving the laity as well. It was, in effect, a second Reformation.

In 1694 a new university was founded under Spener's influence in Halle, a Reformed town on the Saale in Saxony. This soon became the fountainhead of European Pietism, especially under August Hermann Francke, Spener's principal successor in the movement.[7] Here too, in 1727, Count Nicholas von Zinzendorf guided the renewal of the Moravian church; he was Spener's godson and pupil, and later, as we shall see, he and Beissel would confront each other on a distant Pennsylvania frontier.

Pietism appealed to both the emotional and intellectual dimensions of Beissel's personality, and its local conventicles, secretive though they were, gave him a chance to find himself and express himself. The Neckar Valley was predominantly allied to the Reformed church, and Heidelberg's university was then the academic heart of the Reformed establishment, but Conrad found no enlivenment in it. He gave up regular church attendance, forsook his former worldly cronies, and joined the local Pietist circle — actions that brought him under the suspicion of local authorities.

Luckily, he had now reached the end of his apprenticeship, had learned his trade well, and was promoted to journeyman status by the local bakers' guild. This meant that he had to set out for other towns to prove himself, and his *Wanderbuch* would have to be signed with commendation by the local guild in each town before he could return and become a master baker. His friend George Stieffel urged him to depart quickly, for the civil magistrates, prodded by the local clergy, were ready to take action against him for nonattendance at church and the errors of Pietism.

So in 1710 or 1711 Conrad Beissel set out on his Wanderjahre.[8] He headed southward to stop for specified periods at various towns designated by his home guild. Journeymen normally lived in the homes of their masters, and, with or without their connivance, Conrad continued to seek out the conventicles of the Pietists, though he lapsed back into the worldly life from time to time.

Conrad arrived at Strasbourg at a time when a battalion of journeymen bakers was being recruited for a massive campaign against the Turks in Hungary and the Balkans. He determined to volunteer but, probably because of his small stature and frailty, was refused. Some time later the news allegedly reached him that the battalion of four hundred bakers had been massacred to the man.[9]

In Strasbourg, Conrad's fertile mind was opened to the mystical, occult, and millennialist underground of European Christendom. One of the masters he worked for was evidently an intimate of the Pietists of the city, many of whom, we may assume, were drawn to even stranger religious movements. Conrad soon found himself in a circle of Inspirationists and the Society of Philadelphians. Inspirationism was a pan-Europe movement that renewed an ancient tradition of religious fervor, exaltation, and prophecy comparable in intensity to that which swept through the primitive church. The Inspirationist believed himself possessed by the Holy Spirit, and this psychic state was ignited and validated by visions, speaking in tongues (glossolalia), miracles, and prophecy. Inspiration endeavored to free the full, direct power of God in the human spirit, unshackled by forms, dogma, tradition, and mere reason. The Society of Philadelphians took its name (as did the city of William Penn on the Delaware) from the Greek word meaning brotherhood of love: *philos,* to love; *adelphos,* brother. It was a mystical fraternity owing its inspiration to the theosophic writings of Jakob Boehme (1575–1624), who is still regarded as the greatest of German mystical philosophers. The visions and writings of this poor cobbler of Görlitz circulated widely in the religious underground; Jane Leade of England propagated the Boehme vision. It reached Holland and from there spread through the intellectual and religious underworld on the Continent.[10]

Even under French rule, unjustifiably continued by the Ryswick settlement, the city of Strasbourg held to its privileges as a "free town." It had welcomed the Reformation; its great cathedral was still the focus of the city. It became a sophisticated intellectual center where the whole spectrum of religious interests was exhibited. The young, imaginative journeyman baker who came here must have found it an exciting place to be. The local Philadelphian Society was by then well established under the leadership of Professor Haug of the city's university. In 1712 it had published its own collection of religious poetry, which, according to John Joseph Stoudt, contained "more than six hundred hymns in the flowery and rich style of the later Ephrata poetry."[11] (In later years Haug became one of the editors of the Berleburg Bible, of which more later.) Before Conrad arrived, another member of the group was Michael Eckerling (sometimes written Eckerle or Eckerlin), a distinguished city councillor, who in 1709 had to flee with his family for his Pietist activities; his four sons would eventually pose the most serious threat to Beissel's leadership at Ephrata.[12]

It seems likely that at Strasbourg, Conrad became acquainted with the writings of Boehme, Johann Georg Gichtel (a Boehme disciple but, unlike Boehme, a Separatist), Spener, and Gottfried Arnold.[13] He may also have been introduced to the mystical system of the Jewish Kabbalah, which had considerable currency at this time, and to the spiritual symbolism of alchemy. (The last and greatest of the European minds cast in the alchemical tradition, Paracelsus, who died in 1541, first attained fame in Strasbourg.)[14]

We know little else about Conrad's personal affairs in Strasbourg, but it seems evident that he gained not only social polish but also intellectual enrichment there. It was a heady experience for a journeyman baker. When he traveled on to his next stop, Mannheim, the *Chronicon* notes that he was "temporarily brought low in the spirit." His master at Mannheim, a man named Kantebecker, soon grew very fond of him and accompanied him to the secret conventicles. Kantebecker's wife also grew very fond of Conrad. The result seems to have been a lusty affair, and, as in the sophisticated society of Strasbourg, Conrad vacillated between the callings of the spirit and the flesh. Apparently the calling of the spirit again overcame him, and Mistress Kantebecker became intensely jealous. In the words of the *Chronicon,* she "broke out in violence." Conrad, for his part, called her a painted Jezebel. After a violent quarrel, the mistress in despair confessed to the master, and the journeyman thereupon took hurried leave from both the house and the city. In the suggestive words of the chronicle, Conrad "bade good-night to earthly woman."[15] His mind now focused on the mystical Virgin Sophia, the divine wisdom, and thereafter became permanently convinced that human copulation was shameful, physically debilitating, and spiritually smothering.

His next stop was Heidelberg, almost as broadening an experience for Conrad as Strasbourg. There he worked for a master by the name of Prior, whose family, particularly the female members, saw in Conrad a charismatic saintliness. Family meetings he held in the master's house were devoted to Bible study and theosophical inquiry, and we are told that he converted the entire family to a Pietist life. At least one letter in Beissel's 1755 Letter Book indicates that the family continued to be grateful to him for many years after he left Europe.[16] Although there is no indication that sensuality played a role in his influence on the Prior women, the letter is but another indication, to be confirmed many times over, that Conrad had an unusual effect on the opposite sex. Moreover, in an emotionally charged religious experience, the line between sensuality and spiritual elation is not always sharp and clear.

Conrad also gained his first and only real prosperity in Heidelberg. Whether he learned a new formula for baking bread from some ancient or esoteric source or from certain illuminations of his own is not clear. But the new bread, prepared in accordance with Mosaic laws using oil instead of pork lard, was a huge success. The chronicle says that he became the most celebrated baker in the city. The new product made a good deal of money for Prior and for Beissel himself, who was now elevated to the status of a master and placed in charge of the Prior bakery.

Conrad's new-found fame as a baker was matched by his growing popularity among the Heidelberg illuminati. Although Pietism had taken root in the city's great university and even in several of the local churches, underground religious movements were still banned by civil authorities acting on behalf of the religious establishment. Two of the city's Reformed pastors were Pietists, and Conrad was so taken with them that he began to attend church regularly, while at the same time meeting with the more radical Pietists and theosophists in their secret conventicles. The latter tried to sway him to give up church attendance once and for all. Finally, a "powerful enlightenment of the spirit" convinced him to cut the last ties to the church and cast his lot with the *collegium* of Pietists and mystics.

One historian implies that the local *collegium* was a front for the Brotherhood of the Rosy Cross (Rosicrucians), whose influence may have infiltrated the Philadelphian underground.[17] Whatever the case, the local religious underground held its meetings at night in the mountainous forest glens outside the city, partly to escape detection by the civil authorities and partly to heighten the mystic character of their rites. To the uninitiated, the rites and complex symbolism of the Ancient Mystic Order of Rosae Crucis must remain something of a mystery. Even its history is not clear. It has been popularly assumed that the order was founded in Cassel and spread through Germany early in the seventeenth century, but a much older brotherhood existed in the medieval world. Paracelsus, for example, was initiated into the secret rites in 1530. The early Rosicrucians absorbed the symbolism of alchemy and experimented in the transmutation of metals, but their principal objective was the attainment of a higher consciousness. Conrad himself, while at Heidelberg, apparently progressed from neophyte to the rank of Adept, perhaps even to that of Magus.

Conrad's status and fortune in Heidelberg were too good to last. He was now about twenty-five years old, a prosperous baker, the familiar of the city's intelligentsia, a prominent participant in the religious underground and in a rarified secret society. He was evidently highly respected in his guild, for he was chosen as Servitor of the Chest (treasurer). And that proved to be his undoing.

This post in the bakers' guild soon came into conflict with his freshly honed mystical and moral zeal. The roistering at the guild's banquets disturbed him, and he lashed out at their excesses. His criticisms (and perhaps his withholding of funds) provoked other members of the guild, who learned that he had cut his ties to the church and attended secret meetings, to contrive with the city council to have him arrested and thrown in jail. After an indecisive civil trial, he was brought before the ecclesiastical court. He refused to reveal anything about his secret associations, but the die was cast. In due time he received orders of banishment from the whole Palatinate.

It is said that Master Prior offered the city council a hundred Reichsthaler for Conrad's freedom and that a wealthy Jewish woman also interceded on his behalf. Presumably his university friends also stood up for him. All to no avail. The council dealt the final blow by confiscating his *Wanderbuch*, the official record of his journeyman's experience as a baker.

So now he was bereft of both citizenship and a means of earning a living. He was forced to become a vagrant.

He first sought refuge in his brother's house in Eberbach. From there he renewed his friendships among "the pious" and is alleged to have converted one of his brothers, probably Peter, and one of his sisters. (In later years two members of the sisterhood at Ephrata, Sister Eusebia and Sister Sevoram, were Beissels.) But the civil authorities heard of Conrad's tarrying in Eberbach, and, since this was still in the Palatinate, they ordered his arrest. Apparently just in the nick of time, and in the dark of night, he escaped into the forest, probably in the recesses of the Katzenbuckel to the north. He was now a hunted man.

The following months were almost too much for him. The life of a vagrant in those days, when all avenues of life were tightly controlled by the interlinked establishment of church, guild, and government, was extremely austere. En route to Westphalia, where some of the princely houses welcomed dissenters, he earned a precarious living as a wandering peddler; it may be that he also learned the trade of wool-spinning at this time. But the peasant countryside provided little sustenance, and he contracted consumption. His illness no doubt exacerbated the already confused state of his mind. He fell into excessive penitence and fasting. Even years later the trauma of leaving his homeland was still fresh and fierce: a passage in his *Theosophische Lectionen* cries out: "O Palatinate, Palatinate! what are the burdens that rest upon your conscience? . . . Upon how many of God's witnesses to truth have you heaped outrage and torture and made them sigh against you in their wretchedness! . . . For you have not thought upon the time wherein you were afflicted, and have fattened yourself for the slaughter in the day of God Almighty's fierce wrath, and the blood of the poor and wretched lies heavy upon you . . . for the time of His judgment is come, and who can endure it?"[18]

His wandering northward through Hesse to Westphalia must have been erratic and confused. But at last he came to Schwarzenau, where a coterie of Pietists and mystics had already formed a separate communion that in time became known as the German Baptist Brethren (today known in America as the Church of the Brethren).[19]

For the first seven years after its establishment in 1708, the Brotherhood at Schwarzenau lived in the spirit of the first

church at Jerusalem, practicing both a community of goods
and celibacy. In its early days its inspiration came primarily
from the eminent Ernst Christoph Hochmann von Hohenau
(1670–1721), a theosophic wanderer whose views coincided
closely with those which eventually shaped Ephrata. Indeed,
Beissel may have met Hochmann. Like Hochmann, Beissel came
to distrust both church and sectarian attempts to formulate
precise and exclusive creeds. Both men were essentially Inspirationists who felt that creeds set up barriers to the free flight
of the spirit. Like Hochmann also, Beissel rejected the spiritual constriction imposed by the property system and its reliance on marriage.[20]

But by the time Beissel arrived in Schwarzenau, the mer-
curial Hochmann's influence had probably waned. Alexander
Mack, originally a wealthy miller from the Palatinate who had
followed Hochmann in some of his wanderings, now assumed
the leadership of the Brotherhood. Mack gave up his earthly
wealth on behalf of the new faith, but under his guidance the
Schwarzenau movement became a Separatist church with an
increasingly defined form and creed—and by then the community of goods and celibacy were no longer practiced.[21]

The new sect increased rapidly. One branch first settled in
the Marienborn district; when it met persecution there, it moved
to Krefeld west of the Rhine in 1715.[22] There a division took
place on the questions of marriage and the nature of the church.
The more liberal segment of the Krefeld Dunkers (as they were
called derisively for their practice of baptizing by total immersion) migrated to America. In 1719 they settled at Germantown in the province of Pennsylvania under the leadership of
Peter Becker, whom the *Chronicon* identifies as "a spiritual
son of Hochmann."[23]

From a theological point of view, Beissel must have felt at
home with the Schwarzenau Dunkers, but his real inclinations
favored the Inspirationists because of their emphases on the
gift of prophecy and on the free expression of the spirit. As
we shall see in the account of his early American days, his relationship to the Brethren prompted continual soul searching
and uncertainty.

From Schwarzenau, Beissel drifted around the countryside
to the homes of visionaries and Inspirationists generally grouped
as the Awakened, an antichurch movement of individualistic
enthusiasts. Like the Schwarzenau Brotherhood, they were wel-

comed in the territory by the house of Wittgenstein, headed
by Count Heinrich Albert, himself a member of the Philadelphian Society. The same family also ruled over Berleberg, where
less erratic mystics gathered and in the years 1726 to 1742 produced the Berleberg Bible. This differed significantly on some
points from the Bible of Luther and influenced German mystics and radical sectarians in both Europe and Pennsylvania.[24]

Conrad, however, was growing restless. The wild individuality he encountered among the Inspirationists and the Awakened in the Schwarzenau neighborhood seemed to him outrageously undisciplined. He was ready neither for the credal
Dunker Brethren nor for the wilderness of Inspiration. He must
have longed for solitude, for something akin to what Hochmann himself found near the end of his life on a high mountain near Schwarzenau. Moreover, the local governing house's
political interests and alignments were changing; it would not
be long before Alexander Mack's Dunkers would have to flee
to West Friesland, and eventually all branches of the mother
church would migrate to America.

Beissel in these years was still in frail health. At last he found
help and refuge in the house of a baker named Schatz, where
he was nursed back to health by a noted Inspirationist doctor.
The doctor scolded him for meditating too much on the world's
dark side. It is doubtful if Conrad took his advice on this matter. At any rate, he was soon active in a group called the Community of the True Inspiration, led by the fanatical Johann
Friedrich Rock. Their practices and rituals, borrowed in part
from Rosicrucians and Philadelphians, were wild and extreme,
and they were given to spiritualist trances. Though Beissel became one of Rock's assistants, he never joined the community.
It was just as well; at one meeting the presence of Beissel "violently affected" two young sisters, and Beissel was accused of
"touching forbidden fruit." The charge did not stick, but Rock
himself censured Conrad for spiritual pride. Flirtation with the
Inspired had gone too far, and he roamed afield again.[25]

When at last he returned to Schwarzenau, he found his
old friend George Stieffel there. They apparently lived together
for a time, and Stieffel introduced Conrad to Johann Junkerroth, an eccentric and wealthy nobleman and a Philadelphian.
The *Chronicon* says that Junkerroth was "known among the
learned by his strange translation of the New Testament."[26]
The nobleman became Conrad's patron, and there is some

suggestion that he introduced Conrad to the mystical lore of the East.

Probably with a few others, Beissel and Stieffel began dreaming of a New World, and the latter offered to pay Beissel's passage to America. In this daring enterprise they were joined by a youth named Jacob Stuntz (who seems actually to have paid for Conrad's passage) and soon thereafter by Simon König and Heinrich van Bebber. Quite likely they were also joined by others whose names have not come down to us.[27]

Doubtless the example of Peter Becker and his colleagues reinforced Beissel's decision to migrate, but something even more compelling lured him. Somewhere in his wanderings he had heard about the spiritual hermitage of Johannes Kelpius and a band of mystics in the wilderness drained by a stream called Wissahickon in a remote glen not far from Penn's new city of "brotherly love." What he heard answered to his own yearning for spiritual solitude within the uncomplicated framework of a small, celibate, communal society.[28]

We know nothing about the journey of Beissel and his friends to America except that they arrived in Boston in September and in Germantown "toward the close of autumn of the year 1720."[29] The journey from the Rhine had begun in early spring, and the trip in those days could not have been an easy sacrifice for freedom.

The Search for Solitude

FROM GERMANTOWN TO THE

CONESTOGA FRONTIER, 1720–1723

N the eighteenth century Germantown was the focus for most German migration to the New World. Its founding was traceable to William Penn's second missionizing journey to Holland and the Rhineland in 1677 and to his vivid promotional piece about his colony, "Some Account of the Province of Pennsylvania," first issued in 1681.[1] The first Germans to become seriously interested in buying land in Germantown were a group of distinguished Spener Pietists in Frankfurt-am-Main, including several merchants and attorneys. The man who assumed the leadership of the group's Pennsylvania interests was a remarkable young scholar and lawyer, Francis Daniel Pastorius. In April 1683 he arranged with Benjamin Furly, Penn's land agent in Rotterdam, for the purchase of fifteen thousand acres on behalf of the Frankfurt Land Company.[2] That summer, on his way down the Rhine to Holland enroute to America, he also enlisted the interest of a group of persecuted Mennonites in Krefeld, who purchased an additional three thousand acres in Pennsylvania. By August, Pastorius was in Pennsylvania negotiating with Penn for the first German settlement. Although the wealthy Frankfurters did not follow Pastorius to America, the Krefelders (it is alleged that at least some had converted to Quakerism) arrived in force late in 1683, and the so-called German Township was promptly laid out.[3]

It was this little group of first settlers in Germantown, Pastorius and the Krefelders, who in 1688 issued the first formal protest against slavery in America, but curiously the Quaker Yearly Meeting refused to take conclusive action on their slav-   *27* ery petition. Sectarian lines were not then so sharply drawn as in later years, and some of the Krefelders readily allied with the Quakers in the new colony. In 1690, however, a sizable group of German and Dutch Mennonites arrived; in 1708 they built the first Mennonite meetinghouse in America on what became Germantown Avenue above Herman Street. But all kinds of dissidents were arriving in "Germanopolis," as the Latin scholar Pastorius liked to call the place.

In 1691 these early arrivals incorporated the village, giving the corporate members the sole right of the franchise, of legislation and government, and of admitting new members. It was, in effect, an unusual political experiment, an *imperium in imperio* designed as a community in the image of the apostolic church. But most Mennonites refused to accept the offices of civil magistracy, and there simply were not enough officeholders to go around. Then when the queen's attorney investigated the Germantown charter and claimed to find illegalities in it, the original charter was canceled in 1707.

The principal reason that Conrad Beissel's objective was Germantown in 1720 was his desire to join the hermits of the Kelpius commune on the nearby Wissahickon. In this he was disappointed, for there was not enough of a brotherhood left for him to join. Whether his companions had the same idea is not clear. George Stieffel went north to Oley to take up the hermit life, Simon König bought some land on the new Germanic frontier to the west in the Conestoga country, Jacob Stuntz and Heinrich van Bebber, along with Beissel, decided to remain in Germantown awhile. There at least a remnant of the Kelpius hermitage was within reach.

The hermitage had taken shape soon after a remarkably learned band of theosophists—extreme Pietists from Germany still loosely allied with the Lutheran church—arrived in Germantown in June 1694 under the leadership of Johannes Kelpius and Heinrich Bernard Köster. Adherents of Köster drifted away from the core group, held meetings in the house of Jacob Isaac van Bebber (Heinrich's father and an original Krefelder), and attracted a number of English-speaking residents of the colony into a short-lived Philadelphian Society. Kelpius and his adherents established their celibate commune in the neighboring township of Roxborough on the west bank of the Wissahickon in a wild area known as the Ridge. Pastorius secured for them 175 acres in this locale, and here they lived an extremely abstemious life and practiced arcane rituals. They called themselves the Contented of the God-loving Soul but were more widely known as the Society of the Woman in the Wilderness after the millennial imagery in the twelfth chapter of the Book of Revelation, for they were convinced of the imminence of the Second Coming and of the dawn of the millennium.

When Beissel arrived in Germantown, Kelpius had been dead a dozen years and the learned Pastorius since late 1719 or early 1720 (accounts vary), the original Germantown charter had been virtually forgotten, and William Penn's life had come to a tragic end in England in 1718. Only a few of the mystics along the Wissahickon lingered in their hermit cells. One of them, Conrad Matthäi, soon became Beissel's principal spiritual confidant. Another, Johann Gottfried Seelig—who had been Kelpius's chief aide and owned what was alleged to be the best classical library in the whole region—still lived the hermit life. Others abandoned their former ways to seek economic security, and probably more than one engaged in the growing land speculation.

Since the commune had not pretended to exercise an authoritarian discipline, members were permitted to marry and live in town. An eminent example was Dr. Christopher Witt, an English latecomer.[4] He now lived in Germantown and was becoming famous as a physician, teacher, the first of Pennsylvania's many fine clockmakers, planter of the first botanical garden in the colony, builder of probably its first pipe organ, and a skilled musician and artist who translated some of Kelpius's writings. His portrait of Kelpius in 1705 may have been the earliest of its kind in the middle colonies. Although he was also enamored with astrology and magic, the many-sided career of this remarkable man deserves much more attention from historians and biographers.

Germantown itself had changed since the old charter days. It was no longer at the edge of the American frontier. It was regularly flooded with shiploads of German émigrés and dissidents, many of whom stopped only momentarily before proceeding up the North Wales Road to settle new lands to the north along the Skippack and Perkiomen or in the Oley region or westward in the newly opened Conestoga lands. Those who stayed longer soon lost the religious inspiration for their

European exodus in secular and economic concerns. Some joined the Quakers, but many became increasingly apathetic in spiritual matters.

The Dunkers who came over with Peter Becker the year before Beissel were in part affected by the same materialistic virus. Some of the twenty families, who quarreled even on shipboard, went off to the new lands. Becker did not seem able to maintain the unity of the members who stayed in Germantown, and he and Beissel, disenchanted with the "ungodliness" of their countrymen, conspired together to reawaken them in the spirit. But the revival effort did not take hold.

Beissel, who really had no other place to go, was invited into the household and family of Becker, who coaxed him to undertake a year's apprenticeship in his weaving shop.[5] Conrad learned the trade well, and the association must have been economically successful, but he was restless. He had observed the life of Germantown with great care but found it wanting. The Quakers, whose meetings he attended for some time, seemed too involved with provincial politics and economic enterprise. The Mennonites had become, perhaps, too doctrinaire for his taste. As for the Dunkers, they were too disunited to promise a brotherhood in the apostolic sense, and besides, Peter Becker himself seemed to lack the strength and mystique necessary for effective religious leadership. He and Conrad were on friendly terms, but Becker had little background in occultism and the arcane that was so much a part of the Beissel *magia*. The hermit Matthäi urged Conrad to seek out spiritual solitude on the Conestoga frontier, and after his year's apprenticeship he took the advice.

We know nothing of his journey. Evidently Jacob Stuntz, Conrad's former shipmate and benefactor, went along with him. Stuntz had already purchased some land on or near the Mühlbach (Mill Creek), a tributary of the Conestoga. The country west of the Schuylkill was but sparsely settled; only an occasional farm broke the vastness of an unending forest. They may have crossed the Schuylkill upstream at Swedes Ford, followed the great limestone valley south of the Welsh Hills, passed the tract settled by Welsh Quakers, where the Welsh language was still spoken, and followed the wagon trail to the Conestoga.

In that autumn of 1721 most of the area was still Indian trading country.[6] As the Colonial Records show, Frenchmen were

still vying with Englishmen for the rich fur traffic, even as far
south and east as the Conestoga, and at the time at least two
French traders were imprisoned in Philadelphia for such presumption. Shadowy Indian clans drifted through the area. The
so-called Conestogas (probably a mixture of dispersed tribes
mainly including the once-lordly Susquehannocks) had long
since been broken as an Indian power by the Six Nations of
the Iroquois, to whom they paid tribute. But they were especially favored by the Quaker government, and in 1721 Sir William Keith, governor of the province, paid an official visit to
them at their central village on the Pequea, south of the future town of Lancaster. Other drifters from southern tribes—
Conoys (Piscataways), Shawnees, Nanticokes—wandered
through the territory in small clans. They too lived by Iroquois
sufferance.

But white settlement on the Conestoga frontier had begun
a decade earlier. In 1710 a group of Swiss Mennonites led by
preacher Hans Herr had obtained a grant for about ten thousand acres in the region of Pequea Creek and settled hardly
three miles distant from where Beissel and Stuntz built their
cabin. Herr's former home, the oldest building still standing
in what became Lancaster County, is a solid stone structure
near the place called Willow Street. Completed in 1719, it is
known as the Hans Herr House, though it was actually built
by his son Christian. No sooner had the first of Herr's group
taken up land here when they dispatched one of their number
to recruit more settlers from Germany and Switzerland.[7]

For the next several decades the Mennonite tide rolled in.
They were soon joined by like-minded Huguenots, persecuted
French Protestants, the first of whom was the widow Mary
Ferree and her children, who had won the sympathy of William Penn and Queen Anne in England. Some of the more ad-
venturous Dunkers from Germantown also settled in the area.
Scotch-Irish Presbyterians, seemingly always in search of the
farther edge of the frontier, took up less fertile hill lands to
the north and west, and after 1724 English and Welsh Quakers spilled over from Chester County to settle hill lands in the
eastern portion of what became Lancaster County.

When Conrad and Jacob arrived in the Conestoga countryside, it was already autumn, and the two quickly raised a cabin
in the primeval forest beside a spring on the banks of the Mühlbach.[8] In the ensuing months they kept school there for chil-

dren of German neighbors—the first free school in a very large area, for they regarded it as purely a labor of love.

Before the year was out young Isaac van Bebber, a nephew of shipmate Heinrich, joined the two men.[9] Isaac's immediate objective was to visit his father, Isaac Jacob, and his uncle Matthias, who had joined the Labadist commune at Bohemia Manor, Maryland, in 1704 and had lived there ever since. They had been part of a larger group of Mennonites from Germantown who joined the Labadists because their Germantown communion was becoming too "worldly." Isaac talked Beissel into accompanying him, and the two set out in the dead of winter.

The Labadist community was the second radical religious commune established in the Americas. It had been preceded, twenty-two years before its founding, by a short-lived Dutch Mennonite commune founded on liberal Socinian socialist principles by Peter Cornelius Plockhoy, once the friend and associate of Oliver Cromwell and even today regarded as the founder of the British cooperative movement.[10] Plockhoy's society had little chance to prove its durability, for its communal buildings were destroyed "to the very Naile" by the British when they wrested control of the Delaware from the Dutch in 1664. Thereafter, Plockhoy drifted around in limbo for years before appearing in Germantown with his wife. Beissel would have appreciated his gentle pacifism, his mild Socinian theology, and his mobilization of Dutch Mennonites for a daring adventure overseas, but he would just as firmly have rejected Plockhoy's encouragement of marriage and the family system and his rationalist view of social development. (See table 2 in the Appendix for a summary of religious communes in America, 1662–1800.)

The Labadist commune, on the other hand, influenced Beissel deeply. This in spite of the fact that Petrus Sluyter, who had long since proclaimed himself bishop, was then an old man, and the commune itself was slowly disintegrating. Its regimen, however, was as severely ascetic and otherworldly as ever. Even though it permitted marriage between those regarded as truly regenerate, it was a celibate community; the sexes lived, slept, and ate apart, and all desires of the flesh were sternly subdued. The cells were unheated even in the severest weather, and there were few amenities. The life of poverty was trea-

sured. Evidently, however, agriculture, milling, and trade produced a substantial common fund.[11]

The community's origins dated from 1683, when Petrus Sluyter and Jasper Dankärts came upon the area in their search
for land for a colony to be sent out from the Labadist headquarters at Waltahouse in Wiewerd, Holland. Through one
of their converts they obtained 3,750 acres from a much larger
holding called Bohemia Manor. The Labadist tract comprised
four necks of land at the head of the Chesapeake, where the
Bohemia and Elk rivers empty into the bay. The Labadists took
their name and direction from the teachings of Jean de Labadie
(1610–1674), an ex-Jesuit, mystic, and theosophist from France,
who, after banishment from several territories in Europe for
seditious teachings, established a society in the image of the
primitive church. The Princess Palatine Elizabeth, a friend of
William Penn, is said to have been a follower of de Labadie,
and Penn himself tried to visit the mystic but was apparently
rebuffed.

In spite of the decay of the society, Beissel's imagination must
have been stirred by the practice of "holy poverty" and simplicity; by the spiritual unity; by the rigorous internal discipline, which by then was habitual; and by the Labadist literature, both printed and manuscript, which the aged Sluyter
allegedly passed on to him. Some of the seeds of Ephrata were
planted on that occasion, though a dozen years would pass
before they germinated.

As to the future of the community, Sluyter died about a year
after Conrad's visit; a decade later (or less) the Labadists of
Bohemia Manor divided up their accumulated wealth and property, and the commune disbanded. As we shall see, however,
it was not to be the last of Conrad's encounters with Labadists.

Soon after Beissel and Isaac van Bebber returned to Jacob
Stuntz at the Mühlbach cabin, they were joined by George Stieffel, who had evidently tired of his lonely hermit life in the Oley
region. It is unlikely that a formal, organized unity was now
established in the household of the four men, but it is quite
probable that they resolved together to adopt a communal pattern and purpose, an echo perhaps of the Labadist influence,
in the mode of a primitive Christian cell.[12] Activities of this
tiny brotherhood concentrated on the cabin school, which
added religious instruction to the three Rs, and on missioniz-

ing journeys through the backcountry. The Beissel *magia* was already at work, and the more ardent spirits in the new settlements found their way to the Mühlbach cabin door. The Beissel personality soon loomed large on the frontier, and an unorganized disciplehood began to form around him as early as the spring of 1722. One of the pupils of the cabin school, Barbara Meyer (later Sister Jael), "became so enamoured of his angelic life that she became a steadfast follower" for the rest of her days. Although this was typical of his curious effect on young women, one is constrained to add that the Beissel charisma stirred young and old regardless of sex.[13]

Beissel's preachments in these early years "were but little tinged with that mysticism and speculative theology which characterized his hymns and writings in after years."[14] The time and frontier conditions were not ripe for that. Carving homes and fields out of wilderness is physically exhausting and spiritually deadening, and Conrad saw that the arcane dimensions of his mind were far less useful now than his innate charisma. His plain Gospel missionizing in this period, however, had a remarkable impact on the renewal of religious consciousness in Pennsylvania, so much so that there is some justification for saying that he was the first to herald what became, two decades later, the "Great Awakening" throughout colonial America. The earlier Beisselian awakening spread from the Conestoga eastward through Philadelphia and its hinterlands and did much to prepare the Middle Colonies for the fervor of the 1740s.[15] We know little about Beissel's preachments in the 1720s, but their style and spirit must have been substantially different from the pathological and often frightening rhetoric of the 1740s. Revivalist Calvinism was quite different in tone and purpose from Germanic Pietism.[16]

In the 1720s Beissel was still in the process of finding himself. The visit to Bohemia Manor opened new prospects, and his association with the Mennonites on the Conestoga frontier more and more confirmed him in the simplicity of the "plain" lifestyle and the principles of mutual aid as a social ideal. Soon after his return from the Labadists, Beissel was also attracted to the Baptist Sabbatarians in Chester County. In due time he publicly announced that he would henceforth observe the scriptural—that is, the Jewish—Sabbath rather than Sunday as his holy day. This not only caused the first sharp disagreement with his colleagues at the cabin but flew

directly in the face of provincial law, with what consequences
we shall see.

We do not know whether or to what extent Beissel was influenced in this daring decision by the presence of a small Jewish community across the hills that now mark the boundary between Lancaster and Lebanon counties. Although present scholarship finds little or no real evidence of an established Jewish settlement there, a strong tradition persists that at Schaefferstown a few orthodox Jews were active in the Indian trade as early as 1720.[17] It is conceivable that they married daughters of nearby German pioneers; at any rate, Judaistic ideas began to spread on the German frontier, and some settlers, it is said, actually returned to the "old dispensation." During his *Wanderjahre,* Beissel likely became acquainted with the Kabbalah, the source of medieval Jewish mysticism and well known to the European religious underground. Judaistic ideas played an important if secretive role in his spiritual development, and his decision regarding Sabbatarianism was of deep psychological import to him — as it was to Boehme and many another mystic.

Unlike New England and the southern colonies, the province of Pennsylvania had established a new kind of tolerance for religious freedom and dissent. Individualism in religious matters prospered as never before. This was less true within the surveillance of the Quaker theocracy in Philadelphia, of course, than in the rural and frontier areas. In the latter neither Quaker nor Anglican order predominated, and the Germanic established churches, Lutheran and Reformed, were not yet sufficiently well organized or supported from Europe to impose credal and church order. What thus took place was a growing indifference to formal religion coupled with a proliferation of erratic individualized or community sects. People jokingly referred to the chaotic religious scene in the province as "the Pennsylvania religion."

An extreme case in point was the so-called Newborn in the Oley region of what became lower Berks County. This movement grew out of the fevered mind of Matthias Bauman, an uneducated day laborer. After a serious illness in which he claimed to have been "translated" to heaven and given the power of prophecy, he found his way from the Rhenish Palatinate to Pennsylvania in 1719. There he preached a doctrine of regeneration that could free men from all sin, thus canceling the need for Bible or church guidance, for the sacraments, or indeed for matrimony, since by regeneration man returned to a unigenite Adamic state. After Bauman's death in 1727, his followers were mostly absorbed by the Dunkers and later the Moravians, but the short-lived movement was one of many evidences of the religious flux in the province.[18]

On the other hand, a growing religious malaise caused many to abandon the radical religious beliefs that led them to leave Europe in the first place. In Philadelphia, deism, with its rejection of credal rigor, spread through the more sophisticated classes. On the frontier the hard work of hewing a home out of the wilderness took so much energy that little was left for the spirit. But once the houses and barns were built, fields cleared, and crops harvested, many once again felt that something was missing from their lives. They were ready for an Awakening. And Beissel was just the kind of personality that could spirit them out of their doldrums.[19]

Beginning in 1722 he trod from cabin to cabin, settlement to settlement, to reinvigorate the religious consciousness of his compatriots. He was soon the prime spiritual power on the Conestoga frontier. Separatists without a church home, even Mennonites with one, flocked to hear him. That he was unallied with any particular communion made no difference, indeed may have been an advantage. The evidence suggests that Conrad could release powerful spiritual energies.

Although participants in the revival movement, his three colleagues at the cabin could not keep up with him. Half the time they did not know where he was. He was unpredictable and given to sudden leadings of the spirit. Nor was he responsive to practical obligations at the cabin. Since he was dedicated to a life of poverty, he was perhaps too free with the few assets the four men held in common. The breaking point came when he insisted that they make another "offering" to the remaining hermits on the Wissahickon, though their own little group was hard pressed at the time. George Stieffel could stand it no longer. He returned to his lonely hermitage in the Oley region; later he joined the Skippack Brethren (another passing sect known as the *Vereinigte Skippack Brüder*), then joined the Moravians at Bethlehem, where he died in 1748. Young Isaac van Bebber, whose health was being impaired by the ascetic life, decided it was time to leave also, though he and Beissel took leave of each other affectionately. Isaac went

off to sea to regain his health; years later he froze both hands
and feet in a shipwreck and was put under the care of Dr.
Christopher Witt in Germantown.[20]

Finally, one day when Beissel had characteristically wandered off, Jacob Stuntz, who had capitalized the Mühlbach
venture in the first place, sold the cabin to Joseph Gibbons,
whose father now owned the tract on which it was located.
Jacob justified his action as a way to repay himself the money
he had advanced to Beissel over the years. Beissel for his part
regarded those funds as a loan to be repaid—sometime. Stuntz
himself may have been conscience stricken by his action; he
left hurriedly before Conrad returned.

It was now the summer of 1723. Thus deserted, homeless,
and quite penniless, Beissel resolved, according to the *Chronicon,* "never again to borrow from men on God's account."[21]
He packed his few belongings and trekked a mile farther into
the heart of the forest. There beside a fine spring known as
die Schwedenquelle (the Swedes' spring), he built a small log
cabin with his own hands.

Solitude at last! He was determined to live in utter seclusion—
but he did not reckon with his own magnetism.

Birth of a Spiritual Community

FORMULATION AND FRONTIER

HARASSMENT, 1723–1733

N his new-found solitude, Conrad Beissel was soon visited by a delegation of the Wissahickon hermits. He still regarded them as his spiritual mentors, and they probably regarded him as a frontier extension of their own kind. Then came Michael Wohlfahrt. He had visited Beissel on the Mühlbach in the fall of 1722 while on a missionizing trek to the Carolinas, and at that time asked Conrad's permission to rejoin him on his return. The two were to form a friendship that lasted until death. Michael, who had been born in Memel on the Baltic, became an extreme Pietist evangel in Germany, came under the influence of the Inspirationists, wandered to America, and joined the Wissahickon brotherhood. Now he sought a commitment to a spirit broader and deeper than his own.

Years later Wohlfahrt would be remembered by Benjamin Franklin on two occasions, most notably in his *Autobiography,* as "Michael Welfare." The passage begins with a misunderstanding of the Quakers for having "published it as one of their principles that no kind of war was lawful, and which, being once published, they could not afterwards . . . easily get rid of," and this reminds him of "a more prudent conduct in another sect among us, that of the Dunkers":

> I was acquainted with one of its founders, Michael Welfare, soon after it appeared. He complain'd to me that they were grievously calumniated by the zealots of other persuasions, and charg'd with abominable principles and practices, to which they were utter strangers. I told him that this had always been the

case with new sects, and that, to put a stop to such
abuse, I imagin'd it might be well to publish the articles of their belief, and the rules of their discipline.
He said that it had been propos'd among them, but
not agreed to, for this reason: "When we were first
drawn together as a society," says he, "it had pleased
God to enlighten our minds so far as to see that
some doctrines, which we once esteemed truths, were
errors; and that others, which we had esteemed
errors, were real truths. From time to time He has
been pleased to afford us farther light. . . . Now we
are not sure that we are arrived at the end of this
progression, . . . and we fear that, if we should once
print our confession of faith, we should feel ourselves
as if bound and confin'd by it, and perhaps be un-
willing to receive further improvement, and our successors still more so, as conceiving what we their
elders and founders had done, to be something sacred, never to be departed from."

This modesty in a sect is perhaps a singular in-
stance in the history of mankind, every other sect
supposing itself in possession of all truth.[1]

Soon after Michael arrived at Beissel's cabin, another strange
character asked permission to join them. It was probably in
early 1724 that Johannes Stumpf (Joseph Stump), an erratic
and somewhat demented visionary, was accepted into the cabin
with some reluctance. He was a difficult man to deal with and,
in Sachse's words, "on account of his unsettled mind he caused
them much trouble."[2]

Meanwhile, Peter Becker, not to be outdone by his ex-
apprentice and perhaps prompted by the Beisselian Awakening on the frontier, was also busy in Germantown and the
Schuylkill Valley reawakening the apathetic among his fellow
German Baptist Brethren. He had the advantage of represent-
ing a specific creed refined by an identifiable brotherhood and
confirmable by the rite of baptism. Six Brethren now asked for
rebaptism in accord with the spirit and beliefs of the Schwarzenau heritage. On Christmas Day 1723 Becker and the six
applicants — accompanied by seventeen already baptised Brethren and assisted by Conrad Matthäi and other "Hermits of the
Ridge" — marched down to the Wissahickon to perform that

holiest of sacraments. Becker himself broke the ice on the stream, and Martin Urner of Coventry in Chester County, formerly of the Kelpius band, was the first to be thrice immersed in the freezing water.[3] The other five, including Jan Meyle, of whom we shall hear more, followed in a spirit of religious excitement and perhaps with a sense of making religious history. In a way, this was the real beginning of the Church of the Brethren in America.[4]

Beissel, meanwhile, kept to his solitude. Although we are led to think that his mysticism attained new heights in these days so that he was able to reach the "automatic trance" of inspiration and blessedness that was the goal of theosophy, it is also apparent that he was troubled. What troubled him was that his spiritual peace and power existed in a vacuum, unaligned to a formal communion and unsanctified by rebaptism. His pride made him reluctant to accept the ministrations of a spiritually weaker and less committed person like Becker. He tried to baptize himself, but the act did not bring him peace.

In early November 1724 Elder Becker and his revitalized Brethren — after conducting revivals on the Skippack and at Falckner's Swamp, Oley, and Coventry — proceeded to the Conestoga and the farm of Rudolph Nägele, a Mennonite preacher and later Ephrata monk. They sought out the help of Beissel in their missionizing enterprise, and it was freely given. Beissel evidently felt the need to humble himself now, and on November 12, in the midst of baptismal ceremonies in Pequea creek, he allowed himself to be baptized by Becker along with four others.[5]

Not much more than a week went by, however, before the first signs of a schism appeared between the Germantowners and the more avid of Beissel's followers. The fiery Michael Wohlfahrt was evidently in the forefront of the arguments, the substance of which remains unclear. Becker and party soon left the area in some confusion, but they nevertheless assumed that a congregation owing allegiance to the mother church in Germantown had been founded on the Conestoga frontier. Indeed, on November 26 the congregation was formally organized, with Beissel presiding. The whole group seems to have agreed to observe the Jewish Sabbath, but, as the *Chronicon* points out, this was not "publicly adopted" nor were worship meetings held on the seventh day until 1728.[6]

With Beissel as their "God-appointed" leader, the original

founders of the Conestoga congregation included Heinrich Höhn, Sigmund Landert, John Meyer, Joseph Schaeffer, Brother Jonadab (family name unknown), Maria Eicher, and Veronica Friedrichs. Four other Sisters are unidentified, but they may have been wives of the men, and one may have been young Barbara Meyer, Conrad's adoring pupil at the cabin on Mill Creek.[7] Early in May 1725 Conrad conducted his first baptismal rite. In the chilly waters of the Pequea he baptized Johannes Landis, Hans Meyle, Rudolph Nägele, their wives, and Michael Wohlfahrt. In the same month Jacob Gast, who became Brother Jethro, arrived on the scene. Gast was a prominent German Baptist who had settled in the Conestoga Valley, and it was he who apparently kept the diary of the congregation and later of Ephrata, from which years later, it is said, was extracted much of the *Chronicon Ephratense*.[8]

The congregation now began to grow so rapidly that Beissel's followers erected another cabin for him on Nägele's land so that he could be closer to them. Shortly the vicinity was dotted with other new cabins built by those who felt they had to be near the master. These new "Solitary" were dedicated to giving up "the ways of the world" and the marriage bed, and hence looked upon themselves as solitary spirits cut off from the world. They are called thus throughout Ephrata's history. The male Solitary now began to form an amorphous group which they called the "Brothers of the Angels." The Beissel *magia* was certainly at work.

This magnetism was not without its problems, however. They came to a head when two attractive young women, Anna and Maria Eicher, enamored of the Beissel charisma, left home to cast their lot with the master. Virulent gossip about this spread quickly throughout the area, and to prevent further scandal mongering Beissel's followers promptly built a cabin for the sisters on Mill Creek and placed them under the care of Brother Jethro. Thus Anna and Maria became the first of the future sisterhood to adopt the solitary life. Nonetheless, the harsh gossip was but little allayed, and we shall hear much more of the two sisters as our story proceeds.

Sometime in 1726 Simon König, another of Beissel's shipmates in the migration to America, bought a large tract of land in the Mill Creek area to be near the new congregation. Parts of it were then resold to two other remarkable men with a like motive. One was Johannes Hildebrand, whom Sachse identifies as "the most learned man in the early Dunker movement in America," a Germantown Baptist who stayed with the Germantowners for a while but who came to play a significant role in the fortunes of Ephrata.[9]

Another who took up a piece of the Nägele land was a poor German tailor who had arrived in America in 1724. He failed to succeed in his trade in Germantown and in other trades as well, but he eventually gained fame as one of the most remarkable printers in colonial America. This was Christopher Sauer the elder, who was accompanied to Mill Creek by his talented wife, Maria, and a five-year-old son, Christopher the younger, who would one day continue his father's famous printery.[10] It is probable that Maria, attracted by the Beissel *magia* like so many women, was converted and baptized by Conrad after the congregation's love feast on Christmas Day, 1726.

The relationship with the Germantown Brethren continued to be disharmonious. And yet when Beissel and his associates attended the first general conference of the Brethren at Martin Urner's in Coventry in May 1727, Beissel took charge (in Becker's absence), preached with great power, and baptized eleven new members in the Schuylkill. He also introduced antiphonal choral singing, an event that may mark the birth of the great Ephrata music tradition.[11] Later in the year another series of general meetings was less harmonious. At one of them Beissel preached against servitude and slavery, remarks that may have been aimed at Peter Becker to whom Beissel had been formerly indentured. At any rate, the breach between Germantown and the Conestoga widened.

In August 1727 another event occurred that was to have important repercussions on the future of Ephrata. On the urging of Michael Wohlfahrt and Conrad Matthäi, the widow Eckerling sold her unsuccessful plantation near Germantown and came for a visit to the Conestoga with two or three of her capable sons. One of them, Israel, hired himself out to Christopher Sauer as a farmhand. Sauer introduced the family to Beissel, who had first heard of them back in Strasbourg. Israel and his master as well as Jacob Gast were baptized into the congregation on Whitsuntide 1728. Later the widow and her son Gabriel moved into the area, taking up residence in the house of Jan Meyle, where soon the widow died. The coming of the Eckerlings led to one of the most difficult relationships in Beissel's troubled life.

The next several years were significant not only to the future of the little congregation but also to Lancaster County
as a whole. German migration into Pennsylvania, especially
into the Conestoga region where the rich limestone soil beckoned, was reaching high tide. And that troubled the English-
speaking establishment. By 1728 Germans constituted about
three-fifths of the total population of the province, and though
this proportion would decline in the years to come, Pennsylvania would remain bilingual far into the future. Governor
Gordon opened the provincial assembly late in 1728 with the
remark that "I have now positive orders from Britain to provide by a proper Law against those Crowds of Forreigners,
who are yearly powr'd in upon us."[12] Such disparate person-
alities as the aristocratic James Logan, secretary of provincial
affairs, and the young, struggling Ben Franklin feared that Germans would soon assert control over Pennsylvania's destiny.

Ben Franklin should have been grateful. Among the first patrons of his little printing establishment was Conrad Beissel
and the German-reading audience of the province.[13] Beissel's
first work, *Das Büchlein von Sabbath,* a treatise on Sabbatarianism, had been printed by Andrew Bradford in 1728, and
the next year Bradford also issued Michael Wohlfahrt's English
version with the title of *Mystyrion Anomias: The Mystery of
Lawlessness*—but Franklin's shop was not yet operative. Although Bradford also printed Wohlfahrt's *The Naked Truth,*
an address to Quakers about the Seventh Day, thereafter the
field was open to Franklin. In the next year Beissel hired Franklin to print three new works—the *Mystische und sehr geheyme
Sprüche,* a small volume of orthodox moral proverbs and po-
etical musings; the *Göttliche Liebes und Lobes Gethöne,* composed of sixty-two hymn-poems of mystical exaltation, half
of them by Beissel; and a little book against matrimony, *Die
Ehe das Zuchthaus fleischlicher Menschen* ('Marriage, the
prison of sensual men').[14]

It seems apparent that Franklin was paid in advance for
these productions, which undoubtedly helped him through a
difficult period. But the young printer, while happily taking
the money of his German patrons, never did understand the
importance of the transfer of German culture to the province
and apparently regarded it with contempt. Later relations between Franklin and the Beisselians reveal him as opportunistic, tightfisted, and ungrateful.

These writings illustrate the earliest formulation of the spiritual rationale from which the future Ephrata emerged. It was founded on the symbolic significance of the scriptural Sabbath, the intensity of orthodox morality, mystical exhilaration as revealed in the hymns, and the Pauline purity of virginal man. To this combination one must add the practice of the Way of Peace, the rejection of all "unclean" foods, and the spiritual necessity of poverty.

This regimen was too strong for the congregation in Germantown to digest. Beissel, for his part, thought of the congregation as frozen in spirit and hobbled by a dull, flat, unimaginative view of life. The parting of the ways came before the end of 1728. To renounce the authority of Becker's baptism of him, Beissel had his followers thrice immerse him once again. Now an independent entity, the Conestoga congregation continued its missionizing and in the spring of 1728 formed another congregation in Falckner's Swamp under the ministrations of Andreas Frey.[15] This only heightened the tensions with Germantown, for Becker thought of this area as his territory. The situation was not helped by Johannes Hildebrand, who evidently served as a spy for Germantown while at the same time posing as a Beissel emissary. Frey could not unify the congregation, however, and Beissel then assigned Michael Wohlfahrt to the task. Michael was not up to it either and had to suffer the humiliation of Beissel's recalling him. Although the congregation was short-lived, it would not be long before impressive numbers from that area would leave their farms to join the master at Ephrata.

In 1729 the aging patriarch of the German Baptist Brethren, Alexander Mack, arrived in Germantown with his followers from Friesland, where they had gathered after expulsion from Krefeld and Schwarzenau.[16] Peter Becker at once filled the patriarch's ears with lurid tales about the errors and independence of Beissel and the Conestogans. Mack promptly journeyed there to make an effort at reunion. Whereupon Beissel seems to have disappeared, on the grounds that the venerable elder's mind was already prejudiced against him.

A confrontation took place the following year when Mack and his followers appeared at a Beissel meeting at Falckner's Swamp. Confrontation, however, did not heal. Sharp words were exchanged, and the Germantowners once again left in confusion. Hereafter the two congregations maintained a cool degree of communication without real communion, but it is a curious fact that eventually all of Elder Mack's children found their way to Ephrata.

With the increase of migration to the Conestoga territory, local and provincial authorities decided it was time to form a new county government. It was the first to be formed since the three original counties of Bucks, Philadelphia, and Chester were established by William Penn. On May 10, 1729, therefore, Lancaster County was established out of Chester, with uncertain northern and western boundaries.

From the viewpoint of the Penn family proprietors and their investing colleagues, the action appeared overdue. They were doubtless disturbed by so many "Forreigners" on the Lancaster frontier who could live almost untouched by the statutes of the province. Tales about the religious unorthodoxy of some of them, which clearly seemed to flout established British law and custom, rankled in their minds. Worst of all, because it affected establishment pocketbooks, was the problem of squatting — settling on unused land without taking the trouble to register patents, file claims, make specific purchases, or otherwise make one's presence known at the distant courthouse in Chester. This was a common and understandable practice. After all, the frontier looked limitless. But the London Company, which had received huge grants in the Conestoga and other areas, did not see it that way.[17] Nor did the proprietary government, which expected to receive quit-rents on the land occupied.

By now, the wedge of territory formed by Mill Creek and the Conestoga was dotted with squatters' cabins built by the increasing throng of Beissel disciples. With their Anabaptist communitarian background, many of them were simply not property-conscious in the traditional sense. God would provide. But the London Company stockholders, armed with the power of the new county government, were not to be denied. In August 1730 handbills were posted throughout the valley, serving notice to squatters on company lands to vacate them within a month and make good all damages or face the force of the law. Apparently, no evictions or legal actions immediately ensued, but Beissel and his disciples began to think of finding other territory.

The new county government was ill disposed toward the Beisselians from the start. The new officials, mostly non-

German, were suspicious of a religious movement they did not wish to understand, and they were appalled at observance of the Scriptural Sabbath and working on Sunday, contrary to the law of the province. They were equally distressed by the movement's attitudes toward property and government. Unhappily, developments in the Beissel community provided a pretext for applying the heavy hand of the law.

The gossip about the Eicher sisters taking up the spiritual life with Beissel turned into allegations of whoremongering, and rumor spread that Conrad and Anna had brought a child into the world. A local justice thereupon issued a king's warrant for the arrest of both Eicher girls and later one for Beissel himself. Hailed before the magistrate, Beissel demanded witnesses, and when the gossips were gathered up by the constable, the allegation was traced to one person who said she had referred to Anna's *married* sister. The magistrate had to beg pardon of the accused, but Anna nevertheless had to pay costs.[18]

The congregation was now wracked with dissension over the issue of marriage. Conrad's little book on matrimony and his fervent preaching about the perils of the flesh, coupled with the fascination his presence held for susceptible women, brought the issue into the open. One faction, led by Johannes Hildebrand and Daniel Eicher, father of Anna and Maria, actually held their own meetings. In spite of this, the wives of some of the anti-Beissel faction continued to be drawn to Conrad.

Christina Höhn was an example. She was a former Quaker who became contorted and ecstatic in her religious devotion, and she used her household funds secretly to support Beissel's activities. "She clothed him anew," the *Chronicon* states, and after her husband's death she took up a life of continence in adoration of Beissel.[19] She and other women were around him whenever they could break away from household chores, and they filled his cabin so full of "offerings" that the congregation had to elect deacons, as in the apostolic church, to distribute these gifts to the poor. Once in his absence they even put a fine featherbed in his room, but Conrad immediately discovered that its warmth aroused his carnal instincts and ever afterward he slept on a hard bench.

Maria Christina Sauer, wife of the future printer, took the next dramatic step. In 1730 she decided to be "rebaptized into virginity," left her husband (who for many years could not forgive Beissel), and took up the solitary life in the forest until a cabin could be built for her.[20] Phillip Hanselmann's wife, Maria, did the same. The husbands in the congregation had good reason to worry. It seems apparent, however, that in the early 1730s most if not all the congregation had assumed the life of continence, though this did not continue indefinitely among the Householders. During the first twenty years there were only two marriages in the congregation, and those were persons of advanced years.

Other matrons from as far away as Falckner's Swamp also deserted their husbands to seek refuge near Beissel. Sometimes indeed their husbands followed the same course. For a number of the women it is very likely that annual childbearing and sexual slavery under cheerless conditions impelled them toward the solitary life. At any rate, the congregation now seems to have accepted the practice of celibacy for those so motivated. Beissel thereupon organized the community into three "orders" — the married Householders, the Brotherhood of the Angels, and the Spiritual Virgins. The triune organizational structure was, in a sense, a stroke of genius; it persisted for two-thirds of a century.

Meanwhile, harassment by the new county government for flouting provincial law about working on Sunday kept recurring. It became so oppressive that Beissel, along with Michael Wohlfahrt and Abel Noble of the Sabbatarian group in Chester County, called on Governor Patrick Gordon in Philadelphia to plea for official toleration.[21] Evidently the governor agreed not to enforce the law against Sabbatarianism. The three men took the cause to Quaker meeting on the following First Day. Both Beissel and Wohlfahrt were dressed in plain Quaker garb, which, thanks to the women devotees, had been adopted as the standard dress for the Solitary. When Wohlfahrt rose to speak, however, he, Beissel, and Noble were summarily thrown out of meeting.

Governor Gordon, who was appointed in 1726 by William Penn's heirs (who did not follow in their father's Quaker footsteps), was a rough-hewn military man and, in spite of his eighty-two years, a competent administrator until his death in 1736. But he neglected to pass the word of toleration along to local government officers. It so happened then that some of the Solitary men were apprehended for working on Sunday. (The town of Lancaster was just being laid out in 1730, and the county jail and seat of justice were still at Postlewaite's Tavern about four miles south.) The horses and oxen of those arrested were sold by the authorities to pay their fines, but nonresistance finally won out. Those imprisoned sang hymns in jail, refused food for a number of days, and otherwise worried the jail-keepers, until in some desperation the authorities released them and remitted their fines. For some time thereafter the local government left them alone; magistracy had learned that nonresistant Christians committed to a higher power than the law were not an easy lot to deal with.

By early 1732 the congregation in the Mill Creek area—mostly descended from the Mennonites, as the *Chronicon* remarks—had grown to such an extent that Conrad Beissel could no longer call any of his time his own. Both Solitary orders required instruction in the esoteric and mystical aspects of their commitment; the Householders asked for counseling also; and threats of the London Company still hung over the congregation's head. Beissel, who had taken up carpentry, was also busy with other members building new cabins, not only for members but also as an act of charity for needy new settlers who were not a part of the congregation. Then, of course, the distribution of alms through the deacons needed supervision. Preaching, writing, and missionizing also took time. Perhaps, Beissel thought, the world had pressed in too much.

Some of the congregation now urged that the Solitary of both sexes move further into the wilderness to build their own spiritual commune. Perhaps this was not what Conrad had in mind. He still longed for an untroubled solitude of his own. Moreover, the Beissel *magia,* continuing to produce spiritual excesses in others less well founded in the mysteries, generated its own problems. For example, after Conrad designated Hans Landes to take Wohlfahrt's place at Falckner's Swamp, Landes's wife became enamoured and followed Beissel to Mill Creek to take up the Solitary life. Hans was angry, especially when he heard that she stayed overlong in Conrad's cabin and gave up all thought of their household. He soon came from the Swamp, attacked and nearly choked the nonresisting Beissel, and later, in a fit of rage, "worked his will" on his wife.[22]

Jan Meyle, meantime, was set mentally adrift by the Solitary regimen and mystical exercises, and one night, completely naked, he forced himself into the cabin of a neighbor and into

bed with his wife. The neighbors at last delivered him to a
justice, who soon returned him to Beissel for safekeeping. Jan's madness continued for awhile, but later, as Brother Amos, he became the baker for the Solitary and for fifty years would serve the commune faithfully and well.

Weighed down by such vagaries and the pressures of gossip and public harassment, Beissel called a meeting of the congregation in February 1732. He designated Sigmund Landert and another Brother as Elders, Maria Sauer as matron in charge of the women Solitary, and then, to everyone's surprise and "with tears coursing down his cheeks," Beissel resigned as *Vorsteher* (leader) of the congregation. At last he was free for the solitary life again, or so he thought. The move, however, left the congregation agog, and its subsequent meetings proved far from harmonious.

Winter though it was, Conrad gathered up his little store of books and papers and once again journeyed into the unbroken forest alone. He headed for a crude cabin, previously built by Emanuel Eckerling, eight miles north on the banks of a stream called by the Indians Hoch-Halekung or Achgookwalico, meaning "snake hole" or "den of serpents." It was far from any other habitation, and the area was generally avoided by settlers because indeed there were innumerable snakes infesting it. An Indian village had been situated on the creek less than a decade before Conrad arrived. There seemed little likelihood that even ardent devotees would follow. The Cocalico, as the English called the stream, could have been considered "out of bounds."[23]

When spring came, Beissel, with Emanuel Eckerling, cleared some land, planted a garden, and prepared timbers for building his own cabin. The joyful respite of the months of solitude were reflected in one of the poignant hymns he composed at the time: "O blessed solitary life, / Where all creation silence keeps!"[24] He seems to have spent all his spare time in this period preparing a new book of hymn-poems, the *Vorspiel der Neuen Welt* (Prelude to the New World). The book included all the poems of the 1730 hymnal plus seventy-seven new ones, many of them written by Beissel. The remainder were by Michael Wohlfahrt and others. In addition, it contained an appendix—a mystical ABC of twenty-four sentences somewhat like Conrad's earlier proverbs. Samuel Eckerling arranged for it to be printed by Franklin in Philadelphia on a cash-in-advance basis. The printed sheets appeared later in 1732 and were then bound at some unspecified establishment.[25]

Beissel no doubt felt that he was entering a new world indeed, a world of the spirit remote from time and turmoil. But it was not to last for long, for a steady migration from Mill Creek to the Cocalico soon began. The first to arrive were three of the Solitary Brethren—Jacob Gast, Martin Bremer, and soon thereafter Samuel Eckerling—who built another cabin for themselves in order to be near Beissel. Then Anna and Maria Eicher arrived. Remembering the charges of scandal, the men at once built a cabin for them on the *other* side of the creek. In the months that followed, numbers of would-be mystics from the Wissahickon, Falckner's Swamp, and Oley and Sabbatarians from Coventry began to head for the Cocalico, some to stay for the rest of their lives.

So Conrad was now once again the fulcrum of a new society, requiring him to assume spiritual leadership and to reestablish the rules of its order. Following the standards and procedure already adopted by the Solitary on Mill Creek, cabins were built by mutual aid, without cost, and had the same dimensions: 20 by 25 feet, with an inside joist 8½ feet high and a sheltered doorway usually facing south. Personal possessions were discouraged, as befitting a community that rejected the basic idea of personal property. A new and more austere garb was adopted—prompted, it is said, by descriptions in Gottfried Arnold's book *The Primitive Christians*.[26]

Curiously, the members of the new settlement simply identified it as *das Lager der Einsamen,* the Camp of the Solitary. It seemed to have come into being all very naturally, with no grandiose plan or preconceptions. The term *Lager* denoted what today we might call a "happening" without regard to permanence or the future.

As a Beisselian congregation of Householders (those not ready for a "solitary" life) began to take up lands in the neighborhood, the extended settlement was roughly divided into four areas, each with a separate identity, a biblical name of special significance. "Kadesh" is believed to have signified the present cloister grounds, "Zoar" the area now occupied by the village of Reamstown, "Hebron" (a name later used for one of Ephrata's monastic buildings) perhaps denoted the site of the present borough of Akron, and "Massa" possibly the area between the present Ephrata and Denver.[27] Out of this rather amorphous beginning, in the complex matrix of a single strange personality, blossomed one of the most remarkable communities of early America.

Metamorphosis from Camp to Commune

ON THE COCALICO, 1733–1736

Y 1733 the flow of migration to Lancaster County was at flood stage. Most of those who came were Germans like the first pioneers, but now the majority were Lutherans and Reformed, "church people" rather than sectarians like Mennonites and Dunkers or Separatists, who scorned a church affiliation. Many of the newcomers also took the precaution of purchasing the land on which they settled. And so the squatters on Mill Creek, who came to the wilderness without making obeisance to the institution of property, were in effect forced out of their holdings. Many of them followed the immemorial Indian path, which Beissel had taken in 1732, and settled in the Cocalico district.

Within two years the new "camp" of the Solitary was surrounded by farms of the so-called Householders. They were Sabbatarians who still lived "in the world," raised families, and took out legal papers on their property but nevertheless clung to the vision of holiness that Beissel and the Solitary put into practice. The Solitary, on the other hand, refused to take out land patents, because "the English with political influence through bribery and graft got control of the patents and forced the legal owners off the improved lands."[1]

It became apparent, however, that Beissel and his colleagues would have to face up to this incursion of civilization known as property rights. Accordingly, Beissel deputized two men to call on Thomas Penn, son of the founder of the province who was at that time in Philadelphia, to ask official permission of the proprietors to lay out a communal settlement on the Cocalico. Evidently the request was granted, and Thomas

Penn is said to have promised his protection to the society.[2]
Later, however, certain members of the commune saw the
need to take out patents—which, as we shall see, led to many
complications.

Other neighbors of the new settlement were far less tolerant than Thomas Penn. Once in 1734 these frontier ruffians
started a brush fire at night in the direction of the Cocalico
cabins in an obvious effort to wipe out the Beissel commune.
Providentially, the wind changed direction, turned the fire
around, and is alleged to have burned the barn and outbuild-
ings of the chief instigator of the plot.[3]

Coarse gossip about "free love" among the Solitary revived,
and settlers warned each other about the danger of their wives
being seduced by the mystics. Several times Brothers were attacked at night and severely beaten. Civil officers were prodded into arresting more of the Solitary for working on Sunday. Then in 1735 two men sneaked into Beissel's cabin when
he was sleeping and beat him "with a knotted rope and leather
thongs," leaving him covered with painful bruises.[4]

Such attacks were repaid by the Solitary in the only way
they knew, with charity. The school for the children of indi-
gent German settlers was continued, and one of the first under-
takings of the Cocalico Solitary was the building of a granary
for storage of corn and rye and of a large, brick bake oven
for the primary purpose of feeding new settlers who were arriving every week in the territory.[5] The commune's pumper-
nickel bread was distributed without charge. The members also
continued the charity of building cabins for the new arrivals.

Beissel now appointed Samuel Eckerling to take charge of
the internal economy of the settlement. From the outset, it appears that charity, rather than development of a profitable internal economy, was the first priority. Dissonance arose within
the community only after that priority was changed. Jan Meyle,
who had by now recovered his sanity, was given the important responsibility of chief baker, perhaps under the tutelage
of Beissel, but under the direction of Samuel Eckerling. Between the bakery and the almonry a cabin was erected for
Eckerling.

As the population of the settlement increased and none of
the cabins could any longer accommodate meetings for worship and business, the Eckerling brothers and a few others built
a house on the hillside west of the creek that could not only

harbor meetings and love feasts but also provide some cells for Solitary Brothers. It was called the *Berghaus*.[6]

Meanwhile, Beissel and his associates were busy promoting a powerful religious revival throughout much of German Pennsylvania. In the midst of this the patriarch of the Dunkers, Alexander Mack the elder, died in Germantown on the last day of January 1735. The Cocalico Solitary attended the funeral *en masse*. With the Hermits on the Ridge they alternately chanted the *De profundis* and sang a hymn especially composed for the occasion. Lines of communication between Germantown and the Cocalico were renewed on this occasion, but as Sachse remarks, the Dunkers "became more or less unsettled, with a strong leaning toward the stricter observance of the Ephrata movement."[7] Within four years this would lead to a wholesale desertion to the Cocalico.

In 1734 the Schwenkfelders began arriving in Pennsylvania from their native Silesia in eastern Germany. They were a closely knit, long-persecuted religious society dating back to the very origins of the Reformation.[8] The group settled as a unit in the Perkiomen and Skippack watersheds of what later became Montgomery but was then still Philadelphia County, and they are concentrated in this small region to this day. Beissel was naturally intrigued with missionizing prospects among them, but he found them too closely welded together.

He turned again to Skippack and Oley, but this time he netted only one recruit, Maria Heidt, the daughter of his host at the latter place. Maria was then twenty-two and betrothed to a man she thoroughly disliked, so the story goes. She evidently put him completely out of her mind after she met Beissel and, without the consent of her parents, followed him back to the Camp of the Solitary and took the vow of virginity as Sister Berenice.[9]

More converts arrived from Falckner's Swamp north of the Perkiomen, and by mid-1735 nearly all the countryside within several miles of Beissel's cabin had been taken up by his spiritual kindred. Many of them, of course, remained Householders, but the real core of the community were the Solitary orders whose cabins clustered close to Conrad's.

Beissel reaped his greatest revival prize of this period from an area called Tulpehocken. This is an upland region, then on the outer rim of the Pennsylvania frontier, situated between the upper reaches of the Swatara, which drains into the Sus-

quehanna, and the creek called Tulpehocken, which flows into
the Schuylkill. It was settled by German Lutherans and Reformed who had to take a long, troubled, and circuitous route to get there. In London in 1709, they had first been lured by Queen Anne to settle on the Schoharie and the Mohawk in New York province. There they were disappointed by title difficulties and the amount of land they could acquire. In 1723 about thirty-three families pulled up stakes, pushed their way through the wilderness to the headwaters of the Susquehanna, and floated downriver to the mouth of the Swatara and thence to their new home. Given the circumstances at the time, it was a daring, difficult undertaking.[10] More Schoharie Palatines came to the Tulpehocken in 1728 and 1729, including Conrad Weiser, a devout Pietist who was destined to become the most important Indian interpreter and liaison in the American colonies. Weiser became the Lutheran *Vorsteher* of the community as well as its schoolmaster.[11] Then in 1731 another brilliant Pietist, Johann Peter Müller (hereafter Peter Miller) arrived on the scene. He was already an accomplished linguist and savant; "he speaks Latin as we do our vernacular tongue," the examiners of the Philadelphia Presbytery reported.[12] Miller was fresh from the University of Heidelberg, where he had enthusiastically absorbed Pietist notions. At Tulpehocken he took charge of the union Lutheran-Reformed congregation, while Weiser, in league with him, led the Pietist circle within it. But due to the predominating orthodoxy, religious quarrels multiplied.

It is probable that the writings of Beissel were already known among the Pietists at Tulpehocken, along with the works of Spener and Arnold, even before Conrad journeyed among them in 1733. The Pietists, however, were confronted with the sometimes violent contempt for the Cocalico commune expressed by orthodox parishioners who wanted nothing to do with Beissel. But he came again in the spring of 1734, and this time Miller and Weiser "accompanied him over the mountain for six miles" on his return.[13] Later the same year Weiser, Miller, and several others withdrew completely from the Tulpehocken communion. The end result was that Beissel, overcoming their initial hesitation, baptized Weiser, Miller, and six others from the Tulpehocken settlement in the Cocalico in May 1735.

The newly baptized, however, returned to Tulpehocken, where they found the orthodox violently shocked by their defection. Some accused Beissel of witchcraft, some threatened physical violence. Warnings were even passed on to religious authorities in Germany, where Conrad's *magia* was already known. But the Pietists were not to be put down, and in a fit of pique they publicly burned some orthodox catechisms and other works.[14]

Beissel came again to Tulpehocken and tried to organize the defectors into his own kind of Sabbatarian unity. He dispatched Michael Wohlfahrt as their teacher, but once again the job was too much for him. Then, after Emanuel Eckerling also failed, Weiser himself took the leadership. Peter Miller was so upset by the tension that he sought a holy solitude in the mountains, donned pilgrim garb, grew a beard, cleared some land, and started an orchard. "Melancholy temptation," however, pursued him, and after a half-year of severe penance and fasting he fled to the company of saints on the Cocalico.[15]

Weiser's case was somewhat different, although fasting and penance had altered his looks so much that he was hardly recognizable. But he had a very masculine temperament and found the adoption of celibacy extremely difficult, especially since his wife remained unbaptized in the new faith. In this extremity he called on Beissel for help. Beissel persuaded Frau Weiser to accept baptism and with it a life of continence. Man and wife then lived apart, broke up their home, and, with their elder son and elder daughter, took up the Solitary life on the Cocalico. The sequel shows how difficult such a commitment could be. Wieser's wife was soon impelled to return to her younger children, who remained on the Tulpehocken farm. Weiser himself, whose emaciated appearance shocked old friends, continued six more years with the Solitary. But he obviously could not resist a frequent return to the Tulpehocken farm, for during those years of the celibate vow four more children were born to the Weisers!

Unresolved sexual tensions no doubt plagued the first years of the Camp of the Solitary, but there were other sources of tension also. The camp was surrounded by hostile and sometimes violent neighbors; accusations of scandal continued; internally it was bedeviled by occasional spiritual excesses and madness; even the lay congregation was rent by factionalism. Among the Solitary the policy of intentional poverty must have required both a psychic and physical change of life, while their ill-affordable charities sometimes left their larder almost bare.

Since it had virtually no structured government of its own, it is remarkable that the camp survived at all. Yet it did more than that; it grew and waxed strong. Adversity and poverty combined with Beissel's magic to knit the commune together so that nothing could shake it from its uncommon aspiration.

In the hard winter of 1733–1734 the Solitary produced their first manuscript hymnbook, a collection not meant to be shared through the printing press but one that expressed the depths of their own hearts to themselves. The *Paradiesische Nachts Tropffen* (Teardrops of a Night of Paradise) contains not only hymn-poems by Beissel and the Solitary but also by older Pietists and reformers in Germany. The memorable thing about the *Tropffen,* however, is that the hymns were copied and decorated in the cold winter months as a collective act of devotion and spiritual unity—an exercise that prefigured the development of Ephrata's finest art form, the *Frakturschiften,* hand-decorated or illuminated writings.[16]

About 1735 the *Nachtmetten,* or midnight watch meetings, of the Solitary were initiated. They were akin to the strange ritual practiced by the Kelpius hermits on the Wissahickon, but here both sexes participated. Midnight was the hour when the religious mystic anticipated the advent of Judgment, and these meetings were essentially penitential. Beissel allegedly would not allow anyone to pray, sing hymns, or worship at them without first forgiving those with whom they had quarreled and unburdening themselves of any bitterness. At first the sessions lasted four long hours, but the heavy physical labor and severe regimen of the commune soon required that the time be cut in half. The ghostly processions, no matter what the weather, were graced by polyphonic hymn singing. In time they became famed throughout the province, but in the early years they produced allegations of sorcery, Jesuitism, and scandalous intermixing of sexes. Nevertheless, they helped weld the camp together.[17]

By mid-1735 even the Berghaus on the hill could no longer accommodate the expanding congregation for its *agapae* or love feasts, an institution of the ancient church that held deep meaning for the radical sects. Furthermore, solitary cabin life, especially for females, began to lose its charm and purpose as collective unity grew stronger. So in July of that year the erection of *Kedar* was begun, a structure, as Sachse says, "different from anything then existing in the New World."[18] It was a large, three-story wooden building with cells or *Kammern* on the first floor for selected Brothers and on the third for Sisters; the middle floor contained spacious halls for meetings and love feasts. To the top floor Beissel assigned Maria Hildebrand, daughter of Johannes; Barbara Meyer, the enamored early convert, now twenty-two; Maria Stetler; and the runaway from Oley, Maria Heidt. That signaled the true founding of the Order of Spiritual Virgins. The ground floor of Kedar was at first inhabited by four of the "strictest" Brothers, including Michael Wohlfahrt and Jan Meyle, but in a short time they were reassigned back to cabins, and the Sisterhood took over complete possession. In due time Maria Eicher was designated prioress and Maria Christina Sauer became subprioress.

Some of the women welcomed the closer association of the convent and its severe discipline, but this was not always the case. Maria Hildebrand (Sister Abigail), for example, ran away to Germantown and married Valentin Mack, son of the patriarch. And yet later the couple, with daughter Elizabeth, who became Sister Constantia, felt drawn back to Ephrata.

With the development of the Kedar convent, the tempo of internal activities increased. Time took on more meaning, prompting the installation on Kedar of what was probably the first tower clock made in America, a product of the clever hands of Dr. Christopher Witt. It seems plausible that the first of Ephrata's gristmills was built in the same year as Kedar. Although it would not be long before the fame of its excellent flour would spread far beyond the area and bring a lot of business to the commune, the first mill was certainly intended only for grinding grain raised by the congregation. The early economy was clearly meant to provide subsistence for the commune, not to compete at the marketplace, where the evils of possessiveness lurked.

Probably sometime in 1736 the mystical Zion Brotherhood began to take shape among the more fervent Brothers of the Angels. Beissel appointed Daniel Eicher, father of Anna and Maria, superintendent of all the Solitary, just as he had appointed Samuel Eckerling, who continued to take charge of the internal economy. Beissel, of course, continued as the spiritual engine of the whole congregation and gave special attention to the condition of the laic order of Householders. The Eicher appointment, however, was not successful. It alienated Hildebrand, who presumably thought he should have had that

distinction, and he moved back to Germantown for a while.
It may have also alienated Michael Wohlfahrt, still suffering
from his failures at Falckner's Swamp and Tulpehocken, for
Michael took up the hermit's life in Zoar. Eicher himself was
apparently over-proud and did not do well in soothing internal differences, so he was soon dismissed from the post. The
emergence of the more disciplined Zion Brotherhood was, under the circumstances, fortuitous.

The Zion Brotherhood was strong medicine. It was a secretive, select mystical society, perhaps a Rosicrucian order, whose
formulae for initiation and regeneration made incredible de-
mands on both the body and the mind. Today we know little
about those rituals and trials. We do know, however, that the
enormous strains resulting from the system of penance and regeneration led some into mental illness and psychic imbalance.
This is especially apparent in the strange tale of Jean François
Régnier, a French-Swiss visionary who had arrived in the settlement in the summer of 1734. Régnier may indeed have been
on the edge of madness when he arrived. He made grandiose
claims to holiness; he even tried to talk the Brothers into giving up living under roofs and eating cereal grains. He urged
an acorn diet, for the oak was a sacred tree in Rosicrucian lore
and even much farther back in history (as any reader of Fra-
zier's *Golden Bough* can attest). He constructed a very rude
shelter in the woods and seemed to survive on *Eichelbrod* (acorn
bread), acorn "coffee" (which was supposed to be both "mystical and medicinal"), and even some kind of acorn whiskey.

At least two of the Eckerling brothers, who were now assuming leadership of the Zion Brotherhood, and some of their
associates were impressed with Régnier, but Beissel, a keener
judge of men, evidently warned against encouraging him. Not-
withstanding, Régnier insisted on being put through the most
severe rituals without taking the precaution of being led through
the maze step by step. The strain was too much, and at last
he had to be confined to a madman's cell in the Berghaus. His
condition got worse, and he was removed to a yet darker cell
and lashed and beaten in a crude attempt to shock him back
into sanity.

After many experiments and continued rejection from membership in the Brotherhood, Régnier partly recovered a semblance of sanity, but, as he himself wrote, "not without many
lapses." Eventually he found his way to Georgia, where he

joined the Moravians. They in turn sent him to Count Zinzendorf in Germany where, according to Moravian custom, he
was given a wife by lot. Finally he accompanied the Moravians to Bethlehem, the town they founded in Pennsylvania,
but again in 1756 he knocked at Ephrata's door—with what
sad results we shall see.[19]

Precisely when the name Ephrata was first applied to the
Cocalico settlement is not known. The first public mention
of the name is recorded at the end of the preface to yet another new hymnbook as follows: "Ephratha in der Gegend
Canestoges, den 27. April, 1736." The hymnal, again printed
by Franklin, was issued under the title *Jacobs Kampff- und
Ritter-Platz,* which has been translated awkwardly as "Jacob's
Joust and Knightly Resting-Place."[20] This Beisselian title in its
curious way signified to Conrad that the birth struggle of his
little Israel had ended in peace at last. The imagery is suggestive. One must remember that the Ephrata of the Old Testament was the pre-Israelite name for what became Bethlehem.
It was on the way to Ephrata that Rachel, wife of Jacob, died
giving birth to Benjamin. And it was Rachel who "did build
the house of Israel."[21] Perhaps Conrad Beissel dreamt that the
Spiritual Virgins were building a new Israel in a new world
in which the Brothers of Zion could find peace.

Backcountry Zion

CULTURAL BLOSSOMING AMID INNER

TENSIONS, 1736–1741

HORTLY after Kedar was completed, a new structure called the *Bethaus* (house of prayer) was built adjoining it. The size and character of the Bethaus signified the rapid growth of the congregation. Although no picture or plans of the new structure have come down to us, it was evidently a building of stately dimensions with a large hall (*Saal*) for general meetings and worship services and commodious rooms for the love feasts. Sachse reported on the basis of contemporary references that "the Saal was the largest and most imposing room for public worship in the Province."[1]

The ambitious undertaking, completed in 1737, was made possible by Sigmund Landert's sale of his farm on Mill Creek so that he and his two daughters could join the Solitary. He vowed to donate the proceeds from the farm sale to the building of the house of prayer as well as of a house for Beissel in due time. Landert was, as the *Chronicon* puts it, "a skilled mechanic" and became the commune's chief builder and architect.[2] Herbert Zinn and other Householders followed Landert's example — evidence of Conrad's unusual influence on the community's "third order."

The Bethaus afforded a more orderly development of the community's spiritual life, and this was further sharpened by the growing influence of the Zion Brotherhood. Beissel himself could once again afford to penetrate beyond the "plain Gospel" evangelism of the earlier period, and his revivalism was tinged again with mystical and arcane content. The minds of the Solitary and Householders alike were turned more deeply inward by their leader.

One of the innovations of 1736 was an open confessional system, which took shape in the so-called *Lectiones*. Ernst described them as "exercises in mysticism. . . . On a Friday evening every Solitary examined his heart before God in his lonely cell, and then wrote a report on his spiritual condition on a slip of paper and handed it to Conrad, who read it at the Sabbath service on Saturday morning. The most unlearned state their inward condition in an artless, terse, reserved and simple way that is truly astonishing to the layman. Of these several hundred were later published in 1752 as *Theosophische Episteln.*"[3] There was also a private, "secret" confessional routine that was inaugurated back in Mill Creek days, but though Beissel required it of all the Solitary, it was fully observed only by the Sisters to their "spiritual Father."

After the conquests at Tulpehocken and Falckner's Swamp, missionizing was renewed again. In May 1736 Beissel led a group of twelve on a long journey by foot through Nantmill and Coventry to Skippack, Germantown, and Philadelphia, where they preached from the courthouse steps. From there they proceeded across the Delaware to Hunterdon County in New Jersey, where a small German Baptist settlement was located at Amwell.[4]

The Ephrata style of pilgrimage attracted a lot of attention. The disciples, carrying the pilgrim staff, clad in pilgrim garb, and walking on bare feet in all but the coldest weather, proceeded in single file in complete silence, heads bowed in meditation. It was an impressive affair, and many people would gather — some in awe with mouths agape, some with jeers and catcalls — to watch the stately procession.

Although Amwell would prove to be promising territory, a yet more interesting pilgrimage of 1736 established the first contacts between Ephrata and the Moravians; these would eventually end in serious disagreements and mutual rejection. The meetings took place in the house of Christoph Wiegner in the Skippack region. Here Peter Miller and several other Beissel deputies met with two of the Moravian bishops — the learned theologian August G. Spangenberg and David Nitschmann. Wiegner had been one of a group of Schwenkfelder exiles harbored on Count Zinzendorf's estate in Germany and had been sent to Georgia by the count with two other Schwenkfelder leaders, but at the last minute the three men went on their own to Pennsylvania instead. Spangenberg's mission was to woo them and the whole Schwenkfelder settlement into the Moravian fold. But little love was lost between the two parties.[5]

However, Spangenberg was evidently fascinated by the Ephrathites. As the *Chronicon* remarks, "At first sight there was felt by both parties a magnetic attraction between their spirits; for both were yet in their first love."[6] At Ephrata, Spangenberg had friendly meetings with Beissel. He was much impressed with the love feast and the night watches, with the free school and works of charity, with the mysticism of the Zion Brotherhood, with the alternative lifestyles of Solitary and Householders, even with the Ephrata mode of baptism, which he is said to have copied later on St. Thomas. The visit augured well, and a delegation of Brothers accompanied him on his way back as far as French Creek, where they parted amid mystic rites.

In 1736 Ephrata confronted the authority of government again. A township constable invaded the commune to collect the single-man's tax, which was primarily levied for poor relief. Beissel thereupon called a council of the community, and discussion revealed that opinion was split. Some Brothers paid the tax, but others, led by Peter Miller, refused on the grounds that Ephrata voluntarily gave more to the relief of the poor than any other agency of the county. He cited examples of monks and hermits being exempt from taxes in primitive Christian times. This had no effect on the constable, who summoned some anti-Ephrata neighbors and arrested six Brothers who would not pay the tax — Miller, the four Eckerling brothers, and Martin Bremmer, the community's beloved tailor. The six refused any conveyance to the county jail and once there refused to have bail posted for them. Public sympathy for them seems to have gained momentum, and, in some fear of a riot on their behalf, an aged former justice posted their bail on the promise that they would appear in court when called. So after ten days they were released.

In the May 1737 court session the six men continued their refusal to pay the head tax. Their loyalty to the king was challenged, but they argued that they had "already pledged allegiance to another King in heaven." As to the head tax, in the words of the *Chronicon,* "They acknowledged no worldly authority's right over their bodies, since they had been redeemed from the world and men." After further debate it was agreed that the Solitary would be taxed as one spiritual family at the rate of forty shillings a year for their real estate rather than their persons. It is said that thereafter the neighbors who had egged on the constable feared further Beissel "witchcraft" and hurriedly moved away. This seems to have been the last real conflict between Ephrata and the county government.[7]

Whether or not this resolution resulted in the decline of tension between commune and county, the amicable "state visit" of Governor George Thomas and other dignitaries to the Cocalico in 1736 must have dignified the commune's position in the area and solidified its legal standing. Thomas and his large retinue, including officials from Maryland and Virginia, were impressed with the commune's free school, its charitable work, its newfound discipline and organization, its music, its simple economy, and some of its remarkable personnel.

The governor particularly had his eyes on Conrad Weiser, who was already noted as an Indian interpreter. Weiser knew as much as any white man about the unpenetrated frontier of New York and Pennsylvania and the Indian tribes that inhabited it. While growing up on the Schoharie, he had run away from a harsh father and got acquainted with Iroquoian life, language, and customs—and it was the Iroquois confederacy that controlled the frontiers beyond the settlements of the white man. Thomas, acutely aware of increasing tension on the frontier, needed a man like Weiser in the official family.[8] As a first step the governor offered Weiser a commission as justice of the peace, which was then a much more prestigious position than in our day. Weiser, however, was still wedded to the mysteries and the angelic life, and he had become an important member of the Zionitic inner core of the community. He agreed to accept the appointment only if the Brotherhood approved. When a council of the community was about to prohibit him from becoming an agent of the state, it is alleged that Beissel came to his defense, asked him whether he could accept appointment in good conscience, and, when so assured, Beissel persuaded the council to grant him full liberty to do so.

Although Weiser was not commissioned officially until 1741, he hereafter served both his community (until he renounced his fellowship in 1743) and the provincial government. At one time he accompanied the chiefs of the Iroquois to Philadelphia as government interpreter. On another occasion he nearly died of exhaustion on the first of several incredibly difficult journeys as a government messenger through the wilderness to On-

ondago in the distant western region of the upper area claimed
by the New York colony, where the Six Nations maintained their central council.

With the conventual organization of the Sisterhood and consolidation of the communal economy, Ephrata took on characteristics in which strangers sometimes saw the markings of secret "Romish" institutions. This was a provocative label in those days. The accusation of Catholicism increased in the mid-1730s, when a new kind of garb for both men and women was adopted. Heretofore clothing of the Solitary was patterned after the plain garb of early Quakers. A few adaptations had been made, and both the English Sabbatarians of Chester County and the German Dunkers then adopted the Ephrathite pattern, the "old order" of the latter continuing it into the present century. With the excuse of wanting to emulate earlier Christian monastic garb, the Solitary asked Martin Bremer, the community tailor, to design a mode of dress that would hide the contours of the human body more completely. Brother Martin designed a habit based on the style of the Capuchins or White Friars but somewhat modified by Beissel and others. Sachse, who made a careful study of the garb, described it thus:

> This distinctive dress was designed to be made of unbleached linen or wool according to the season of the year, and consisted, for the brethren, of a shirt, trowsers and a kind of vest, together with a long gown to which was attached a pointed cowl or monk's hood. The habit of the sisterhood differed only in the substitution of a narrow skirt for trowsers, and some little peculiarity in the shape of the hood or cowl, it being rounded in place of pointed. A belt or girdle was also used when the gown was worn. In addition, the sisterhood, as a distinguishing mark of their spiritual betrothal, wore a large apron which covered them entirely in front and extended down the back as far as the girdle. . . . When the different members of the Order attended public worship they wore in addition a special short cloak which reached well down to the waist; this garment also had a cowl attached which could be pulled over the head.[9]

The laic Householders at first enthusiastically adopted a somewhat similar gown but of gray color to distinguish them from
the Solitary. This was worn only at worship and at all public
occasions. But other settlers criticized them for aping the Solitary, and in the course of a few years their use of the habit
was discontinued, never having been required.

The new garb signaled the completion of the communal-
conventual scheme. The Sisterhood in Kedar now held all things
in common. The male Solitary were well on their way to a
similar mode of life, and the limited production of their agricultural and milling operations was already communalized. As
with the Labadists at Bohemia Manor, the common table was
adopted, at least for a time. The Solitary allowed themselves
only one regular meal a day; diet was carefully controlled,
severely abstemious, and vegetarian. Those whose bodies demanded more than a simple supper were permitted a limited
ration at other hours, but all strove to reduce the body to its
lean and hungry essentials. It was, indeed, a communism of
intentional poverty aimed at defeating the calls of the flesh and
heightening the claims of the spirit.

Spiritual expression continued in the form of writing hymn-
poems and the music (still of an unelaborated character) for
them. Just when the manuscript of hymn-poems *Geistliches
Blummen-Feld von Rosen und Lilien* (Spiritual Flower-Field
of Roses and Lilies) was prepared is not known, but this occurred possibly in late 1739 or within several years thereafter.
The work was virtually unknown until Betty Jean Martin discovered it in the New York Public Library. The manuscript,
containing fifty-five new hymns mostly by Beissel, may have
been intended only as a temporary expedient, for all the poems
later appeared in the 1747 *Turtel-Taube*. In any case, it was
an augury of greater works to come.[10]

The problem Ephrata faced was finding a responsible and
cooperative printer who knew the German language, ideally
one who would be sympathetic to Ephrata's goals. Obviously, Ben Franklin was not the man. Relations with him,
though not always lacking cordiality, were probably roiled by
his showing contempt for things Germanic (as did other Philadelphia tradesmen), by his distrust of Ephrata in insisting on
payment in advance, and by his sometimes cavalier attitude
toward the texts submitted (his failure to capitalize German
nouns, for example). Although ever alert to a new market for

his shop even if he was unsympathetic to his client, his finally obtaining a German or gothic font only proved to be an
abortive effort to corner the German-reading market in the
province.

Christopher Sauer, Franklin's future and successful competi-
tor for the German market, had meanwhile returned to Germantown in 1731. After dabbling in carpentry and cabinetwork,
clock making, bookselling, and learning the apothecary trade
from Christopher Witt, Sauer decided to take up printing — an
art about which he knew little. Sachse seemed to have thought
that the Sauer's first press might have been obtained from Germany through the good offices of Jacob Gast at Ephrata, but
more recent research suggests that Sauer, an ingenious mechanic, may have built the press himself.[11] There was no love
lost between Beissel and Sauer — Sauer deeply resented that his
wife, Maria, had been caught in the Beisselian spiritual net
and his loss on that account had required him to give up farming on Mill Creek — but he kept in touch with Ephrata and,
knowing of its substantial literary output, hoped to gain its
support for his printing enterprise.

Once the press and type were obtained, Sauer still had problems. Agreement had been reached between him and Beissel
for printing the next Ephrata hymnbook, but no printing paper
was available. Franklin had cornered that market and, loath
to lose the Ephrata account, flatly refused to extend any credit
to "the Dutch" for obtaining a supply, even on his own in-
flated terms.[12] Finally Conrad Weiser came to the rescue, journeyed to Philadelphia in July 1738, and purchased the paper
for Ephrata on his personal credit.

Although a very resourceful man, Sauer still knew next to
nothing about printing a book. Beissel thereupon delegated
Peter Miller as supervisor of the undertaking and chief proof-
reader, with Samuel Eckerling and Michael Wohlfahrt as assistants. It was a slow process, and a *cause célèbre* intervened
before the *Zionitischer Weyrauchs Hügel* (Hill of Zionitic Incense) was completed in mid-1739. The trouble arose because
Sauer, already estranged from Beissel and an independent Separatist full of his own strange visions, set himself up as a censor
of the hymns. He grew increasingly petulant over their imagery and implications. When the four-hundredth hymn was being set up, he objected strenuously to the following verse (the
English translation by Samuel W. Pennypacker):

Sehet, sehet, sehet an!
Sehet, sehet an den Mann!
Der von Gott erhöhet ist
Der ist unser Herr und Christ!

Look and look and look intent,
See the man who here is meant.
He is raised by God the high'st,
He's indeed our Lord and Christ.

From such lines Sauer was convinced that Beissel and his disciples were imputing the very attributes of Christ to Brother Conrad. He absolutely refused to proceed with the production and let Beissel know his reasons in no uncertain terms.[13] Beissel's reply, slow in coming, was full of bitterness. "Thou wast not fit for our community," he scolded, and he implied that Sauer's mind was simply too coarse and narrow to understand the meaning of the poems. He did not condescend to refute the charge, and, considering the effect his *magia* had on his devotees, it is possible to imagine that he may secretly have had some messianic delusions. Yet it is presumptuous to try to dissect the magical complex of an inner spirit and psychic engine of a man like Beissel. The resulting Sauer-Beissel feud simmered for almost another decade, until sometime after Maria returned to her husband in Germantown in 1745. Meanwhile, the printing of the hymnal proceeded in the hands of the Ephrathites at the Sauer printery.

The *Zionitischer Weyrauchs Hügel* was a remarkable production. To the German mystic, incense is a symbol of prayer, and the "hill" of the title reminds us of the high places that were, since time immemorial, sought out by the worshipper in order to feel the transcendent significance of the rising of the sun. With its introduction, explaining the musical system employed, and its appendix, along with 691 hymn-poems, the complete volume contained some eight hundred pages of mystical imagery.[14]

During this period and the following years the Sisters were busy producing a variety of remarkable music manuscripts for the *Weyrauchs Hügel* poems. Of the nine manuscript collections identified by Betty Jean Martin, the most magnificent—and the finest work of *Fraktur* produced in America—is now treasured (along with other Ephrata manuscripts) in the Music

Codex is, to use Martin's words, "one whose beauty no description or facsimile can adequately portray." Another handsome manuscript of music for the *Weyrauchs Hügel,* perhaps
predating the above, is preserved at the Historical Society of
Pennsylvania. It is beautifully illuminated and also contains
a *Vorbericht* (introduction) describing Beissel's musical system with harmonization charts; it may have been Beissel's own
notebook.[15]

The symbolism of Zion was much in the minds of Beissel
and the male Solitary in these times. The Zionitic Brotherhood,
the inner core of adepts, appeared more distinctly organized
by 1738. Thanks to funds provided by Brother Benedict Jüchly,
an ardent neophyte and scion of a rich Swiss family in the district of Berne, a splendid new chapterhouse, the so-called Zion
Saal, was completed in October. Although the Eckerlings
wanted it located in the meadow near the creek, Beissel thought
it best to remove it farther from the temptation of Kedar, and
so it was built on a hill overlooking the valley, which he
named Mount Zion.[16]

The development of the Brotherhood and even the construction of its chapterhouse owed much to the influence of the remnant of the Kelpius commune on the Wissahickon. It is alleged
that Johann Gottfried Seelig, the learned successor to Kelpius,
cast the horoscope to determine the orientation, dimensions,
and even the precise time for the building of Zion. The building was conceived in the likeness of the original Wissahickon
tabernacle as a heavenly watchtower to welcome the dawn of
a new dispensation. Sachse's description of it reveals the new
level of mystic life it was intended to serve:

> This curious house was three stories in height, the
> lower floor consisted of one large room, known as
> the refectory, connected with which were three small
> ante-chambers *(kabinettchen),* two of which served as
> pantries for storing the provisions and necessaries
> for use during the forty days' seclusion, and the re-
> maining chamber constituted the receptacle for such
> paraphernalia as was used by the brethren in their
> ceremonial. The second floor was arranged so as to
> form a circular chamber, without any window. . . . In
> the center of this chamber there was a small table

or pedestal, on which was placed a lighted lamp, which, during the practice of the rite, was kept burning continually.

Around this pedestal were arranged thirteen cots or pallets, like the radiating spokes of a wheel. This chamber was used by the secluded votaries as their sleeping room. . . . The third or upper story was the mystical chamber where the arcana of the rite were unfolded to the secluded. It was a plain room measuring exactly eighteen feet square, with a small oval window in each side, opening to the four cardinal points of the compass.[17]

A second tower clock, along with a church bell, was received about this time from Peter Miller's father, a Reformed pastor in the Palatinate, and was mounted in Zion.

Zion was not for all the male Solitary. Some continued to live in the Berghaus, some in cabins. The new building was reserved for the inner circle of adepts and novices, who now began to assume a separate and special status in the community under the leadership of the Eckerling brothers (though, strangely, Israel did not move into Zion until Beissel appointed him prior in 1740). As nearly as we can tell, the Brotherhood departed somewhat from the pure Philadelphian and Rosicrucian principles and rites as Beissel and his chief lieutenants like Miller and Wohlfahrt understood them. Especially in the Zionitic "ordeal of regeneration," it seems plausible to identify the new movement as a revival of the "strict observance" of the ancient Egyptian cult of Freemasonry.[18]

Freemasonry had just entered the New World through Philadelphia, probably on the tide of deism and anticlerical enlightenment that was sweeping through eighteenth-century Europe. Ben Franklin was admitted as a member in 1731, and it is possible that he influenced Samuel Eckerling in this direction. In 1734 Franklin issued "The Constitution of the Free Masons" by special order of the Pennsylvania Grand Lodge. The Grand Lodge followed a more modern, less ascetic pattern than the ancient strict observance of the Eckerling group at Ephrata, and indeed there is no proof of any real connection between the two.

It is likely that Beissel remained somewhat aloof from the new developments in Zion, for though the Zion elitism evolved from his own theosophy, it was moving in a different part of the spiritual compass. And at an early date, he probably foresaw trouble brewing in Zion.

Beissel had already tried to dissuade Régnier from undergoing the full Zionitic regeneration process. Obviously he had good reasons, and as a matter of fact it is unlikely that the Brotherhood applied the extreme rites as a general rule. In the strict observance there were two processes involved, each lasting no fewer than forty days. The first and most demanding was a physical regeneration aimed at restoring the votary to the state of man's original physical innocence. The neophyte was placed in a hut or shelter in the forest, where he had to subsist on herb broths, hard ship biscuit, and rainwater. At one point in the ordeal several ounces of blood were taken from him and a secret elixir was administered. This was repeated at another interval, after which the votary took a grain of "materia prima." Whether this was some secret drug dredged up from alchemical lore we do not know, but it was very powerful, allegedly causing loss of speech and recollection, and, after another grain, a delirious fever and loss of skin and hair. Very few could have survived mentally unscathed.

The second part of the process was gentler but also rigorous. This was the spiritual regeneration, during which an alleged intercourse commenced between the votary and the archangels, which was supposed to conclude in complete moral and spiritual purification as unigenite man. Spiritual regeneration was less shocking to the body and mind, but it required forty days of the strictest regimen of meditation, prayer, ritual, and communion behind locked doors, with the most meager of diets.[19]

Such experience was, of course, held in secrecy, at least from Ephrata's growing public. Knowledge of the extreme regenerative process would have discouraged the steady flow of new devotees arriving in Ephrata during the late 1730s. Some of the new arrivals came directly from Europe, where the Beisselian phenomenon was gaining more and more attention. Others were lured by the continuing missionizing activities of Beissel and his lieutenants. And from 1738 to 1739 the Germantown Brethren witnessed a mass desertion to the Beissel banner.

Ephrata was also easier to get to, for the frontier had moved farther west. The Paxtang Road, which led from Philadelphia all the way to the ferry across the Susquehanna that John Harris started in 1733 at the present site of Harrisburg, was opened in 1737 and passed the edge of the Ephrata settlement. Five years later, as the westward movement began in earnest, the Ephrathites built a stone bridge over the Cocalico to assist the travelers.

Ephrata was slowly changing, too, though the changes were hardly discernible except for the increase of membership. The Eckerling brothers were increasingly active in Zion and assumed a larger role. Martin Bremer, the beloved tailor whom the Ephrata register recorded as "a peculiar spiritual person," was the first of the Zionitic Brotherhood to enter eternity. In March 1738 he was carried to his grave in a torchlit mystic ritual.[20] Younger Solitary spirits were now approaching maturity, and the Sisterhood seems to have gained new stature and greater independence in this period.

The Germantown Dunkers meanwhile were split into factions. Those more inclined to their theosophic and inspirationist origins, conscious of the examples of the long-departed Kelpius and of Beissel, established their own "camp of the Solitary" in a forested ravine of the Wissahickon. It was a "weird, dark and ghostly" place, to use Sachse's adjectives, and indeed the stream seems to have had a strange power on the minds of sensitive people. Their leader, Stephen Koch, whose theosophic illuminations of this period are explored in the *Chronicon,* was joined by the younger Alexander Mack and Heinrich Höcker, and later by Johannes Riesmann and other dissidents.[21] They built a community house of logs in 1737, but the next year most of them moved on to Ephrata. (The house was replaced about 1750 by the fine stone mansion of Joseph Gorgas, who with his wife joined the Solitary at Ephrata in 1761. Thereafter the mansion was a haven for Ephrata pilgrims; it is still preserved in Philadelphia's Fairmount Park.)

Heinrich Höcker's brother Ludwig arrived in Ephrata in the late 1730s with yet another Germantown contingent. Being a well-educated man, he was promptly assigned as schoolmaster. Under his direction the Ephrata school, heretofore a rather amateur charitable enterprise, raised its standards and became an institution of some consequence. Ludwig (Brother Obed) stuck to his task for many years; he lived until 1791 but served his last years in the printery. The school began to attract young scholars from many faiths and from as far away as the seaboard cities. Brother Obed also started a Sunday School—

perhaps the first in the world—"for children of "church people" in the area who had to spend Saturdays and weekdays working on their farms.[22]

The Thoma family, consisting of parents, three sons, and two daughters, arrived in 1736 direct from their home in the Canton of Basel, Switzerland. One of the daughters, Margaretha or Anna, took the name of Sister Tabea; later, after dismissing her bridegroom to take up the solitary life, she was known as Sister Anastasia. She was a remarkably talented young lady and allegedly quite beautiful. Beissel had a profound influence on her life, and she was perhaps more than spiritually enamored of him. She poured out her love in creating the finest *Fraktur* of her time.[23] She was also an excellent singer, and much of her time was spent decorating and transcribing the Ephrata music manuscripts that today are so highly prized. To Beissel she remained ardently faithful until his death. Thereafter she left Ephrata for Germantown to marry the prominent Philadelphia merchant, John Wister.

Both a singing and a writing school were started for the Sisterhood toward the end of the 1730s. It is said that Beissel himself designed the Gothic letters used in the latter, but prime credit for the workmanship must be assigned to Sister Anastasia. Direction of the singing school first came from another new Ephrata recruit. Ludwig Blum, of unknown origin, arrived in 1738 or thereabouts and, with his family, took up a farm in the community as a Householder. Evidently he had had a solid formal musical training and so was placed in charge of the singing school when it started. Mention has already been made that Beissel himself introduced antiphonal (and probably polyphonic) singing to the Baptist Brethren in 1727, replacing the chantlike monophonic Psalter singing that most congregations still followed. Conrad undoubtedly had a fine ear for music but lacked the more professional understanding of it that Blum now supplied.[24]

The singing school was at first made up exclusively of women Solitary, and even after the Ephrata hymnody had fully evolved, women sang all the parts except the upper and lower bass. But the Sisters in attendance soon grew restive under Blum and longed for Beissel to take personal charge. They even agreed to "steal" Blum's professional secrets and knowledge for Beissel. The *Vorsteher,* knowing a good opportunity when he saw it and genuinely loving music, went along with the plan, or at least did not obstruct it. Not long thereafter Blum was dismissed, and it is said that he took such offense that he soon left the settlement. Nothing is known of his later life.

By this time the Solitary orders of Ephrata consisted of about thirty-five Brothers and nearly an equal number of Sisters. Between thirty-five and forty families could be numbered among the Householders, so that around 1740 the total population of Ephrata would have numbered something over two hundred.[25]

Ephrata was still reaching beyond the bustling borders of the settlement. In December 1738 Beissel and his associates began another pilgrimage to Amwell in New Jersey.[26] As in Germantown, the Dunker settlement there was split between those who followed the lead of Peter Becker and those who were enlivened by the Sabbatarian mysticism of Ephrata. The Sabbatarian faction, probably prompted by Beissel, now began to think of establishing its own cloister life. To assist the process, Beissel appointed Emanuel Eckerling their teacher and elder. But as at Tulpehocken, acceptance of the eldest of the Eckerling brothers was short-lived. Brother Elimelech, as Emanuel was known, was extremely long-winded and repetitive, and his sermons sometimes lasted up to five hours. He also tended to be dictatorial, and when he insisted that all attend the newly instituted night watches, the congregation dismissed him and returned him to Ephrata. He did, however, bring with him several families from Amwell.

We must now begin to reckon more closely with the Eckerling brothers, for in the Zionitic Brotherhood, which they were primarily responsible for founding, they began to exert a powerful leadership throughout the community. The eldest was Emanuel, followed by Samuel (Brother Jephune); the third was Israel (Brother Onesimus), the most powerful and talented of the four; and Gabriel (Brother Jothan) was the youngest. Their view of what Ephrata could become was significantly different from Beissel's. Under their collective leadership an economic system evolved that, from Beissel's point of view at least, threatened to alter and overtake the spiritual objectives of his life and of the commune that he had founded and nurtured.

The complicated history of the duel between the spiritual forces centering in Beissel and the new economic character developed by the Eckerlings now begins to take shape. The clash is easy to oversimplify as a battle between spirit and economics. For the Eckerlings were mystics, too; they were princi-

pally responsible for the increasingly monastic character of the
Brotherhood and introduced a number of elements into its mystical regimen. Israel, it is said, introduced the *Nachtmetten* ritual (literally a predawn mass or matins) and also, along with Alexander Mack, promoted a Mary cult that led the Brothers to adopt the Virgin Mary as the patroness of their order.[27] The latter was kept quiet at first, but word seeped out and exacerbated both internal and external suspicions of "Romish" leanings of the commune. The suspicions were further heightened when Onesimus (Israel) instituted the "cutting of the tonsure" (the shearing of the hair) of all the Brothers, a practice that, though it prompted much ridicule, Beissel then passed on to the Spiritual Virgins.

It was Israel, too, who proposed addressing Conrad as Father, not merely as Brother or *Vorsteher*.[28] Just what Brother Onesimus had in mind in this context is not clear, but it is possible that he saw the need to separate the spiritual function from the internal operations of the Brotherhood and the management of the economy. Use of the term *Father* may have been one subtle way of effecting this separation. This change was endorsed by formal action of the Zionitic council. At first it caused much unfavorable comment, especially among the Housefathers, so it was decided that the laic order could continue to address Beissel as Brother while the Solitary were to call him Father. Beissel thereupon took a new monastic name, Friedsam Gottrecht, which may be liberally translated as "the seed of peace in the righteousness of God."

With the organization of the Zionitic Brotherhood the last vestiges of individual property ownership faded and a fully communal order emerged. Up until this period the society's government and economy were the creatures of Beissel's personal decisions. These may have been frequently ignored, since there was no method of enforcing them, but the Beissel "dictatorship" had thus far provided a reasonably benevolent if loose-jointed regime. However, he was not equipped, either by skill or interest, to manage financial and in-kind resources, and he was more inclined to be charitable to others than to his own community. Evidently no accounts had been kept, and Ephrata's resources had not notably cumulated. Nor had Beissel enforced the principle of common property with any apparent rigor or uniformity; that was a voluntary matter.

All of this time Beissel lived in the cabin of Emanuel Eckerling as a common Brother; even when Zion was built he did not move into the Brothers' house. In their midst he probably felt somewhat out of his element, for Zion was not really of his own creation. It was quite a different matter with Kedar and the Spiritual Virgins; their Order was his doing and most of them adored him. And so, unconventional as he was and scornful of the cynical and evil-minded, Father Friedsam now remodeled quarters in the Sisters' house and moved in. It was a daring and indiscreet move, though the Sisters were apparently delighted. Perhaps too delighted. They interrupted him often and interfered with his meditations and writing. He stuck it out for awhile, perhaps because with them he not only felt needed but could help in developing the music and *Fraktur* activities. Eventually a new cabin was built for him nearby; it is still standing and demonstrates what a sense of grace there is in extreme simplicity.

Stresses and strains, heightened by hasty tempers, might have been expected in a time of transition from cabin-cloistered individuality to monastic and propertyless obedience. Beissel's appointment of Johann Heinrich Hagemann and Peter Miller to the joint priorship of the Order of Zion was not a success. A dual responsibility simply did not work, and Beissel knew it soon enough. He next appointed Gabriel Eckerling as the first regularly constituted prior. But Gabriel was too young and inexperienced for the task and applied his newfound authority too rigorously at a time that called for tact.

Quarrels multiplied. Finally Gabriel's brighter and more experienced brother Israel was appointed to the post in 1740. As Prior Onesimus, Israel was to show remarkable qualities of organization and management over the next five years. But those qualities were sullied by an overweening ambition, a dictatorial style far less benevolent in application than Beissel's, a quite startling misunderstanding of the Ephrata aspiration, and, finally, base political treachery.

The Count Versus the Peasant

CONFLICT WITH THE MORAVIANS

IN THE PENNSYLVANIA SYNODS,

1741–1742

URING the first half of the 1740s a steady increase of tensions, from within and without, produced a condition that can be best described as Ephrata's period of *Sturm und Drang*. It was an odd time for strife. The province as a whole was relatively peaceful and prosperous; most of the aboriginal race, stripped of their hunting grounds, had moved to the western mountains and beyond; a healthy, self-sufficient agricultural enterprise, thanks especially to the German migration, combined with a prosperous trading establishment in Philadelphia to produce a lively economy. Ephrata's strange way of life was well established by 1740, its numbers were steadily increasing, and it was certainly making a distinct impression on the province as a whole.

Then two confrontations determined the commune's future. The first—although each interacted with the other—turned the society inward and shut out the siren song of spiritual ambition through a larger unity. The second, purely internal in nature, once and for all determined that at all costs the commune's spiritual meaning was to be preserved from the temptations of materialism and economics. Each confrontation in its way was classic, one might even say epic, in that it demonstrated a clash of deep-seated impulses in an earlier America.

It was the grandiose ambitions of the Moravians, newcomers to the Pennsylvania frontier, that precipitated the first, outward confrontation. They presented Ephrata (as well as other sectaries) with the choice of preserving its own spiritual iden- *77* tity and communal lifestyle or of merging with a broader religious association under the leadership of "the renewed church" of the Moravians and their charismatic leader, Count Nicholas von Zinzendorf.

The Unitas Fratrum, more commonly known as the Moravian Church from its principal point of origin in eastern Europe, had undergone severe trials ever since the fifteenth century, before the beginning of the Lutheran Reformation.[1] Its original inspiration is traceable to the purifying and reforming efforts of John Hus, who was burned at the stake at the order of the Council of Constance in 1415, and of Gregory the Patriarch, who survived extreme torture in Prague and formulated the principles of the Unitas Fratrum. In time the central group absorbed scattered groups of Waldensians of a still older reform movement who had been driven out of northern Italy and southern France after vicious persecution. The whole Unity was for years forced from refuge to refuge in Moravia, Bohemia, Poland, Prussia, and other parts of Europe. During the years of "the Hidden Seed," as they called this period of their history, they were nevertheless assiduous in maintaining a line of succession of bishops and "apostolic" authority. Finally, in 1722, when Czech and German fugitives of the movement found refuge on the estate of Count Nicholas von Zinzendorf in Saxony and built their village of Herrnhut, "the renewed church" could again emerge into the light of day.

The arm's-length confrontation between the Count and Conrad Beissel provides a fascinating array of problems suitable for a psychological case study. Zinzendorf was a member of the European elite and came from a family of wealth and nobility, of which he was sometimes inordinately proud. Beissel, on the other hand, was of peasant stock and turned poverty into a way of life. He too was unduly prideful of that other end of the spectrum and stubbornly resisted encroachments upon it. If relations between the Moravians and Ephrata, so warmly opened in 1736 at Skippack, could have proceeded between Beissel and August Spangenberg without the Count's dominance, a quite different chapter in the history of American religious radicalism might have been written.

Zinzendorf, a godson of Spener, the "father" of Pietism, grew up to be an intensely religious but clever and prideful young man. At the University of Halle, the center of Pietistic Lutheranism, he was a student of August Hermann Francke, Spener's spiritual successor. Although he eventually drifted away from Halle's influence, the young Count remained Lutheran to the core, in spite of his warm affection for the Moravian Brethren and his involvements in other sectarian movements. He even warned the Moravians against regarding themselves as a separate church. Yet under the auspices of an ecumenical Lutheranism, and inspired by a "Christocracy" that excessively emphasized the blood-and-wounds imagery, he simply assumed the leadership of the Unitas Fratrum. His largesse and his protection of them made that inevitable.

Zinzendorf, however, was increasingly disliked at the court of Saxony, where he was councillor to King Augustus the Strong. A royal investigation of Herrnhut branded the Moravians as fanatics and finally ended with the banishment of the Count. Thereafter, on another estate beyond the range of the court, Zinzendorf formed the Brethren into a "Congregation of Pilgrims." In the years that followed, it sent out numerous Moravian settlements to far corners of the earth.[2]

When the Count and his daughter Benigna arrived in Philadelphia with six other Moravians in December 1741, he was intent on two objectives. One was the establishment of a Moravian colony like Herrnhut on the Pennsylvania frontier. Already a few Moravians had taken up some lands, and others arrived from the first settlement in Georgia.[3] Life had been uncomfortable there because, due to their nonresistant principles, they were molested by both English and Spanish militia. The following July, the first large "Sea Congregation" arrived from Europe. The resulting Moravian establishments at Bethlehem and Nazareth (Northampton County) and later at Lititz (Lancaster County) developed a General Economy, as it was called, with intriguing parallels to Ephrata's communal system. Although the Moravian communal system was abandoned under complex circumstances after twenty years, it must be reckoned one of the most successful utopian communal experiments in American history. (The Moravian Archives at Bethlehem attest to their many remarkable achievements.)[4]

Zinzendorf's second objective was to fulfill a grandiose dream of establishing what he called a Congregation of God in the Spirit, an ecumenical unity embracing all the sectarians and German Lutherans and Reformed—under the count's aegis and with Moravian leadership. It was an ingenious proposal by which the various communions could unite with the Moravians while still retaining their own peculiar church traditions, practices, and fundamental beliefs. Whether or not it was also a thinly veiled maneuver to gain status and power throughout the American-German establishment, there is no reason to doubt that Zinzendorf was sincere about his ecumenical proposal, and he acted with astonishing dispatch to set the stage.

Zinzendorf's ecumenism had already been rebuffed by groups in Europe and by the Schwenkfelders in Pennsylvania. But he did find support from the so-called Associated Skippack Brethren, a diverse collection of individual Separatists, and it was under the signature of their leader, Henry Antes, that the call to the first ecumenical synod was issued only two weeks after Zinzendorf arrived in America.[5] Lutherans, Reformed, Mennonites, Dunkers, Ephrathites, Quakers, and a diversity of Separatists and Inspirationists were represented in the first meeting at Germantown. Schwenkfelders generally ignored the call.

Beissel may have appreciated the potential significance of Zinzendorf's ecumenism but had good reason to feel suspicious of his real objectives. In July 1741, for example, the Moravians sent the elder David Zeisberger and Anna Nitschmann, the bishop's wife, to inspect Ephrata. The principal purpose, to scout out possibilities for a union, may have appeared all too transparent. Moreover, there is some indication that the bishop's wife represented herself at the time as the count's daughter Benigna. Some of the Spiritual Virgins considered her a spy. At any rate, Anna apparently got into some boisterous arguments with them about theology and marriage and later claimed that most of the Ephrata Sisters really wanted to desert the single state if they could find another retreat. Evidently Anna also talked at length with Gottlieb Haberecht, a former Moravian who had joined Zion, in an abortive effort to woo him back. The Sisters and Beissel were outraged, and by the time of the first synod, Beissel had his guard up.[6]

Nevertheless, Beissel met with the inner circle of the Zion Brotherhood, and they agreed to send a delegation of observers—not associates—to the synod. Prior Onesimus (Israel Eckerling) arrogated to himself the leadership of the delegation, and along with him went Johannes Hildebrand and Heinrich Kalkglässer, as well as Conrad Weiser, whose official business as well as personal inclinations frequently took him away from Ephrata.[7]

The first synod, which began its deliberations on January 1,
1742, set the ground rules, considered Zinzendorf's proposal for a Congregation of God in the Spirit, and actually adopted a confession of faith. The latter was heavily flavored with Zinzendorfian ideas, language, and imagery. Since the count had his eyes set especially on Ephrata, that delegation was given the place of honor next to him. Prior Onesimus, duly impressed with such attention from nobility, even agreed to hold the next synod at Ephrata. But he forgot to reckon with Beissel, who, when he heard of the invitation, wrote a friendly letter to Henry Antes revoking it. "I shall remain your devoted patron and well-wisher," he wrote, but as to the idea of an ecumenical congregation, "I stand still, and will neither further nor oppose it."[8]

Six more Pennsylvania synods were held during the first half of 1742, but they became increasingly acrimonious. At the second, transferred to Falckner's Swamp, Johannes Hildebrand and perhaps the other Ephrata observers prompted a heated debate over the religious sanction of matrimony. They suspected that the Moravian system of marriage by lot, then followed with enthusiasm, was only a justification of the carnal instinct. The third synod crackled with still more acrimony over the institution of marriage and spread to the issues of infant baptism and the eucharist, rituals that Zinzendorf, as a faithful Lutheran, accepted. In the midst of it all, the count fell into a temper tantrum, that led to his temporary dismissal as chairman. The Ephrata delegation walked out and withdrew permanently. That was a blow to Prior Onesimus's ambition, and evidently he tried to soften the effect of the walkout to preserve his relationship with the count.[9]

Zinzendorf did not give up easily. Before the next synod he visited Ephrata and was warmly received in Zion by the prior and Peter Miller. But when it came to seeing Beissel, both men, the noble and the peasant, stood on their dignity, each assuming that the other should call on him—and so the two never met at all. Afterward Zinzendorf wrote Beissel complaining of the latter's spiritual pride and that his representatives at the synods were mere tools in his hands. Beissel's reply is a clever piece of studied aplomb that avoided the issues entirely: "I hardly know what induces me to issue this mite unto you, without perceiving some inner deep and very secret draughts of love, which urge and challenge me. Should it strike in the spirit, it would be well if in future the heavens would make truth and justice drop down from above and honesty grow upon the earth and the children of man be taught the truth. Then there would be some hope of recovery."[10]

The count's pride and petulance caused him other problems also. Just before the next synod he had the affrontery to address an epistle to the Schwenkfelders asserting that both their spiritual and temporal care had been entrusted to him as "the appointee of Jesus as Reformer of the Schwenkfelders."[11] Understandably he was rebuked.

The remaining synods lacked the electricity of the first three and became mired in tiresome doctrinal discussions and specifically Moravian concerns. The old fire flared up in the fifth synod, however, when that incorrigible Separatist, Christopher Sauer, entered into a bitter quarrel with the count; he later refused to print any of the Moravian diatribes against Ephrata. In the end, nearly all other churches and sects had deserted the synods, and the Moravians were left virtually alone to ponder their future.

The last synod formulated a Zinzendorfian assessment of the various religious groups in Germanic Pennsylvania. It pronounced that Ephrata was "founded only by the devil to hinder the approaching Kingdom of Jesus Christ" and proclaimed: "May the Lamb shortly trample this Satan underfoot." Assessing this disputatious experience as a whole, a historian of the Moravians in America, Jacob John Sessler (who is responsible for the English translations used throughout much of this chapter), had this comment: "Zinzendorf realized the failure of his ideal, and seeing the 'handwriting on the wall,' he could not forego a last opportunity to sit on the judge's bench. A diametrically opposite result from that originally intended was obtained. Instead of stopping the slanderers and gossipers the Synods had greatly increased their numbers, among whom Zinzendorf was chief. . . . The so-called Church of God in the Spirit, which had as its aim the harmonizing of discordant voices, added still greater to the existing Babel."[12]

What followed thereafter was an exchange of vituperative tracts. Sauer printed several against the Moravians; these came principally from the hand of Johannes Hildebrand.[13] The Moravians continued their covert and overt attempts to proselytize both Solitary and Householders from Ephrata. Benigna Zinzendorf even made a three-day visit to Ephrata with this rather obvious intention, but the Sisters in Kedar foiled her efforts by seeing to it that she spoke privately to no one.[14] And for years thereafter no love was lost between these two remarkable communities; their respective leaders seemed to ignore each other and go their own ways.[15]

The petulant disaffection between the two communions should not obscure the remarkable achievements of both. The Moravian establishment in America has had a durability, and a capacity for adjustment to changing conditions, that Ephrata did not. As a result, Moravian congregations are still very active and have an historical continuity both here and abroad, while Ephrata died out as a distinctive society very early in the nineteenth century.

The real glory time of the American branch of the Unitas Fratrum was the last six decades of the eighteenth century. The brotherhood's mission stations among the Indian nations stretched from the Delaware Valley through western Pennsylvania and the Ohio country to what is now northern Michigan and Canada. The brilliant work of David Zeisberger and John Heckewelder on various Indian languages and lifestyles and Frederick Post's journals and government missions to unexplored regions of the West achieved fame on both sides of the Atlantic. The Moravians, in fact, had greater success among the aborigines than did any other group in colonial days, no doubt because of their deep respect for the Indian.

As at Ephrata, music played an integral part in Moravian community life. Group singing, in fields and workshops as well as in worship, and the composition of hymns established a tradition of festive religious music since Christmas Eve of 1741, when Zinzendorf founded Bethlehem, until our own century, when the great Bethlehem Bach Festivals became internationally famous. Unlike Ephrata, however, the Unitas Fratrum used a wide variety of fine musical instruments, and the beautifully toned "tracker action" organs made by David Tannenberg are still played and honored by some of the world's great organists.[16]

Also as at Ephrata, the arts and architecture of the Moravian settlements had intrinsic communal qualities unjustly neglected in our annals. Moravian architecture, however, was more akin to the classical style of the eighteenth century than Ephrata's, whose most distinctive features echoed the medieval spirit. But in both cases the architectural style was uniquely related to their communal character and community purpose.[17]

In the fine arts Ephrata had no one comparable to Bethlehem's Valentine Haidt, whose religious paintings and many portraits of Moravian leaders place him among the greatest of American "primitives." On the other hand, the Moravians never equaled the distinctive folk arts of Ephrata as exemplified in lavish *Frakturschriften* produced by the Sisterhood.

Nor did the Moravians develop a complete printing establishment or produce books of rare quality like the Ephrata imprints. Literature produced by the Moravians tended to be of a more practical character and lacked, for the most part, the mystical flights of imagination and poetry of Ephrata.

It is curious that after the synods very little cultural or personal interchange between the two communities took place. Bethlehem may have gained an occasional Ephrata deserter; Gottlieb Haberecht, thanks to Anna Nitschmann, was an example, but then Haberecht had been a Moravian before going to Ephrata and becoming psychically destabilized by the Zionitic discipline. On the other hand, Ephrata gained the curious Thomas Hardie from Bethlehem. Hardie was allegedly "of gentle if not noble birth," something of a drifter and seeker who as a youth ran away from home in England and went eventually to Bethlehem, where, like Haberecht at Ephrata, he seems to have lost his bearings. When he recovered he went to Ephrata, adored Beissel as a "high priest of God," joined the Zion Brotherhood, and, as an exceptionally well-educated man in both languages and law, became a translator, perhaps as an assistant to Peter Miller. Here too the Zionitic regime may have been too much for him, and evidently the Brotherhood reassigned him as a teacher to backcountry settlements. It is said that he wandered off to Pittsburgh but that before his death he was back again at Ephrata.[18]

The Moravian establishment, in spite of its multiethnicity, seems to have been more integrated, perhaps more disciplined even if less demanding, than that at Ephrata, thanks in large part to the exceptional organizational and administrative abilities of August Spangenberg.[19] But its communal character was perpetuated for only two decades, until 1762, two years after Zinzendorf's death and Spangenberg's return to Herrnhut in Germany, the world center of Moravianism. Its abrogation was due to a variety of reasons, but the principal cause is traceable to the church-sponsored marriage system and increasing internal pressures for family unity, self-direction, and economic private initiative. For years thereafter the Unitas Fratrum settlements continued to be exclusively Moravian, and church gained ascendance over community. In the process, spirituality in imitation of primitive Christian ideals lost ground to economics.

As we shall now see, Ephrata went in a quite different direction—but not without pain and struggle.

The Fall of the Eckerlings

SELF-DESTRUCTION OF A MATERIALISTIC

WORK ETHIC, 1742–1745

LOSE upon the heels of the abortive Pennsylvania synods, a time of crisis arose in the life of the Ephrata community. The sense of spiritual crisis was dramatically heightened by an event that allegedly took place around midnight of February 22, 1742. It was a cold, clear, moonless night. The bell had just sounded for the *Nachtmetten,* the night mass and processional, and the Solitary were just beginning their mystic march when a fiery comet lit up the heavens. It had a great tail like a bundle of switches to scourge mankind. Beissel was sent for at once; he ordered that the bell be tolled again to gather the whole community to Peniel, a new structure named by him after the place where Jacob wrestled with the spirit and received the name Israel after having "seen God face to face" (Genesis 32). The prayer session was intense.[1]

With today's scientific view of astronomical phenomena, it is difficult to understand what a powerful effect such an event had on much of the world in 1742, and particularly on the mystics of Ephrata. Many of them remembered how the comets that appeared years before in the Palatinate seemed to presage the French invasions that devastated the homeland. Celestial phenomena took on astrological and apocalyptic significance; they were omens of the coming of a changed order of things, perhaps even of the end of the world or of the long-awaited millennium that Michael Wohlfahrt prophesied just before his death in May 1741. Samuel Eckerling, the community's "astronomer" (astrologer would be more accurate), carefully observed the course of the comet. Beissel and others were moved to a prophetic state and began to write some of the most mystical and apocalyptic hymn-poems of their literature.

Yet another comet appeared just after sunset on Christmas Day, 1743. It grew in magnitude and brilliancy and stood in the heavens for two months, prompting still more excitement and prophecy. According to Sachse the Zion Brothers on this occasion identified it as "the star" prophesied in the Zohar, most important of the Kabbalistic works and a mystical commentary on the Pentateuch attributed to the second century. The "star" was to stand as a warning for seventy days, and then a great religious or political revolution would take place, "ending with the establishment of God's kingdom in the New World." Some believed this New Jerusalem would take form around the Zionitic Brotherhood. Older members asked Beissel for rebaptism. A period of fear compounded with expectation and mystic yearning hovered over the commune.[2]

Back in Germantown, Christopher Sauer, whose German almanac and newspaper were first issued in 1739, probably spoke for many Pennsylvania Germans in his newspaper comment on the 1743 comet's omens: "All of which are to me plain tokens that the destruction of the religious Babylonian governmental order is near at hand."[3] By that he probably meant the merchant-dominated Quaker establishment in Philadelphia, for which he had no affection. Actually, his prognostication of the downfall of Quaker government (if that is indeed what he meant) was not off by many years.

With or without celestial omens, Ephrata was increasingly ill at ease, and the reasons for it seemed to multiply and take on their own dynamic. Even the building of Peniel proved ominous. This large, striking, medieval structure resulted from the largesses of two Householders — Rudolph Nägele, the former Mennonite preacher, and Samuel Funk — after a son of each was received into the Zion Brotherhood as a neophyte. Its first floor chapel was designed to serve the worship needs of the whole community. The second floor consisted of a large hall for the *agapae* and *pedelavia,* the ancient Christian rites of the love feast and the humbling "maundy" or washing of each other's feet before communion. The third floor contained a number of cells reserved for the Brotherhood. The fact that the Brothers considered this building their own, where they could perform their mystic rites undisturbed, was bound to chagrin the Sisterhood. The Householders, for their part, were glad to see it built so that the midnight marches of the Brothers could be diverted from the *Saal* of Kedar and the Sisters and thus dampen the spread of scandalmongering.[4]

What made matters worse was that, as soon as the construction of Peniel began, Father Friedsam ordered the beautiful Bethaus torn down. The precise reasons for this apparent vandalism are unknown. The Bethaus, allegedly the finest house of worship in the colony, had been erected only six years before with much toil and sacrifice. The Eckerlings may have put Beissel up to it to emphasize the dominance of the Brotherhood. And there was some suspicion that the Bethaus was used as a trysting place by some of the young Spiritual Virgins and their male friends.

Following the dedication of Peniel, Beissel invested Israel Eckerling, Conrad Weiser, and Peter Miller to the priesthood "according to the ancient Order of Melchizedek." This was a high calling of great mystical significance. It was the priesthood of perfection, without beginning or end, like that of the High Priest Melchizedek in the Book of Genesis, to whom Abraham paid his tithe. It existed without lineage or descent, and as the Apostle Paul wrote, it had "neither beginning of days, nor end of life; but was made like unto the Son of God." Melchizedek was also "King of Salem"—that is, king of peace—and those who took up the priestly office in his image could only be those whose inner peace transcended all conflict. Alas for Ephrata, it was not to be so.[5]

Discontent in the Brotherhood during Prior Onesimus's regime grew increasingly bitter and intense. The prior applied a heavy hand, demanded obedience, cut sleeping hours to six out of every twenty-four (ten to midnight, one to five), and instituted a virtual slavery of work in both Solitary orders. Many longed for a return to Solitary cabins in the forest. The most disgruntled walked out of Zion. Two of them, Alexander Mack and Johann Conrad Riesmann, headed west, perhaps to explore possible sites for a mystic colony of their own.[6] Father Freidsam kept out of the internecine squabble, but nursed a growing suspicion of the Eckerlings.

Prior Onesimus fell ill (or feigned illness) in March 1742, about a month after the Ephrata delegation stalked out of the third synod and gave up the Zinzendorf dream for good. What the illness was we do not know, but there is some reason to suppose that it might have been psychosomatic. After all, Onesimus had sat at the right hand of the count, had represented himself as the high priest of Ephrata, and had probably divulged too much to Zinzendorf both orally and in letters. When dreams of union were shattered by the count's tempestuous temper and presumption, it was a serious defeat for the prior.

Samuel Eckerling, less provocative and dictatorial than his brother Israel, took the prior's place for about three months. That settled nothing, and monkish squabbles multiplied. Then when Onesimus was ready to resume his duties as prior, Beissel supervised an election in the Brotherhood and found that Israel lacked a majority. Thereupon Beissel, dreading the possibility of anarchy, claimed two votes for himself and swung the election back to Israel.

There is little evidence that the prior now took stock of himself and his position in the community, as he might well have done, but he did spend a good deal of time writing. His brothers were steadily employed at this time in copying and editing the prior's work. Some of the results were read at dreary length when the prior tired of preaching. Like Emanuel's sermons, his own were frequent and interminable. Many begged relief from them. The unsympathetic *Chronicon* claims that "many cried unto God for release from this spiritual tyranny" and also notes that Israel's writings were "confused and unclear."[7] Few of them have survived to give us clues to the mind of this remarkable man.

Jealousy and mutual distrust had already developed between the Sisterhood and the Brotherhood. Hardly several months had passed since the dedication of Peniel when the two orders, to all intents and purposes, closed their doors to each other. Then each began to hold its religious services independent of the other, and indeed the secular congregation itself followed suit.

The matter of the ownership of the communal lands was probably another cause for suspicious whispers at this time. What happened in this matter is clouded today, though it does appear evident that the Zion inner circle made efforts to assure its control of the cloister's lands. Even though Thomas Penn earlier granted proprietary permission to Beissel and his associates to occupy and live on them, proprietary agents had soon thereafter sold the lands to outsiders. Beissel had to send deputies to Philadelphia to urge the authorities to withhold the land titles. Then, on what grounds we do not know, Jan Meyle evidently took out a patent for the 180 acres of the commune in 1737.[8] Two years later he and his wife sold the title to Israel, Samuel, and Emanuel Eckerling, Jacob Gast, and Peter Miller, a transaction that was witnessed by Heinrich

Hagemann and Conrad Weiser. The intention, obviously, was to safeguard the property for the commune as a whole under the auspices of the Brotherhood's inner core. Some believe that they kept the transaction a secret, even from Beissel himself. This is difficult to believe, but the fact remains that Father Friedsam had nothing to do with it, and if he knew about it he deliberately ignored it.

Prior Onesimus took the matter into his own capable but over-eager hands. Discovering that the Meyle transaction was invalid, he petitioned the proprietors, who in turn granted, in his name, about 240 acres in trust for the Zionitic Brotherhood. This occurred in May 1741, apparently with the knowledge of the Brotherhood's inner circle. The new transaction also seems to have been hidden from Beissel.

Meanwhile, the Eckerling circle lost no time in reconstituting the economy of Ephrata. An intensive agricultural effort extended the production of wheat, flax for oil and linen, millet for hay and seed, pasturage for livestock, hemp for fiber making. By late 1741 water rights on the south side of the Cocalico were obtained to power additional mill works. The community had had its own gristmill since 1736, but now, under the driving direction of the prior, yet another gristmill was constructed, along with a sawmill, a linseed oil mill, a fulling mill for cloth preparation, and a paper mill, the latter the fourth such in Pennsylvania and the seventh in the colonies.[9]

What resulted was an entirely new kind of industrial and market-oriented commune under extreme pressure to produce, very different from anything visualized by Conrad Beissel. Shortly the markets for Ephrata produce extended to Philadelphia and Wilmington, and a substantial trading system, with outside agents, developed. Ephrata products became known for their excellence, and the community's treasury, now discreetly removed from Beissel's control, grew fat. No longer did the Solitary need to depend on voluntary contributions of the Householders. Ephrata was becoming an economic force to be reckoned with.

Father Friedsam, who did not understand these things and did not wish to try, nevertheless began to observe that a significant change had taken place. He sincerely believed that a life of intentional poverty was the only way to holiness. To his way of thinking, money and property and trade were loaded with danger and evil, even if their benefits were shared on a communal basis. What did it profit a society, a communion, to grow financially strong and rich if in the process its spirit and soul are lost?

He must have felt painfully lonely as the tide shifted in a different direction. There was no one he could really confide in now that his most faithful disciple, Michael Wohlfahrt, had died.[10] Brother Agonius had been upset even by the building of large common houses and chapels, and he would have been aghast at the new regime. Without that Jeremiah of the province, Beissel's Ephrata could never be quite the same.

But the work of the spirit was not altogether cast aside. The year of the Christmas comet, 1743, marked the publication of Christopher Sauer's German Bible, and Ephrata contributed a great deal of work to it. Except for John Eliot's Algonquian translation, issued in 1663, the Sauer Bible was the first non-English edition published in the colonies. Johannes Hildebrand and Jacob Gast, and probably Peter Miller and two of the Eckerlings, assisted in the monumental task.[11] For the most part the excellent paper it was printed on was manufactured in Ephrata's new paper mill. However, Sauer flew directly in the face of British authority, which reserved the right to produce a Bible to the king's printer or the universities of Oxford and Cambridge. The arch-Separatist was lucky; the government did not interfere.

But Sauer did encounter difficulties with the German population of the province. Most of the sectarians and separatists wanted a Berleburg Bible translation, whereas, probably with sales in view, Sauer duplicated the thirty-fourth edition of the Halle Bible in the Luther translation. As a conciliatory gesture to the sectarians, he did insert an appendix to the Apocrypha according to the latest Berleburg version, a "Brief Compend" that he and Johannes Hildebrand may have authored. As to the "church people," Heinrich Melchior Muhlenberg, recently sent out by Halle to bring order to the Lutheran establishment in America, denounced the Sauer edition from his pulpit at Trappe (in what is now Montgomery County). After all, Muhlenberg was prepared to furnish a plentiful supply of Halle Bibles cheaply as part of his assignment, and these were unsullied by the unorthodoxy of any incorrigible Separatist.[12]

The Sauer production required fifteen months of effort and resulted in a massive quarto of 1,267 pages. But the 1200 copies were not sold out for nearly twenty years, five years after Sauer's death. Today any copy that comes on the market sells at a high premium, but, thanks to the help of Ephrata, Sauer was able to advertize that "for the poor and needy there is no price."

During the first half of the 1740s, the Brotherhood of Zion grew in riches and influence, thanks in large measure to the enslaving work ethic imposed by Israel Eckerling as well as to his considerable talents in management. It was Prior Onesimus who conceived the beautifully balanced economy of productive mills and workshops combined with a diversified agriculture in tandem with a profitable marketing system. That he persisted successfully in these ventures against considerable odds, some of his own making, was an achievement of some genius.

One of the odds against his scheme for economic development resulted from the Householders' discontinuance of their tithing to the Solitary orders because the tithes were now being used as investment capital for developing industry and trade. The Householders, of course, had their own farm economies to nurture. As long as their tithes went toward support of the commune's religious objectives and charitable work, the Householders were more than generous. But they did not want their hard-earned tithing tarnished by materialistic investment and profit.

The prior must have been shocked by the action of the Householders. His mind then became fixed on developing his own purely temporal and self-sufficient economy. This required the forced coordination of the total economic affairs of both Solitary orders, for which the help of the Sisterhood was indispensable. Onesimus then secretly won over the allegiance of Prioress Maria Eicher. The total effect of what one might call an economic dictatorship has been summed up thus: "So there was now instituted into the commune a worldly economy for the sustenance of the natural life which represented a ducal court-economy wherein Brethren and Sisters became servants. Thus much primitive simplicity was lost and in its stead a wide outlook into the world came, for the Brethren whose intelligences had been widened by conversion set up several mechanical trades which brought in profits so that in a short while the treasury which was no longer in Beissel's hands became so rich that money came to be loaned."[13]

At full tide, then, Ephrata may have been the single most comprehensive economic-industrial system in the colonies prior

to the Revolution. With quite limited land available for agriculture, cultivation was simply intensified, livestock was introduced, the entire property was ringed with fruit trees, and
a vineyard was set out on the hillside. But it was the mills
that made the difference.[14] Of these the gristmills and paper
mill were especially profitable. A large share of the writing and
printing papers used in colonial Pennsylvania was Ephrata-
made, and the paper mill also produced the only high-grade
cardboard in the colonies. A large-scale tannery produced superb leathers that in turn supplied an extensive shoemaking
enterprise and one of the largest colonial bookbinderies. The
fulling mill prepared materials for the "cloth house" (still standing), where various textiles were woven and prepared. The
sawmill processed logs not only for Ephrata's building needs
but also for a large regional market. The oil mill processed
flax seed for conversion into oils to make much of the printers' ink used in the province.[15]

The Sisters were soon thoroughly enmeshed in the economic
scheme of things. They prepared garden and farm produce,
cloth and cloth products, managed the free school except for
the older boys, made sulphur matches and wax tapers and
household remedies, illuminated manuscripts and music, carried out the works of charity, and performed many other functions. Some were even assigned to the heavy work in the mills.
A new and demanding division of labor increased the tempo
of their lives to just this side of the breaking point.

So too with the Brothers. They were organized into specialized cadres that worked fixed, long hours at hard tasks under
the supervision of watchful, hard-driving foremen. Gradually,
too, outside hired help was introduced to the production lines,
and special training was set up in the various mechanical trades.
There was little time or energy left for nursing religious experience and mystical speculation. The "saints" were turned
into work slaves as the harsh, Puritanic work ethic, which soon
lost its "voluntary" character, took over.

One of the more offensive aspects of this new regime was
the external trade system developed by the Eckerling group.
The shrewd prior soon began to buy grain at low harvest-season
prices and store it in the Ephrata granaries. Then when flour
prices soared in periods of short supply, he had the flour milled
and sold it in the Philadelphia market at high prices. Doubtless the Philadelphia merchants did the same, but in a society

whose life was based on charity to the poor and on the vow of voluntary poverty, this seemed like usury of the worst kind.

To move the mounting stores of Ephrata produce, the Eckerlings procured horses and wagons, another innovation. Three teams were almost constantly on the road between Ephrata and the seaboard. Heretofore, Ephrata had moved solely on human feet, and indeed Beissel and others rejected "animal slavery" as well as human slavery on religious grounds. Virtually all the work of the commune until now had been performed by human backs and muscles.

On their own authority, the Eckerlings also contracted with agents in Philadelphia and elsewhere to handle the purchase and sale of Ephrata materials and products. And they chose the agents shrewdly: among them were John Wister (Johannes Wüster), a prominent merchant of Philadelphia and Germantown; the young Christopher Marshall, who in later years became a close friend of Peter Miller and the ambivalent, conservative Quaker diarist of the Revolution; and Wilhelm Jung, a sharp Philadelphia factor whose relations with Ephrata in time became badly tarnished. Of course, like the hired hands in the mills, these men were not chosen for their consonance with Ephrata ideals (Marshall may have been something of an exception). At any rate, to the Beisselians the institution of agents appeared to be an abrogation of Ephrata's functional rationale.

Future events would prove that the Eckerling ambition was too heady and all-encompassing; it quite undervalued the psychic power of the spiritual forces that, after all, formed the foundation on which the brothers built. The tide began to shift against the Eckerlings as a result of a scheme they conceived for incorporating the Householders fully into the communal economy. The principal instrument for accomplishing this was the building of Hebron.[16] (As events turned out, this building became the still-standing *Schwestersaal* or "Saron" of the Sisterhood.)

The name Hebron refers to the area in ancient Israel regarded as the common tomb of the Patriarchs. Abraham was buried near Hebron. Generations later, David was crowned King of Judah there, and to his court came representatives of the northern tribes, leading to the formation of an enlarged kingdom with its new capital at Jerusalem. Perhaps Ephrata too saw in its Hebron the emergence from a tribe to a kingdom. To Ephrata it also symbolized the ending of conjugal attachments.

The Hebron scheme was a thinly disguised plot of the Eckerlings to lure the Householders into the celibate commune in order to acquire control of their economic resources. The farms and other property of the Householders were to become communal property, which would more than make up for the loss of their tithes. As an added attraction, the plan proposed that those who accepted it would be granted complete security and relief from farmhold responsibilities, and older members would be absolved from all labor. Actually, if the little economic kingdom of Zion was to continue to grow, use of the property of the Householders now seemed a necessity. The increase of raw materials from these holdings might double or treble the output of the mills and shops—and who knew how far the profit margin could climb?

At first Father Friedsam went along with the plan enthusiastically. He exercised a commanding influence over the "third order" and may have seen in Hebron a further fulfillment of his ministry. He would have welcomed the extension of the blessed state of propertyless celibacy. Moreover, with an underdeveloped sense of property and family ties, it is unlikely that he could have foreseen the problems growing out of the experiment. Separation of man and wife to take up the Solitary state was not uncommon among Householders; the step had been taken recently, for example, by Rudolph Nägele, Ludwig Höcker, and the community's building foreman, Sigmund Landert, and their wives. In Beissel's view, Hebron simply made the process more encompassing, and the presence of his faithful devotees in the third order might help to modify the empire building of the Eckerlings.

The dimensions and architectural character of Hebron were again developed in accord with theosophic and Rosicrucian symbolism. The building was ready for occupancy by Christmas 1743, when the second brilliant and provocative comet appeared in the heavens. The building was situated immediately adjacent and at right angles to Peniel, and the two structures constituted a mystic harmony. It was a large structure, seventy by thirty feet, and was carefully divided into two parts so that the men in one part could not communicate with the matrons in the other. The tiny cells, with doors only five feet high and twenty inches wide, were clustered around common rooms on each floor. They were equipped with narrow short wood benches for sleeping, to enforce the "mortification of the flesh." A fat man or woman would simply have to reduce to negotiate them.

The impressive ritual dedication of Hebron was followed by rebaptism in the frigid waters of the Cocalico. More important for Ephrata's future was the distribution of letters of divorce to the new occupants. These had been drafted by Prior Onesimus and signed by the housefathers and matrons. From that extralegal action all kinds of complications ensued. Civil authorities began to investigate, urged on by Lancaster County neighbors who began to see Ephrata emerging as an economic monopoly in their midst. The mass divorce procedure, without the slightest obeisance to constituted public authority, was outrageously presumptuous, to their way of thinking.

Conrad Weiser evidently felt the same way. It is likely that even before the building of Hebron he was restive with both the Eckerling work ethic and Beissel's seemingly messianic pretensions. He was certainly suspicious of the latter's free access to the house of the Spiritual Virgins, and he played a questionable role in the so-called Anna Eicher affair, which caused great embarrassment to Father Friedsam.[17]

The story goes that Anna's mind became disoriented by a more than spiritual affection for Beissel and perhaps by jealousy over his appointment of her sister, whom she came to dislike intensely, as prioress of Kedar. At any rate, Anna suddenly asked Beissel to marry her. When he refused, and then again refused to let her bear his name without marriage, she went to Weiser and accused Conrad of infanticide, alleging that she herself had given birth to the Beissel-sired victim. Weiser promptly sent the astounding information to the governor and apparently was about to institute charges when several Brothers convinced him that the charges were false. But the wheels of justice had already been set in motion, and the charge was aired in a formal hearing. Finally, Anna herself realized that she was trapped in her own lie and withdrew the "confession." Beissel was completely vindicated.

Over the years Anna had become increasingly cold and austere as her sister Maria became gentler and more saintly (though not without designs of her own). Anna suffered frequent temper tantrums and at one time beat Maria unmercifully. Re-

jected by Beissel, she had tried to ruin him. Now all was gone
from her life; the whole community turned against her and she seemed to hover on the edge of madness. Finally in 1748 she agreed to marry a man named Musselman, but just after the vows were completed she suddenly died—perhaps of a broken heart.

As for Weiser, he must have been sorry for his role in the tawdry affair. Was he also sorry for proceeding against the Hebron divorces? When the case finally did come up, he withdrew himself from any part in the proceedings. The case was dropped, but Conrad Weiser had had enough of Ephrata.

Beissel had circulated an acerbic letter of Weiser's calling for a thorough reformation of Ephrata, but others took no notice of it, "for," says the *Chronicon,* perhaps unfairly, "every one knew that it had been written during temptation."[18] Then in September 1743 Weiser addressed a bitterly worded letter of resignation from Ephrata to "Worthy and Dear Friends and Brethren." The adjectives were clearly meant sarcastically, perhaps the nouns, too.

Some historians have interpreted Weiser's break with Ephrata as a strong personal reaction against Beissel, but the evidence would seem to indicate that he was even more deeply perturbed by the pretensions of the Eckerlings and the Zionitic Brotherhood. The letter makes no direct mention of Beissel, but its principal charges reveal an Ephrata that, under the Eckerling influence, had altered its course so drastically that Weiser's spiritual attachment to it was crushed:

> It cannot be denied at Ephrata that I and several
> other members of the community, partly gone to
> their rest, partly still living, were compelled to pro-
> test for a considerable time against the domination
> of conscience, the suppression of innocent minds,
> against the prevailing pomp and luxury, both in dress
> and magnificent buildings; but we achieved about as
> much as nothing; on the contrary, in spite of all pro-
> tests, this practice was still more eagerly continued,
> and following the manner of the world, the attempt
> was made to cover such pride and luxury with the
> man of God. It was most zealously defended. . . .
> Whole assemblies were held in honor of the loath-
> some idolatry, while the leaders have indulged in

the most fulsome self-praise by all kinds of fictitious stories.

For these and other reasons, . . . I take leave of your young but already decrepit sect, and I desire henceforth to be treated as a stranger, especially by you, the presiding officers (superintendents). . . . You will no doubt know how to instruct, as usual, the other, partly innocent, minds, as to what they have to consider me. I make a distinction between them and you, and hope the time will come when they shall be liberated from their physical and spiritual bondage, as also from the thraldom of conscience, under which they are groaning. I protest once more against you, the overseers, who feed yourselves and do not spare the flock, but scatter and devour them.[19]

The reference to pomp and luxury refers to another innovation of Prior Onesimus. Puffed up with his own increase in power at the expense of Beissel, the prior ordered new ceremonial and ritual robes for himself and Prioress Maria. They made a lavish display — rich, colorful, gaudy, extraordinarily presumptuous. The robes were patterned after those of the high priest in the Book of Exodus, complete with jeweled breastplate and tinkling bells at the hem. Prior and prioress now reveled in ecclesiastical pomp and show such as never before graced a Protestant establishment.[20]

Meanwhile, the Hebron plot was coming apart; it lasted for less than a year. It soon became apparent that many of the newly celibate Hebronites were not about to give up their landed estates. Perhaps they had not clearly understood the implications of the scheme. At any rate, regardless of how much the prior preached against the sin of Ananias and Sapphira (who had withheld part of their property from the "common goods" of the first church at Jerusalem), the property assets of the Brotherhood did not increase as expected. Moreover, parental feelings soon reasserted themselves in Hebron, and the women openly longed for the children they left at home to struggle with the farm. It is astonishing that the Eckerlings had failed to foresee this problem and had not provided for the care of minors. When finally the whole matter was aired with Beissel, he showed his complete independence of Zion by unhesitatingly advising each couple to return to their former condition.

It was, of course, a bitter pill for the prior. In the first months of the Hebron experiment, Beissel, still yearning for the peace of solitude and perhaps sensing a turning of the tide, asked to be relieved from leadership responsibilities in Hebron. The prior then proposed his own name as *Vorsteher* there and thought he had won the day. He was then principal overseer of the entire community. But when Hebron fell apart, he quickly had to settle the claims of the Householders who wanted their contributions to the common assets returned. It was another sharp blow to the prior's ambitions.

Hebron was being deserted by November 1744. A convocation of all orders was then called, and the prior's letters of divorce were ceremoniously burned in the angle formed by Hebron and Peniel. Hebron was turned over to the widows and poor of the community, and Beissel organized the women into an Order of Holy Matrons and Virgins. In mid-1745 they were moved into Kedar, for the Sisterhood, newly reorganized as the Order of the Roses of Saron, had moved into what had been Hebron and renamed it after their own order.

In January 1744, whether because of the untidy Anna Eicher affair or from worry over the increasing materialism of Zion and the Hebron plot, Beissel became ill, or perhaps pretended illness. It may have been psychosomatic, as in the case of Onesimus nearly two years before. During the two months of his illness, the Eckerlings usurped the government of the commune. They even prepared a tombstone for Beissel, who, regardless of any wishful thinking, survived.

In the same January, Sister Berenice (Maria Heidt of Oley) died. Evidently she had never got over her affection for Beissel, and it had been alleged that she died of consumption induced by his rejection of her. Later in the year, shortly after Weiser's resignation, the subprioress, Sister Marcella, known to the world as Frau Christopher Sauer, decided to return to her husband after about fourteen years of voluntary celibacy. It is said that she was persuaded to do so by Dr. George de Benneville, founder of Universalism in America, who was preaching in Lancaster County at the time.[21]

Meanwhile, Beissel continued his outward support of the prior; at least the antagonisms between them were kept hidden from public view. But Beissel was now leading a very retired existence. On hindsight there is some reason to believe that he was simply giving the prior enough rope to hang himself. He even gave up his own cabin to Onesimus and moved into Peniel. Father Friedsam became merely a humble Brother again. Perhaps subconsciously to engender sympathy for his reduced state, he moved from place to place, four times all told, and always in humbling circumstances. To the prior and his adherents, with their pomp and power, the contrast with simple Brother Conrad was all too obvious; his humiliation by the new order was now complete.

Too complete. Indeed, it may have been a part of Beissel's grand strategy to reassert the authority of the spirit. It must have been a shock to the Eckerlings to watch the humbled peasant reassert his authority as spiritual director. Finally, in an all-night session with the Brothers of Zion, he was able to demote the prior to assistant overseer in Peniel and to raise his brother Emanuel to overseer in Zion. "The war for the cap," as it came to be known, was now out in the open.

And everyone knew it. Sensing the mounting resentment against his ambition, the erstwhile prior decided that now was not the time to force the issue; instead he would cool it off by going on a missionizing pilgrimage. Beissel gave his consent, and to accompany Onesimus he appointed his brother Samuel as physician and astrologer for the party, Alexander Mack, Jr., to represent the secular congregation and German Baptists generally, and Peter Miller to serve as interpreter and principal theologian.

Beginning on September 12, 1744, it was the longest and most varied pilgrimage in Ephrata's history. The first phase of the journey brought them to the Seventh Day Baptists at Nantmill and Coventry in Chester County; then they crossed the Schuylkill to the Skippack and headed south to Germantown, where they visited those two ancient mystics of the Wissahickon, Conrad Matthäi and Gottfried Seelig. They sojourned briefly with agent Wilhelm Jung in Philadelphia, then proceeded upcountry across the Delaware to Amwell, where the old Ephrata spirit had atrophied. From there they walked across the pine barrens of New Jersey to Barnegat Bay, where a few Sabbatarians from Connecticut and Rhode Island had recently settled, then crossed the bay to the settlement of a cluster of New England sectarians known as Rogerenes after a "Quaker Baptist" from Rhode Island. And they sought out the aged hermit John Lovell, "an old Pythagorean" who lived for years without human contact.

At New Brunswick the party boarded a sailing vessel for New England, landing at Black Point, Connecticut, some six miles from New London. On their single-file procession to a Rogerene congregation at a place still called Quaker Hill, their cowled, bearded, monkish appearance caused a sensation. England and Spain were then engaged in the so-called War of Jenkins' Ear, and the Ephrathites were soon arrested as Jesuit agents spying for Spain. Through the efforts of local Rogerenes they were soon released, but people kept following them everywhere. Their revival meetings were crowded and popular, for the New Light movement launched by the great revivalist George Whitefield, who once was associated with Zinzendorf and in a way set the stage for the Wesleys and Methodism, was now at its height.

Evidently their invasion of New England was a success (though it left no permanent mark), for a huge assembly gathered for their departure for New York. There they were again arrested as Jesuit spies in the pay of Spain, but a local justice came to their rescue. At last they found haven again at Wilhelm Jung's house in Philadelphia, and from there they walked the eighty-six miles to Ephrata. When they returned, they discovered that Beissel had moved into the very citadel of Zion.[22]

On the last day of 1744 Beissel instructed Israel Eckerling to move back to Zion from Peniel and to assume again the position of *Vorsteher* in the Brotherhood. If his brother Emanuel was diappointed in this, at least Israel was prior again—or was he? There is a significant difference between being overseer and being prior, and Beissel was not about to clarify the matter. This time Israel was overseer on Beissel's terms, not his own. Even that was not to continue for long.

Israel chafed under the new arrangement and steeled himself to avoid the disaster that seemed to threaten his grand ambitions. No bumbling peasant-saint was going to be allowed to dismantle the thriving economic empire that he had created out of virtually nothing. There was still hope. The Brothers still did his bidding, and Conrad Beissel, for all his spiritual pride, was merely an ordinary Brother and cell-mate. Now if only the Sisters could be brought out of their beloved independence and into league with Zion, Beissel's *magia* could still be vanquished, or at least brought to heel. Prioress Maria actually seemed to be leaning in that direction. She cooperated efficiently on economic matters; she had accepted the priestly robes with Onesimus, and there were probably some secret schemes between them. But now it was a matter of all or nothing. In the end, the issue might be decided by the Sisterhood.

But Beissel thought the same thoughts and moved more quickly. He may have convinced Maria of the danger of Zion taking control over her Order; at any rate, when the issue became clear, she opted for Beissel. Their first order of business was the thorough reorganization and reorientation of the Sisterhood, partly to broaden the range of its capabilities, partly to secure it against the designs of the Eckerlings. In the process the Order changed its image from that of a cold, celestial virginity to one of warm devotion and love. No longer the Spiritual Virgins but now the Roses of Saron, as in "the song of songs which is Solomon's":

> I am the rose of Sharon, and the lily of the valleys.
> As the lily among thorns, so is my love among the
>   daughters.
> As the apple tree among the trees of the wood,
> so is my beloved among the sons.
> I sat down under his shadow with great delight,
> and his fruit was sweet to my taste.
> He brought me to the banqueting house,
> and his banner over me was love.

So the Order of the Roses of Saron (the German dropped the *h*) came into being at the height of Ephrata's greatest internal crisis. The sensuous imagery of the poem will shine through the Sisters' luxuriant *Fraktur* and Ephrata's angelic singing. In the sublimated imagination of the Sisters, Conrad Beissel appeared as "the fair beloved." He was fifty-five years old now, but his unique *magia* must have seemed as young and fair as ever.

The Sisterhood was now organized into "choirs" or "classes" according to work activities. Each choir had its own common room in the remodeled Hebron or Saron, surrounded by the cells of its members. Each was governed by a monitor who ruled without question over not only the work program but also the conduct of its members, and she reported only to the prioress. Maria Eicher continued, after some jostling, not only

as prioress but also as "Mother" to the order. Time schedules,
the conduct of "masses" (such is the term used in the diary of
the Order), garb, novitiate procedures, and activity assignments
were all carefully rearranged and newly regulated. Rules governing expulsion, penance, and reentry were clarified. The complete "Rule of Discipline" was put into writing in ornate Gothic
Fraktur in a manuscript entitled *Die Rose,* and this with later
additions and records became the *Schwester Chronicon,* the
Sisters' diary.[23]

Only one man was admitted to their meals, their secret sessions and rituals, and their confidence; that of course was Conrad Beissel. He was now openly and frankly regarded as their
spiritual father and guide. Whatever hopes Onesimus entertained in this context were thoroughly dashed.

By July 22, 1745, Beissel was prepared for the inevitable climax and moved out of his cell in Zion into a solitary cabin,
alleging that Onesimus had "seized his person." No doubt
both Householders and the Sisters stood firmly behind him.
Later the same month the Eckerling fortress of Zion itself was
breached when Peter Miller openly challenged Onesimus's treatment of Beissel. After being rudely repulsed, Miller found another accomplice, Israel's own youngest brother, Gabriel. Then
Peter and Gabriel accompanied Beissel to a meeting with the
Housefathers, at which a host of charges against the prior were
aired. Soon four of the Brothers confronted the prior with the
flat announcement that they could no longer in conscience serve
him or be subject to his directions.

The dike suddenly began to crumble, and Onesimus was
aghast that his own brother and the scholarly Miller, who had
been his most trusted co-worker, formed the wedge of rebellion. The prior's attempt at temporizing did not help; soon
the word was out, and the revolt spread. After five years of
work slavery and spiritual tyranny under the hard-driving
Onesimus and of deep-seated resentment against an ever more
consuming materialism, many believed that the day of libera-
tion was at hand.

On the first Sabbath in August even the prior's preaching
was interrupted, first by young Gabriel, then by Jacob Gast
and Heinrich Hagemann, both stalwarts of the community since
its beginning. Soon more of the Brothers renounced their obedience, and a decision was made to discontinue the prior's
night-watch ceremonies. Onesimus had now lost his control

over Zion. Finally, on August 7, at a meeting of the rebel Brothers, Beissel temporarily appointed Gabriel as Israel's successor and Peter Miller and Jacob Gast as his deputies.

The following weeks were even more humiliating for Israel Eckerling. As his little empire began to crumble, it is said that he took to drink and on one occasion appeared at supper in Zion barely able to navigate. Beissel was there at the time and was sorely grieved by the sight, perhaps even remorseful. But Onesimus did not give up easily. He made harried efforts to bribe Mother Maria with forty pounds sterling that he took from Zion's treasury. Maria accepted the money, but her intercession with Beissel was unavailing. Another effort to bribe a fellow Brother miscarried. Shock after shock led him into pronouncing dark prophecies and judgments about Ephrata to any who would listen, but many now shunned or snubbed him. Finally, before his very eyes the Brothers built a bonfire and publicly burned what writings of his they could collect. Several days later the Sisters, finding additional copies in their own collections, followed suit. Virtually all his writings, accounts, and records went up in smoke.[24]

On August 11 the whole community held a "reformation meeting." Israel and those who still adhered to him were put under the ban, thereby cutting them off from any internal communication with the majority. A week later Israel's "priestly office" was formally taken from him. As an ordinary Brother under the ban, he was seized with sickness, grief, and repentance and pleaded for a lifting of the ban. The others held council with Beissel and, perhaps touched by Israel's despair, decided that he should leave the Order for a time and manage the fulling mill. After Zion was reorganized he could either return to the Brotherhood or they would build a cabin for him and provide for his care the rest of his life. In his misery he promptly accepted the offer, but on the very next day his brother Samuel and he decided to flee to the outermost edge of the frontier.

Alexander Mack, Jr., who once before left Ephrata only to return, joined the two Eckerling brothers when on September 4 they began a four-hundred mile trek to the New River in far southwestern Virginia. Young Mack provided the specific objective of their journey—the cabin of his father's cousin, Wilhelm Mack, on the upper reaches of the river.[25] The area around the cabin, though it had been recently penetrated by a few white settlers, was still predominantly Indian country.[26]

Wild rumors about the departure of Mack and the two Eckerlings quickly spread throughout Pennsylvania German land — that they had deserted to the Moravians to find wives, that Ephrata was in turmoil, even that it had been sold. Christopher Sauer, feeling forgiveness now that his wife had returned to him, scotched the rumors in his German newspaper, ending with the wry remark: "In the future the brethren will be more careful first to consult the father, as all human societies must depend upon their leader, otherwise they cannot endure."[27]

Gabriel Eckerling was promoted from overseer in Zion to prior, but he did not fare much better than his brother. He too was overweeningly ambitious and aggressive and tried to force "reforms" on Zion without consulting either his peers or Beissel. The Brothers had had enough of that, and on December 5 he was deposed and assigned to the widows and poor in Kedar. Ten days later, for windy preachments about celibacy to the Housefathers, which ruffled the feathers of the matrons, Emanuel Eckerling lost his priestly standing and was moved to the Berghaus, where he was soon joined by Gabriel. One day near the end of the year, before dawn, Emanuel fled Ephrata for a hermitage six miles to the northeast at the base of a mountain in the area called Zoar. Thereafter, to all intents and purposes, Brother Elimelech plays no part in the Ephrata story.[28]

For a brief while Gabriel was the only Eckerling left in Ephrata. But in the following winter months his brother Samuel and Alexander Mack journeyed east again to buy supplies and recruit for their frontier hermitage, which they called the House of David to contrast with Ephrata, which they labeled the House of Saul. The two visited Ephrata again, and Gabriel, having spent a couple of months in bitterness, joined them on the long, treacherous, and cold trek back to the far frontier. So did Jacob Höhnly, who seemed to make a practice of leaving and rejoining the Brotherhood; this was his fifth departure.

Recruits were few and slow to come to the tiny settlement on the New River, formally named Mahanaim after the place where the angels appeared to Jacob after he had escaped the thralldom of Laban (Genesis 32).[29] Here Israel seems to have spent much of his time in esoteric studies and in writing vilifying letters back to Ephrata. Samuel took up the practice of medicine and pharmacy, such as it was in those days on the rough frontier. His outreach to the scattered settlements on the frontier and his practical mind made him the logical choice for the business management of the Mahanaim settlement. Shortly he filed a claim for nine hundred acres of land in the area. Gabriel seems to have provided the brothers' principal economic support by hunting and trapping and probably trading with the Indians, for the furs they sent east brought a high price. But from what little evidence has come down to us, all three brothers for some time secretly longed to return to Ephrata.

As to Alexander Mack, his sensitive, theosophic mind may not have been well adjusted to the rigors of the frontier, but more important, he and Israel Eckerling came to a parting of the ways. In 1748 Alexander wrote his brother Valentin that "Brother Eckerling has not understood me rightly." He left Mahanaim for good that year, and with him went the peripatetic Höhnly. Alexander then returned to Germantown, where he soon married Elizabeth Nice. There he took up his old family relationship with the Dunkers and became an elder among them, though he continued to have an arm's-length association with Ephrata.

In many respects Mahanaim, despite the Eckerlings' self-imposed and acrimonious exile, was but an extension of Ephrata to the far frontier, combining the spiritual form and purpose implicit in the Ephrata society as a religious hermitage with the Eckerling genius for economic development. Evidently the three brothers continued to think of themselves as Ephrathites; Israel, for one, continued to use his Ephrata brotherhood name of Onesimus. Correspondence continued regularly with Ephrata itself, and of course the brothers continued to visit Ephrata on most of their trips to markets back east, where they were usually received in a friendly fashion.

The Eckerling years on the distant Allegheny frontier are thus an integral part of the Ephrata story. We shall meet the brothers again in chapter 10, when Israel and Gabriel suffer a frightful fate in the French and Indian War years. Even after that, Samuel will play a determining role in the destiny of Ephrata. Before those events transpire, however, Ephrata is reformed on Beisselian principles in spite of continued internal tensions, and for all too brief a time it will experience its finest cultural blossoming. Then "the world" moves in again with events, over which it has no control, that begin to smother its uncommon aspiration.

Recovery of Eden

THE TROUBLED RETURN TO A

GOLDEN AGE, 1745–1751

NLY time could heal the deeper wounds incurred
by Ephrata's internal revolution, and in a few
individual cases these festered for years to come.
Taking their cues from these cases, a good many
students of Ephrata in our century bemoan the
expulsion of the Eckerlings and Beissel's rejection of their
economic opportunism. Assuming as it does that economic development is the only true test of community vitality and that
materialism is the only way to measure it, their conclusion that
the Eckerling departure led to the tragic decay of the community is a serious misreading of Ephrata's underlying purpose.
And for that matter, attitudes in young America did begin to
change in midcentury: the opening of the frontier emphasized
individualism at the expense of community and do-it-yourself
free enterprise at the expense of the older and gentler forms
of agrarian cooperation. Ben Franklin's "Way to Wealth" caught
the spirit of the time—and we have yet to outlive it.[1]

But Ephrata did *not* begin to decline after the Eckerling regime was dismantled. Spiritually and culturally it blossomed
as never before. In those respects the revolution against economic opportunism must be regarded as a stunning success.
Tensions and self-imposed poverty remained, of course, but
as an aspiring local microcosm Ephrata attained its richest maturity and gained world fame *after* its internal revolution.

Even in the year of her greatest internal trauma (1745), Ephrata's writers and press were busier than ever before. During
most of the Eckerling regime, very little literature or music was
produced, for the Solitary were daily worn out by the work
schedules. Before the expulsion, a few leaflets and broadsides

from the pen of Prior Onesimus (Israel Eckerling) had been issued, but most copies seem to have perished in the August auto-da-fé. The comet of 1743 produced a spate of mystical and apocalyptic hymn-poems; what may have been the first issue from the Ephrata press, Beissel's lyrical *Cometen-Buch,* appeared in 1745 and reflected the mystical view that the comet of 1743 was a harbinger of the New Jerusalem.[2]

Ephrata's remarkable printing establishment may have been set up as early as 1743 during the Eckerling regime, although the circumstances are unclear and undocumented. Tradition has it that Jacob Gast was responsible for obtaining the press and type from Germany. Apparently, during the frenetic publishing activity of the next several years, the printery obtained a second and larger press to meet the demand. Ephrata could now claim the only complete printing, binding, and publishing establishment in America. Best of all, the Brotherhood included men well experienced in book editing and production — Johannes Hildebrand, Peter Miller, Jacob Gast, and Samuel Eckerling, who before his departure seems to have been the first foreman of the printery — not to mention writers and poets. Ephrata's printing and publishing establishment played a central role in the life of the commune throughout its subsequent history. Beissel and the core of the Brotherhood regarded it with pride and esteem; some considered it a competitive response to the growing fame of the Sisters' art of *Fraktur.*[3]

Two major works of Conrad Beissel were evidently written in the year 1745, though one did not appear in print for some time to come. One is known as a *Wunderschrift* on the Fall and Restoration of Man and on the separation and reunification of the male and female principle through the operations of celestial wisdom, which Ephrata and the ancients personalized as the Virgin Sophia. When translated by Peter Miller in 1765, its lengthy German title was simplified to *A Dissertation on Man's Fall.*[4] It is often regarded as the most important of Beissel's essays, and it gained wide currency among the mystics of Pennsylvania and abroad.

Beissel's Sophianism also shines through his other major work of 1745, a substantial volume called *Zionitischer Stiffts* (Zionitic Foundations). In it he looks forward to the "heavenly tomorrow" in terms of "Irenic Theodicy" — that is, the serene peace achievable between man and God. Thereby Beissel may have been attempting to reassert his own brand of theoso-

Panoramic view of Ephrata. From left to right: Saron, built in
1743 and remodeled in 1745 for the Order of the Roses of Saron;
the Saal, 1741, with upper floors housing the singing and writing schools; and weaving and cloth house, ca. 1750; Beissel's
cabin, 1748; and the bake house.
Photo by Pennsylvania Historical and Museum Commission,
Harrisburg, Pa.

Travelers and newly arrived immigrants were offered food and lodging in the Almonry (foreground, ca. 1732–33). In the background is the rear of the Saal.
Photo by Pennsylvania Historical and Museum Commission, Harrisburg, Pa.

The interior of Beissel's cabin. The five-plate stove at the far left, dated 1756, was fired from the rear of the kitchen fireplace on the other side of the wall.
Photo by Karl G. Rath for the Pennsylvania Historical and Museum Commission, Harrisburg, Pa.

The Vorsteher's podium in the chapel of the Saal.
Library of Congress

phy in Zion. The principal body of the work is composed of his "Theosophischen Episteln."[5]

Ephrata's internal Sophia cult (if one may use that term) undoubtedly owed its inspiration to Beissel, but its imagery was also deeply rooted in the esoteric mysticism of the Zionitic Brotherhood, even before the departure of the Eckerlings. During his *Wanderjahre,* Beissel had become well acquainted with Sophian imagery through the Society of Philadelphians and particularly the writings of Boehme, Gichtel, and Gottfried Arnold. Other Brothers probably had similar early experiences (Johannes Hildebrand especially). Sophianism as a mystical touchstone, however, dates back to the Gnostics, Neo-Platonism, and the philosophic fringes of pre-Constantine Christianity as a symbol of the Logos and the "hidden wisdom" of the Christ-message.[6] The Sophia symbol can hardly be described in terms of present-day rationalism, for Ephrata and the ancients regarded it as the ultimate supramundane transcendence, beyond the scope of mere mind and reality, as the poetic, affective, psychic "inner light" of the spirit.

Also in the year 1745 the Ephrata press issued the first of its productions for the Mennonites, the *Güldene Aepffel in Silbern Schalen* (Golden Apples in Silver Rind), a substantial religious work published for "a few Mennonite leaders." Hereafter for some years Ephrata, which had been populated in part by dissident Mennonites, became the principal American source of religious literature for the Mennonite community.

The next several years were blessed with a renewal of Ephrata music making. Beissel had taken full charge of it around 1740, which resulted in some problems and skirmishes. Several of the singing Sisters, for example, conspired to steal a lock of their director's hair. They also complained volubly about Beissel's stern discipline and his long and sometimes scathing lectures. Finally Sister Anastasia was delegated to tell him that they would not put up with his scoldings any longer. The parting was short-lived, however. Soon the singing school was opened to Brothers as well as Householders, and music became the principal unifying element of all three orders of the community.

Beissel divided the singers into quintets composed of a soprano, who carried the air or melody, an alto, a female tenor, and two men to sing the upper and lower bass parts. The Sisters were further divided into three choirs. On the occasion of love feasts, the singers were seated alternately up and down the table so that they could sing antiphonally in turns.

Perhaps no choral group in history ever equaled Ephrata's in intensity of training, iron discipline, and devotion to its own special art form. Singing class sessions generally lasted four hours and ended in a spectral midnight procession through the night mists of the meadow prior to the *Nachtmetten*. At the heart of the Ephrata music system was the absolute requisite that those who gave themselves to this art form must be pure in heart and spirit in order to address what was divine and holy in life. The art of singing at Ephrata involved the whole of life, not just the vocal chords and the techniques of tone production. All the technical aspects, which were developed by Beissel, flowed from that purity and wholeness.[7]

To emphasize the sacredness of the occasion, the singers were clothed in white whenever they sang, even in practice sessions. The classes were required to give absolute attention and devotion, and any departure therefrom would evoke long and wrathful lectures from their leader. It is said that Samuel Eckerling decided he would no longer submit to this, but when he left the singing class his influence in the community waned.

Even before engaging in this highly spiritualized exercise, the body itself had to be purified, so that the music could take on its special angelic character. Hence each singer followed a rigorous diet, varying perhaps in accordance with the part sung. Milk, cheese, butter, eggs, beans, even honey were forbidden; the devout singer had to be satisfied with wheat and buckwheat breads and dishes along with the tuberous vegetables and plain clear water. Of course, all carnal thoughts and desires had to be obliterated, and the whole personality had to be spiritually sublimated. Beissel was uncanny at detecting any impurities.

From all accounts, the sound that was thus produced was wondrous and angelic, full of an unforgettable spirituality. The sounds were evidently produced with lips barely parted to enunciate the words and were directed upward so that they seemed to hover over and above the auditor, as if descending from heaven. The selfhood and bravura of our modern vocal arts were altogether lacking; everything was sacrificed to the organ-like serenity of the "sound of heaven," unified and bodiless.

As to the music itself, it represented a system original with Ephrata and never since duplicated, except in a faded way at the Snow Hill cloister in Franklin County (see chapter 14). We know a great deal about the composition of the sacred poems that supplied the text for the hymns and chorales, but we know little about how and by whom the original music was composed. The harmonic system was no doubt the product of the inventive mind of Conrad Beissel. It seems logical to suppose, however, that actual composition may have been the result of some system of organized teamwork. Nevertheless, in its totality, this was Conrad Beissel's music and no other's.

Beissel himself wrote a highly technical explanation of the musical system he used and of the regimen and requirements for singing it. William M. Fahnestock, whose family had for generations been associated with Ephrata and Snow Hill, captured something of the unique nature of the Ephrata music in a piece published in 1835:

> Beissel was a first rate musician and composer. In composing sacred music he took his style from the music of nature, and the whole of it, comprising several large volumes, is founded on the tones of the Aeolian harp; the singing, in a word, is the Aeolian harp harmonized. It is very peculiar in its style and concords, and in its execution. The tones issuing from the choir imitate very soft instrumental music; conveying a softness and devotion almost superhuman to the auditor. Their music is set in four, six, and eight parts. All the parts save the bass are lead and sung exclusively by females, the men being confined to the bass, which is set in two parts, the high and low bass—the latter resembling the deep tones of the organ, and the first, in combination with one of the female parts, is an excellent imitation of the concert horn. The whole is sung on the *falsetto* voice.[8]

Ephrata's curious use of musical notation is described by Sachse:

> The chief peculiarity of the Ephrata music consisted in the fact that the music, although barred, was free, and that the accent of the word ruled, rather than the accent of the bar, the music in every case being subservient to the words. . . . The true musical value of the note, as understood in modern music, was not

thought of; the first and other notes were frequently
lengthened . . . and the emphasized words in the
course of the hymns were also frequently lengthened,
so that we find indiscriminately three, four, five, six,
yes, even seven notes in the bar, which in modern
music would have but four.[9]

The sophisticated and worldly Reverend Jacob Duché, Anglican minister in Philadelphia, son of the mayor, and future chaplain to the Continental Congress, paid a visit to Ephrata in 1771, in the fast-fading years of Ephrata music after Beissel had departed, and even then was quite overcome by its choral singing:

The music had little or no air or melody; but consisted of simple, long notes, combined in the richest harmony. . . . The performers sat with their heads reclined, their countenances solemn and dejected, their faces pale and emaciated from their manner of living, their clothing exceedingly white and quite picturesque, and their music such as thrilled to the very soul. I almost began to think myself in the world of spirits, and the objects before me were ethereal. In short, the impression this scene made upon my mind continued strong for many days, and I believe, will never be wholly obliterated.[10]

Soon after the expulsion of the Eckerlings, the Ephrata printing establishment came into full production and produced its first hymnbook. This was *Das Gesäng der einsamen und verlassenen Turtel-Taube* (The Song of the Solitary and Deserted Turtle-Dove, Namely the Christian Church). It was the first Ephrata hymnal to be printed since the Sauer press issued the *Weyrauchs Hügel* in 1739. Hence we must assume that the art did not prosper during the Eckerling regime. The *Turtel-Taube* however, made up for lost time and exploded out of the heart of Ephrata. It contained only original Ephrata material (the first work of its kind in America). The first edition of 1747 contained 279 hymn-poems, of which Beissel is said to have written 212, and more than half of the poems are not found in the earlier hymnbooks. Later editions were expanded to 375 hymns. Some copies have hand-written music written in the margins; one copy at the Library of Congress has a number of such pages as well as other pages with Ephrata names (signatures?) inscribed on them. What also made the printed *Turtel-Taube* significant was the extensive preface, in which Beissel outlined the harmonic system and the singing discipline and technique that he originated, the earliest American essay on music.[11]

While the printed *Turtel-Taube* was still in production, the Sisterhood, presumably Anastasia and Efigenia in particular, were preparing *Fraktur* manuscript music scores for it.[12] As a rule, however, these were not as lavish and brilliant as those for the *Weyrauchs Hügel,* perhaps because Beissel and the Brothers (who were heavily occupied with the new press) were not now so directly involved.

The totality of Conrad Beissel's musical achievement, coupled with the considerable corpus of his hymn-poetry, is awesome. Quite unschooled in the musical arts (if we discount his learning to play the fiddle as an apprentice in Eberbach), he was able in middle age to develop his own unique, even magical, system of harmony and composition, to perform wonders in training the Ephrata singers, and to compose hundreds, perhaps a thousand, poems and pieces of music for them.[13] All this while carrying out many other difficult duties and writing many published discourses, which Peter Miller estimated at sixty-six. The musicologist Hans T. David remarked that "Beissel's method of composing may be said to have been 'as naive as it was original'." Yet for all its naiveté, the final result was as moving as any choral art in our history. As to his poems, John Joseph Stoudt, after much study, arrived at the firm opinion that "Conrad Beissel's poetry is without doubt the most profound creation in Colonial literature, English or German."[14]

It should be remembered that Ephrata regarded the arts of music, *Fraktur,* poetry, and even printing as all of one piece, not as disparate and unconnected disciplines. Fundamentally, however, it was the Beisselian music that integrated them into a totality of expression. The musical system itself had therefore to be of a fresh, unique order. The spiritual character of Ephrata virtually dictated a naiveté that was consonant with the commune's simplicity and purity.

It is fortunate that at least some faint echo of the Ephrata music has come down to our own times. It cannot, of course, be performed today as it was originally intended, for the peculiar Ephrata psyche, spiritual unity, diet, and intensity of discipline that could produce the "angelic" sound cannot be copied in our time. As a matter of fact, as Hans T. David noted, "The music production of Ephrata ceased about 1762"—as Beissel was entering into his last tortured years on earth—and "no hymns seem to have been preserved that were written at Ephrata after 1766."[15]

Without diminishing Beissel's incredible achievement, one must put it in context. Early Pennsylvania German culture was extraordinarily rich in music and religious poetry. It is estimated that there were more than a hundred German hymn writers active during Pennsylvania's colonial era.[16] The hymn writing and choral music of the Schwenkfelders, for example, began in Europe in the first half of the sixteenth century and continued into the following century in Pennsylvania, as exemplified by Christopher Sauer's edition of their hymns in 1762 and by several huge folio manuscripts.[17] The instrumental and choral music of the Moravians is well remembered even today, and their fine instruments and the organs of David Tannenberg were known for their excellence throughout the colonies.

The renascence of Ephrata music was but one sign of a complete realignment of Ephrata's life-style and spiritual direction after the departure of the Eckerlings and a few of their adherents. That realignment began with a festal day of rededication on September 27, 1745. Many were rebaptized to wash away the baptism of Onesimus; tonsures were freshly cut; and at the love feast the following day Beissel was reinvested with the priestly office and full direction of the community.

Before the Eckerlings left, Israel had ordered a large church bell from Germany inscribed with the vain Latin phrase *Sub Auspicio Viri Venerandi Onesimus Societatis Ephratensis Praepositi* (by the authority of the venerable Prior Onesimus appointed by the society of Ephrata). It was an obvious indication that he thought of himself as superior to and, in effect, replacing Beissel. The bell cost the considerable sum of eighty pounds sterling; when it arrived the council agreed to sustain the loss but angrily demanded that the bell be broken up and buried. Beissel, however, invoked a pardon on it, and it was sold to the Trinity Lutheran Church in Lancaster and later moved to Grace Lutheran. There would be no more such pompous nonsense.

Rooting out all evidences of Eckerling influence resulted in some organizational problems. When Gabriel was deposed as prior of Zion in December 1745, Jacob Gast, then known as Brother Jethro, was designated his successor, but for reasons that are not clear he did not prove to be a successful administrator and lasted in the post only until the following March. Then Peter Miller assumed the priorship, but he too could not cope with the job — or with Beissel, in spite of their intimacy. It brought him to the verge of a nervous breakdown, and in September 1746 he turned back the vestments of priorship to Beissel. The two men quarreled, and that brought on a deep despondency to both until the spat was patched over with a poem that Miller inscribed to Beissel.[18] Meanwhile, Brother Jethro was installed as prior a second time, a load he carried until 1749.

The central problem lay in Zion itself and all that it signified. Zion had been primarily the creation of the Eckerlings, and it had to be forgotten and replaced. The male Solitary were thereupon reconstituted as the Brotherhood of Bethania. The Brotherhood was doubtless named for the Biblical town on the slope of the Mount of Olives where Lazarus and his sisters, Martha and Mary, lived and where Jesus had found peace and rest during the closing days of his life. Conrad Beissel probably hoped to gain the same from Bethania at Ephrata.

Before their departure, the Eckerling brothers planned to build a huge wing onto Zion, which was to contain no less than a hundred cells in addition to community rooms and offices. The whole venture was cut short, of course, but a lot of building material had been collected. It was soon put to good use. After Miller assumed the priorship, Sigmund Landert began erecting a new house for the Brotherhood in the meadow near Saron. The design of the structure differed from the other communal buildings in that the basement and main floors provided a buttressing to the second floor and the attic. But like its predecessors (except the Almonry) it was built entirely of wood, even the flues, with half-timber framing filled in with straw-clay-lime wattle. Consonant with theosophic principles, no iron whatsoever was used.

Materials left over from this undertaking were then used to build a brother-saal or chapel at right angles to the brother-house. The large second-floor room was eventually converted for the use of the classical school, for which Ephrata became

noted, and the enlarged printing establishment seems to have
been housed on the third floor. (The brother-saal, "for some
unexplained reason," as Sachse reports, was demolished around
1837, and the brother-house began to collapse and was razed
about 1910.)[19]

During the transitional period of the later 1740s, problems
continued to arise regarding the internal discipline of the commune. The work slavery system of the Eckerling regime was
a thing of the past, and production activity sagged. More time
was now allotted to prayer, meditation, and, in a few cases,
to conduct unbecoming the devotee. A certain Sister Blandina,
whom Beissel had tried to convert from a life of sin, continued
to ply her trade in the Berghaus, now little used. But when
he read her out of the society, he discovered that other Sisters
also used the Berghaus as a rendezvous with both Brothers and
outsiders. Beissel then promptly ordered the whole structure
razed to the very foundation stones—which some took as an
occasion for accusing him of "vandalism."

Although Beissel felt that a wholesale moral reform was
called for, at the time there must have been some alteration
in his view of marriage. At any rate, Friedsam performed his
first marriage ceremony before the whole congregation in
August 1746. Moral reform seems to have proceeded spasmodi-
cally, however. One wonders how it may have been affected
by the beginning of distilling in Ephrata during 1751 and 1752,
when bumper crops of wheat were harvested.

When the internal revolution occurred, the mills were working overtime to fill orders beyond their normal capacity. The
sawmill, gristmill, and oil mill were seriously overloaded, and
the paper mill was so overtaxed that orders could only be filled
in the indefinite future. Hirelings from outside the commune
had been employed by the Eckerling taskmasters, but even if
the industrial system had continued, radical changes would
have been necessary to bring sales and production into balance. Employing outside labor has spelled trouble for more
than one such commune, and the post-Eckerling society wisely
took a different tack. The mills were summarily closed to outside trade, hirelings were dismissed, horses and wagons were
sold, and announcements were issued agreeing to fill standing
orders but canceling all others. Dealers in Philadelphia, Wilmington, and Baltimore were upset; they had come to depend
on Ephrata's quality goods, and the loss of this source hit them

hard. To destroy the image of Ephrata as a shrewd society of traders, the commune returned to a system of subsistence and self-reliance. The paper mill and printery were exceptions to this general policy. They continued in full production.

To clarify the air still more, Beissel announced that any contributions made to Ephrata, whether from internal or external sources, would be repaid on application, and all financial obligations of the society would be honored. He also publicly announced that any of the Solitary would be at liberty to leave if he or she wished. There was to be no implication that the revolutionized Ephrata was any kind of spiritual prison camp. Hence the few remaining Eckerling supporters found the grounds for criticism cut out from under them.

Some historians have given the impression that the Eckerling expulsion prompted a large-scale exodus. The known facts do not support this proposition. Even those who were resentful of Father Friedsam's spiritual "tyranny" remained within the community. The Eckerling departure was not really a schism; it was simply a painful return to the original intentions of Ephrata.

Perhaps all revolutions entail some stupidities and vandalism. Ephrata was no exception. For example, nearly a thousand fruit trees were uprooted one dark night, some say simply because the Eckerlings had been responsible for starting the large orchard. Although the *Chronicon* seems to indicate that Beissel was innocent of this act, suspicion of his involvement persisted in some quarters.[20]

Then on the cold and bitter night of December 5, 1747, a furious fire broke out in the gristmill. The commune was quickly mobilized to fight the flames, but to no avail. The fire not only consumed the gristmill and all its contents and stored grain but spread to the fulling mill and the oil mill and destroyed them both. It was an enormous loss. Sachse claims (without proof) that it was "undoubtedly the work of an incendiary."[21] A number of people in the area, including unsympathetic neighbors, were apparently suspected. Even Beissel himself was; but the culprit was never identified. Some alleged that Beissel had at least some foreknowledge of the event, and in support of that cite the comment, recorded in the *Chronicon,* that he made at the end of the daily meal on the evening before the fire broke out: "I am now withdrawn again from all that has been done and leave it to God, in order to see

what kind of trial will come to me through this whole affair.
For as yet I have no proof at hand by which I know that God
approves it."²² Obviously he was speaking of the now dismantled industrial establishment, and there is no reason to
doubt that he was opposed to what it had done to the commune. But this by no means makes Conrad Beissel an arson-
ist or accomplice.

The winter that followed was a hard one and plagued by
a serious food shortage caused by the destruction of stored flour
and grain. Moreover, the society was once again poor; funds
had been used up erratically in the cashiering of the industrial
system. The secular community, which had continued to prosper, came to the rescue. The lay members agreed to rebuild
the mills provided they were given a half interest in them. When
this was done and the gristmill was rebuilt by the following
February, the lay members magnanimously transferred their
share in it to the Sisters. Probably they did not fully trust the
Brotherhood or its past treatment of Beissel. The gristmill continued to prosper through the years; even in the last tired days
of the commune it was enlarged. Then in 1784 it was set afire
again.

By 1747, when Ephrata's self-imposed poverty had fully replaced the industrial system, Conrad Beissel was fifty-six
years old, and many of those who had gathered around him
in youth were now passing through middle age. Beissel still
possessed much of his unique charisma or *magia,* but the years
were soon to deal more harshly with him. The confrontations
that his strong mind and weak body had endured were sap-
ping his strength. Very shortly after the first mill fire, he asked
the Brothers to relieve him of the title of Father, and once again
he became a mere Brother. Whether he liked it or not—and
it seems quite possible that he wished it so—the Brotherhood
also relieved him of the control of the treasury.

Yet for all its renewed inwardness, the commune blossomed
again, in its educational activities, its missionizing, its music,
and its arts of *Fraktur* and printing. Its free school for the children of the neighboring area had become a more professional
enterprise after Ludwig Höcker took it over about 1739, but
it must have grown beyond his limits, for the Sisters of Saron
took over the school sometime in the 1740s, perhaps after their
reorganization. Schooling for older boys, however, was put
in the hands of the Brothers, perhaps to avoid any sexual con-

notations. As time went on, pressure on the school to extend its program beyond elementary stages mounted. Precisely when its Latin Academy took shape is not known, but it was probably in the late 1740s. The academy was organized and directed by Peter Miller, himself a multilingual Latin scholar, and it was soon drawing students from eastern counties and seaboard cities. (Its fame lasted well after the commune itself had dissolved; the academy building preserved at Ephrata was not built until 1837.)

In the post-Eckerling period, the missionizing of the Solitary more and more pointed westward, but the eastward relationships of the Eckerlings were not easy to shake. A case in point is that of Wilhelm Jung, favorite agent of the Eckerlings in Philadelphia. We do not know how or whether he bilked the Eckerlings, but his subsequent relations with Ephrata mark him as an unctuous scoundrel. About a year after Prior Onesimus was deposed and trading profits from Ephrata had dried up, Jung asked for a substantial loan from the community so that he could settle his wife in a house and shop to allow him to join the Brothers at Ephrata. Although the petition was at first refused, Beissel seems to have overruled the Brothers, and early the following year Jung was baptised at the commune. He thereupon arrogated to himself the role of the commune's chief external agent and recruiter. In the latter he was not without some success; he sent his sister to join Saron, and perhaps a half-dozen new Solitary may be credited to him, including Ephrata's latter-day chief dissident, Ezekiel (originally Heinrich) Sangmeister. In both 1747 and 1748 Jung convinced Beissel to send pilgrimages to his house in Philadelphia to hold love feasts and to recondition Ephrata's image in the capital. He also persuaded Beissel and the Brothers to pay his debts of 200 pounds and to cancel out what he still owed Ephrata—another 123 pounds. He even had the effrontery to bill the community for "damage" to his business caused by observing Saturday as the Sabbath. Having at last bilked the community for more than 600 pounds sterling, the Brothers and Beissel decided they had had enough; the scoundrel's connection with Ephrata was dissolved in August 1748. Jung had, in effect, cleaned out the treasury.[23]

The Jung-sponsored sorties to Philadelphia were among Ephrata's last missionizing pilgrimages to the settled east. By mid-century and even before, most of the German Separatists had become allied to specific sects, and many of the sects had become formalized church bodies or had merged with them. Occasional religious "awakenings," similar to those of prior decades, continued to take place, though probably with reduced fervor, but in the settled parts of the province the excitement of religious revival had faded. With one exception, Ephrata would now turn its evangelical face to the west.

The exception occurred among the English and Welsh Baptists in the neighborhood of West Nantmill (or Nantmeal), a dispersed settlement in northern Chester County. Three inhabitants of the settlement—Israel Seymour, his sister, and Abel Griffyth—actually joined the Solitary at Ephrata as novices. Seymour, however, could not adjust to the stern regimen of the Bethania Brotherhood, and so, since he was a man of remarkable evangelical gifts, Beissel assigned him to take charge of a new conventual establishment patterned after Ephrata at West Nantmill. Initially, this extension of Ephrata seemed to promise success.[24]

Seymour possessed some of the charismatic qualities of Beissel, but he was emotionally unsteady and occasionally verged on madness. One of the Sisters at Ephrata (of the Hagemann family, perhaps Sister Magdelena) fell in love with him. On the pretense of studying English under his tutelage, she followed him back to West Nantmill and moved in with him. Gossip of the affair spread back to Ephrata, and Beissel gave Seymour the choice of either marrying the girl or leaving her. The ensuing marriage was not a success, whereupon the distraught Seymour proclaimed that Beissel, in envy of his gifts as an evangelist, had sent the Sister to bring about his fall. Defections next drove Seymour out of the ministry, and he suffered a period of insanity. Finally, after attempting to defraud the Hagemann family, he wandered off to the Carolinas without a proper divorce and married again, but apparently preached Ephrata doctrine for many years thereafter.[25] However, the West Nantmill hermitage quickly faded.

Thereafter Ephrata's missionizing ventures, such as they were, turned westward—but it was not really the same as in former days. The Ephrathites had grown older; the excitement of earlier times was beginning to fade. The sweetness of life after the Eckerling trauma tended to diminish the evangelistic spirit. True, the westward-moving frontier beckoned, but it was beginning to fester with French-fostered Indian troubles.

Gentle, settled, middle-aged folk are unlikely to rise to that challenge.

There was one more infusion of youth to come from abroad. The new blood began to arrive in the summer of 1749 from the village of Gimbsheim in the Rhine Valley below Worms. The migration is traceable to the impact of Beissel's correspondence through the years to maintain contact with friends and relatives in Germany, especially with his converted brother, Peter.[26]

The story is told that two merchants of Gimbsheim named Lohmann and Kimmel, after experiencing a powerful conversion while drunk in a tavern, joined with Peter Beissel and others in holding secret Pietistic conventicles. The authorities soon found them out, and the ecclesiastical council at Heidelberg found them guilty. Thereuon the civil authority fined them, but the tolerant, aging Count Palatine remitted the fines. The count soon died, however, and the Gimbsheim Pietists lost what little protection they had. Soon some of them were on their way to Ephrata. For two years the Gimbsheimers continued to arrive, evidently with financial help from Ephrata. The real leaders of the group, Lohmann and Kimmel, brought up the rear in 1751. The infusion of new blood, newly freed from the spiritual constraints of the Old World, brought on a dramatic religious awakening within Ephrata itself.

Oddly enough, it was the younger boys — new arrivals from Gimbsheim combined with students of Ephrata's Latin Academy — who gave focus to the awakening. The *Vorsteher*'s young nephew from Gimbsheim, Phillip Beissel, and Daniel Wister at the academy, who was the son of a noted Philadelphia merchant, lit the fires of revival among the older children of the Householders. The youth movement eventuated in the formation of a new order, the Society of Succoth, named in memory of the first encampment of the Israelites after they left Egypt. A separate monastery was planned for it, each of the youthful devotees received a communal name, and they were baptized in the freezing waters of the Cocalico in December 1749. But the movement became unmanageable and caused resentment among Householders. After a year and a half the enthusiasm burnt itself out, and the Order of Succoth disintegrated.

Meanwhile, Jacob Kimmel pushed westward to a beautiful but little-known stream called the Bermudian in the western

hill country of what in 1749 became York County. There he
prepared the way for other Gimbsheimers, including Henry Lohmann and Peter Beissel. A dispersed settlement took shape under rather lax Ephrata auspices. Although the congregation was formally organized in 1758, it strayed from Beisselian and Sabbatarian doctrine. It nevertheless served as a halfway rallying point for Ephrata pilgrims en route to a more promising congregation on the Antietam, of which more later.[27]

In the midst of the Gimbsheim migration and the youth revival, the unique art forms developed by the genius of Ephrata were attaining their finest flowering. The baroque art of *Fraktur* did not originate with Ephrata; it probably came from Switzerland and the Rhine country and was patterned after similar lettering in medieval illuminated manuscripts. In Germanic Pennsylvania it was practiced through much of the eighteenth and nineteenth centuries. The Schwenkfelders, among others, were particularly adept at it, as manuscripts in the notable Schwenkfelder Library attest. But its finest early flowering occurred at Ephrata, where dedicated students in regular classes developed a unique manuscript style with the same intensity that created Ephrata's unusual music.

The masterworks of Ephrata's illuminated music-writing have been widely studied as art forms. The hymn and chorale texts, however, have received less attention as literary productions, and only recently has the Ephrata hymnody been studied in musicological terms. But assessing the music manuscripts without uniting all three elements — art form, literary meaning, and musical quality — tends to obscure what they meant to Ephrata as a totality. John Joseph Stoudt remarked that "each piece of *Fraktur* tells its story. A point is being made, and it is a mistake to separate the point from the designs."[28] At Ephrata, art, literature, and music were not regarded as separate disciplines; they united into one common spiritual experience. Yet the manuscript hymns and chorales (and most lengthier chorales have not even been transcribed) "have never been judged as hymns, only as literary productions."[29]

In 1750 Sisters Anastasia and Efigenia collaborated to produce a calligraphic masterwork, *Der Christen A B C,* a large *Fraktur* stylebook of a series of alphabets in various sizes and styles. The large capitals in this unique work are described by Frances Lichten as follows: "The capitals, supposed to have been drawn by Beissel, are constructed with a series of swinging, voluptuous curves, all interstices of the letters filled with additional scrollings and floral forms. A passionate devotion to the work caused the individual calligrapher to further elaborate all possible areas with minute stipplings and dottings, in the manner of steel engraving. Significant symbolistic motifs also entered into the enrichment of the capitals."[30] However, the claim that Beissel actually drew the capitals seems open to question, though he doubtless tutored Anastasia in the symbolism to be represented.

There is no doubt about the elaborate richness of the large capital letters. Some of them, such as the *A* and the *O*, make use of the human form to portray a provocative symbolism with light lines in the interstices which are sometimes barely discernible. In the *A*, for example, the inner top of the letter shows the garb of a primitively drawn Ephrata Sister and below it the figure of Father Abraham. The *O* suggests Anastasia's vision of Beissel being crowned with the Holy Spirit beneath the form of the dove; it may also reflect her sublimated love for him — and there is little reason to doubt that she was infatuated, in spite of the difference in their ages. Other letters, such as the *Z*, are devoid of the human form but are nested in a profusion of nonrepresentational motifs in the brilliant borders.

The borders are astonishing, even if somewhat less original and wildly imaginative than the letters themselves. In them one finds a profusion of motifs — sunwheels, rosettes, six-petaled stars or blossoms, curious foliage forms, florets — that call to mind some of the design elements of the "hex signs" on nineteenth-century Pennsylvania German barns. We know little about the origins of these forms and motifs except that they must have been developed in the dim Germanic past as symbols of spiritual or mystic elements now lost to memory.[31]

This was a glory time for Ephrata, a recovery of communal confidence. The pain of uprooting the materialism in its midst was followed by a flowering of the communal consciousness, especially in the arts — musical composition, singing, religious poetry, *Fraktur*. The hopes and yearnings implicit in Ephrata's view of itself as a "prevision of the New World" must now have been reaching high tide. But the aspiration would begin to wither all too soon, for a time of change and troubles was already beginning to alter the quality and character of the world in which Ephrata had its being.

Refuge in the Frontier Crisis

AUTUMN OF THE EPHRATA SPIRIT,

AND THE ECKERLING TRAGEDY,

1751–1763

RANCE and England were at war again. After three campaigns, each nation's territorial stake in the New World was still unresolved. The English were confined to the strip of land between the Atlantic and the Alleghenies, and the French, as overlords of lower Canada and the Mississippi Valley, would not permit a farther westward advance by the English. The Indian nations were caught in the middle, but since they had lost their patrimony east of the Alleghenies, thanks to unscrupulous land "purchases" that they did not understand, their anger against the British was rapidly coming to a boil.

The "peace sects" of Pennsylvania understandably worried about the gathering storm. The Mennonites of the Skippack area signaled their concern to their rich Dutch brethren in Europe and asked for help as early as 1745. They noted that "since the flames of war are evidently rising higher," nonresistant Christians faced the prospect that "persecution may come to their house," and they should prepare "for firmness and perseverance in faith."[1] Their prescience was remarkable, but being pacifists they had no other tools to prepare for the danger except the revival of their nonresistant Christian faith. It had carried them through the pains of war and persecution before.

Next to the Bible, the Mennonites treasured above all a vast compendium of the tortures and sufferings endured by Anabaptists, Mennonites, and still earlier *wehrlosen* (nonresistant)

Christian martyrs at the hands of church and state, a huge work called the *Martyrer-Spiegel* (Martyrs' Mirror). The only available edition, prepared by the Dutch Mennonite preacher Thielman J. van Braght, was published in 1685 in the Dutch language.[2] The trouble was that most Pennsylvania Mennonites could not read Dutch. Yet this was the one book the Mennonites on the Skippack wanted above all else to prepare their hearts and minds for the wrath to come.

Naturally they turned to Ephrata, already known for its linguistic abilities and its interest in Christian pacifist martyrology. Perhaps even before working out an agreement on the undertaking, its press had issued "A Memorial of a Holy Martyr," translated from the Dutch by the younger Alexander Mack.[3] Beissel, who was as troubled by current events as the Mennonites, was more than willing to help. A production crew of fifteen men worked for three years under constant pressure from Beissel on the enormous tasks of translating, editing, producing ink and paper, typesetting, printing, collating, and binding. It is said that Peter Miller, chief translator and editor while carrying other heavy responsibilities, averaged only three or four hours sleep each night for the whole period.

Finally in 1748 the huge folio edition of 1,512 pages, measuring ten by fifteen inches, was ready for sale at twenty shillings a copy. Three years later only eight hundred of the thirteen hundred copies printed had been sold. The scant sales seemed to make no difference to Father Friedsam; his "contract" with the Skippack Mennonites was so lax that, in spite of an enormous expenditure of effort, the Mennonites were not obligated to buy a single copy if they did not wish. For Conrad and his associates, this was purely a labor of love.

The *Martyrer-Spiegel* was the largest volume published in America, at least before 1800, and is properly regarded as the greatest product of the colonial bookmaker's art. The translation from Dutch into German was impeccable, as the Mennonite representatives certified at the end of the volume. In the opinion of Governor Samuel W. Pennypacker, a noted bibliophile in his own right, it "easily stands at the head of our colonial books."[4]

The press and the Sisters had produced the wondrous *Turtel-Taube* hymnal at the height of this massive undertaking, and by the time the *Martyrer-Spiegel* was completed the workers

were quite exhausted. Nothing more was produced until 1750,
when two short works came off the press: a 48-page "Remem-
brance" of August Hermann Francke, the famous Halle Pietist,
and a 28-page pamphlet acknowledging "the esteemed calling
of the fathers, friends and patrons in Europe" who supported
the Gimbsheim migration.[5] Another press interlude ended in
1752 with the publication of the *Theosophischen Lectionen,*
a handsome 434-page collection of confessional comments and
poems.[6] Two years later the press issued a German translation of Bunyan's *Pilgrim's Progress* and one of the most treasured of Ephrata's hymnals, the *Paradisisches Wunder-spiel.*[7]
The latter demonstrates a remarkable marriage of the arts
of *Fraktur* and printing, for it was partly hand lettered and
decorated by the Roses of Saron. It incorporated Beissel's last
hymn-poems and choral songs, many of them written in the
chiliastic spirit of the "comet time" a decade earlier. The title,
in the English *Chronicon,* demonstrates with what fond hope
Beissel visualized the role of Ephrata in the New World: "Para-
disiacal Wonder Music, which in these latter times and days
became prominent in the occidental parts of the world as a
prevision of the New World, consisting of an entirely new and
uncommon manner of singing, arranged in accord with the
angelic and heavenly choirs . . . by a Peaceful one, who desires no other name or title in this world."[8]

Evidently, the partly printed 1754 *Wunder-spiel* was several
years in the making, for as early as 1751 the Sisters' writing
school had already prepared a manuscript codex for it, with
music mostly in four parts but some in six or seven. In the
earlier manuscript both the letters and floral and scroll designs
were illuminated with green, blue, brown, and orange washes.
Although the 1754 *Wunder-spiel* contains only forty-nine compositions, it concludes with the grandest of all Ephrata choral
works, the "Lobet den Herrn," for double choir, which ends
in a stunning Hallelujah.[9]

In the years that followed, as the crisis on the Pennsylvania
frontier gathered momentum, the Ephrata press continued issu-
ing relatively small productions of additional hymn-poems as
supplements to the *Turtel-Taube.* At the same time, however,
there was a marked falling off in the production of illuminated
codices of music; whether it was the Sisters' writing school or
its inspiration that faded is uncertain. We simply do not know

how to explain this drying up of a brilliant art. With few exceptions we shall have to wait for its renascence in a somewhat different style in the next century at Snow Hill.

In 1755 the Ephrata press issued a 112-page *Nachklang* (supplement) to the *Turtel-Taube*; this was followed (presumably
soon after) by a 32-page *Neuer Nachklang,* which is undated.
Of the 89 hymns in the two works, only 21 have been attributed to Beissel, suggesting that he too may have been losing
inspiration in this period. A pair of supplements, if they can
be called that, appeared the following year as *Ein Angenehmer
Geruch der Rosen und Lilien* (A Pleasant Aroma of Roses and
Lilies)—one from and for the "lilies," the Brothers of Bethania,
a single *Brüderlied* of 311 stanzas; the other by and for the
Sisters of Saron, the "roses," mainly a *Schwesterlied* of 272
stanzas plus an appendix of ten hymns by Beissel and other
Brothers and Sisters. After this double product of 1756, hymn
production from the press seems to have come to a stand-
still until 1762, when a hymnal of 180 poems—the *Neu-
vermehrtes Gesäng,* yet another supplement to the *Turtel-
Taube*—appeared. It is quite apparent, however, that the mystical aspiration of Ephrata's earlier hymn-poetry was now, like
its manuscript art, entering a period of dessication.[10]

Perhaps too, Germanic Pennsylvania was no longer paying
much attention to the mystics on the Cocalico. Christopher
Sauer was now becoming the principal interpreter of German
affairs, and he had his own reasons for disliking Ephrata. In
1751 he sent a long letter on Pennsylvania German religious
matters to an influential periodical in Weimar.[11] His comments
on Beissel—"He wanted to erect a kind of papacy, and be called
Father"—are still bitter, and he asserts that Ephrata "is on the
decline; it seems that God does not support it." Yet his less
acerbic Weimar editor's introduction was gentle:

> The patriarch and abbess of this society are very dif-
> ferent from those in Europe, for they think little of
> pomp, state, and splendor, but order their religion
> and way of living according to mystical tenets and
> live very meanly. All brothers and sisters from the
> patriarch down to the most insignificant member are
> common people—artisans and uneducated. But in
> their own way—in sermons, in the writing of books,
> and in other artful contrivances—they put to shame

many who have been specially trained. At the same
time they are well versed in the mechanical arts, ex-
celling the best artisans of England.

Sauer himself shows little respect also for Israel Eckerling, who
"ruled as an autocrat" and "did not stoop to ask Conrad's permission." He noted that members of the celibate orders "stick
together to an uncommon degree": "This has become so completely a matter of spiritual participation that they do not withdraw themselves even in death. All the deceased have returned
and are readily visible; for my wife (who has lived for a long
time among the Ephrata Brethren) has seen many and even —
take note — spoken with them." A surprising confession! But
then Sauer too was an Inspirationist of sorts. He further notes
that "there are now only forty single brothers and forty single
sisters, but in view of the still daily building one would believe
they hoped to get a thousand more." Death was beginning to
take its toll on the Solitary orders; after the Gimbsheim migration, few recruits appeared on the scene, but presumably the
Householder community was continuing to increase.

Except for infrequent "official" visits from "people of the
world," few outsiders gained firsthand information about
the commune before 1751. In the decade that followed, however, the fame of Ephrata spread far and wide. For example,
Lewis Evans, Pennsylvania's colonial geographer extraordinary,
noted in his journal that the Ephrathites "live the most retired,
regular, inoffensive lives of any people I know."[12] David Rittenhouse, a remarkable self-taught scientist, visited Ephrata
overnight in 1756. Having been imbued with a sophisticated
rationalism after straying from his Mennonite background,
Rittenhouse was unenthusiastic in commenting to his later biographer, William Barton: "I was there entertained with an
epitome of all the whimsies mankind are capable of conceiving. Yet it seemed to me the most melancholy place in the world,
and I believe would soon kill me were I to continue there;
though the people were exceedingly civil and kind, and the
situation of the place is pleasant enough."[13]

The Reverend Israel Acrelius, provost of the Swedish Lu-
theran church in America, visited Ephrata in 1753 with George
Ross, Jr., later a signer of the Declaration of Independence.
Acrelius's lengthy account appeared in his notable *History of
New Sweden,* where it takes up a surprising number of pages

for something not central to his subject.[14] The result is the best firsthand account of Ephrata by an outsider during the whole of the eighteenth century. At the time of the visit, Beissel was sixty-four years old. Acrelius described him as " a small, lean man" with "gray and bushy hair"; "quick in his utterance as well as in his movements." He found him living "in entire solitude, except when messengers go out and in, or he performs his duties in the congregation." Acrelius saw little of him; his chief informant, with whom he argued religious principles, was the learned Peter Miller. The Solitary orders had declined still further: twenty-five Brothers and thirty-five or so Sisters. What accounts for this reduction from the forty of each reported by Sauer two years earlier is not clear, but there had been further desertions, for the Brotherhood especially was in some disarray.

One is grateful for Acrelius's description of the post-Eckerling division of labor, which succinctly outlines the strict separation of male and female Solitary:

> The business of the brethren outside of the house is to work in the fields, meadows, and woods, as also at their mill. The greatest part of them seem to be brought up to agricultural labors. Others labor inside of the convent at all sorts of handicrafts, such as shoemaking, tailoring, weaving cloth and stockings, and the like, partly for the use of the cloisters and partly for sale, and so as to enable them to purchase other necessaries. Others attend to other domestic duties, such as cooking, baking, house-cleaning, washing clothes, etc., for all the work is done by the brethren without any female assistance in the men's cloister.
>
> The sisters also live by themselves in their convent, engaged in spinning, sewing, writing, drawing, singing, and other things. The younger sisters are mostly employed in drawing. A part of them are just now constantly engaged in copying musical notebooks for themselves and the brethren. I saw some of these upon which a wonderful amount of labor had been expended.

An unidentified British traveler, who in 1759 found that the population of the whole Ephrata community (which certainly included the Householders) totaled 250, commented that "harmony and mutual affection reigns surprisingly among them; every person is industrious, and contented in the task assigned him." Since his article later appeared in Dodsley's *Annual Register* (1759) in London, and still later in the *Edinburgh Magazine* (May 1785), we may assume that it was widely read on the Continent and helped to color the European view of Ephrata with a poignant yearning for "the simple life."[15]

Even the great Voltaire included a garbled mention of Ephrata (absurdly misnamed Euphrates) in his *Philosophical Dictionary* (1764). His translated comments are curiously erratic but essentially apt:

> The example of the Primitives, called "Quakers," has given rise in Pennsylvania to a new society, in a district which is called Euphrates. This is the sect of Dunkers or Dumplers, a sect much more secluded from the world than Penn's; a sort of religious hospitallers, all clothed uniformly. Married persons are not permitted to reside in the city of Euphrates; they reside in the country, which they cultivate. The public treasury supplies all their wants in times of scarcity. This society administers baptism only to adults. It rejects the doctrine of original sin as impious, and that of the eternity of punishment as barbarous. The purity of their lives permits them not to imagine that God will torment his creatures cruelly or eternally. Gone astray in a corner of the new world, far from the great flock of the Catholic Church, they are, up to the present hour, notwithstanding this unfortunate error, the most just and most inimitable of men.[16]

One may smile at his tongue-in-cheek reference to Ephrata's "unfortunate error," but his idealization of its lifestyle obscures the fact that Ephrata affairs were not proceeding serenely. Internal leadership problems continued to plague the Brotherhood. In 1749 Brother Jethro (Jacob Gast) had been removed from the priorship for the second time, an event that caused him great grief.[17] Jacob Eicher (Brother Eleazer), Prioress Maria's brother, was not a notable improvement because of his rough forthrightness, even though he held the job until 1756.[18] Then Beissel appointed a multiple leadership, but such a division of authority failed quickly. Finally Peter Miller (Brother Jaebez, a name he later Latinized to Agrippa) assumed the priorship as the man most in harmony with the sometimes irascible Father Friedsam.

Even then Beissel was not pleased. Internal frictions—some, in part at least, of his own making—continued. In 1753, thwarted by both Eicher and Miller in making additional reforms, the aging Conrad withdrew from Bethania affairs altogether and called for a judgment of God on what he regarded as a perversion of the divine plan for Ephrata. From this point on he withdrew more and more into his spirit realm.

He was troubled, in part, by the increasing lack of inner discipline, and the signs were all too obvious. For example, crops had been unusually bountiful in recent years, and with this bounty, he thought, Ephrata was growing spiritually soft. With a superabundance of grain, the Brothers even began to distill it into spiritous liquors and to eat grain-fattened pork. Then three years of drought followed. Food reserves were used up, and some of the more impressionable Brothers were convinced that Beissel's *magia* was at work in the calamity, that he had a special pact with God to bring Ephrata to its senses. Reconciliation, however, was finally established in the autumn of 1755, and Beissel seems to have promised the Brothers that as soon as the night watches (which had lapsed with the quarrel) would be started again, it would rain. Miraculously, according to the diarist, showers fell the first night of the reinstituted watch. Once again, in 1756, crops were plenteous.[19]

During the last year of the drought a group of Labadists arrived in Philadelphia from Denmark, poverty-stricken and not knowing where to turn. When word reached Ephrata, Peter Miller and others were delegated to visit them. Some of the group, including their leader, a scholar named Ludovic, were invited to visit Ephrata. The visit was cordial enough; both Beissel and Ludovic were impressed with possibilities for starting a new religious commune in Lancaster County. The Labadists finally settled on Pequea Creek, rented a small farm, and had the good luck to be succored by a friendly neighbor, though other neighbors were not so well disposed. Knowing little about farming or self-reliance, the Labadists announced to Ephrata that God expected the Ephrathites to come to their support. Moreover, Ludovic, a rationalist of the Enlightenment, engaged Beissel in controversy. So not much came of the interchange

or of Labadist hopes. Suddenly Ludovic died, and his commune dispersed soon afterward. It was the last sad venture of
the Labadists in America.[20]

The long-anticipated outbreak of violence on the frontier
was now about to become a reality. Violent sentiments against
religious pacifists increased, and it is said that backcountry
roughnecks threatened to burn Ephrata to the ground; even
the governor sent a commission to investigate, though with
no known results. The records do not reveal just how these
events affected Ephrata. We do know, however, that at least
two more Brothers deserted.

Ezechiel Sangmeister, the 1748 recruit of Wilhelm Jung, was
a peculiar, free spirit, a deep mystic in the Beisselian tradition
who nevertheless resented Beissel's aloof "spiritual dictatorship" and attempts at imposing discipline in the Brotherhood.[21]
Ezechiel and his friend and fellow-recruit Anthony Höllenthal
deserted Ephrata in October 1752 and headed for a small, predominantly Mennonite, German settlement on the North Fork
of the Shenandoah in western Virginia, in the area of the present Strasburg. Here they found refuge with the family of Henry
Funk, some of whose relatives were numbered among the Solitary and Householders at Ephrata. The first hard winter the
two deserters quartered themselves in Funk's stable, then in
the following year they moved across the North Fork onto a
loop of land known as Sandy Hook, where they built their
own small house.[22] Brother Anthony tended house and garden while Ezechiel, who was an expert craftsman, earned
needed cash by doing carpentry for surrounding settlers; his
services were evidently in much demand.

At first the objective of the two men was simply to establish
a hermitage of their own, but as a few visitors from Ephrata
began to appear by 1754, the idea of founding a new Sabbatarian "Camp of the Solitary" began to take shape. Ezechiel,
however, was little interested in administration and the disci-
plining of others, so the commune was slow to grow. Moreover, less pacifistic neighbors began to regard them with suspicion, especially when Ezechiel built a tiny oratory on a nearby
hill. The suspicious neighbors thought it a secret hideout for
celebrating Catholic rites and finaly sent a county posse to root
it out, but by then the two men, getting wind of it, had dismantled the structure.

It was not long before regular exchanges were being made

between the Sangmeister coterie on the Shenandoah and the still more distant camp of the Eckerlings. Mahanaim, however, had been deserted in 1752 because of increasing incursions of unfriendly Shawnees in the area. Some considerable time was then spent in searching for a safer refuge. It is said that the Eckerlings explored as far west as the Indian village of Logstown, eighteen miles below the Forks of the Ohio, where they appealed to the chiefs of the Iroquois for permission to settle on the Youghiogheny River. Since permission was apparently not granted, the brothers next settled on a stream flowing into the Monongahela, which came to be known as Dunkard Creek. Here they placed themselves under the protection of the Delaware tribe, but soon their Indian friends urged them to move to a safer area. They then settled more permanently on the Cheat River, another tributary of the Monongahela farther east, in an area henceforth called Dunkard's Bottom.[23]

Although the new location had the advantage of putting the Eckerlings a hundred miles closer to their lucrative markets in eastern Pennsylvania, the brothers were now in an unexplored no-man's land. The whole Monongahela Valley was uninhabited until sometime after the famous scout Christopher Gist penetrated into the area in 1751–1752, just before the Eckerlings arrived on the Cheat. Thereafter we may assume that a few Dunker families settled in or near the Eckerling camp, but if so their origins and names remain a mystery. A few hardy Scotch-Irish also took up lands in the Monongahela country; they became increasingly suspicious of the Eckerlings and their Dunker friends for their friendship with the Indians.[24]

As with Sangmeister on the Shenandoah, the suspicion that the Eckerlings were French spies in league with the Indians gathered momentum. It was not just a matter of their Christian nonresistance toward the increasing pressure of Indian raids in the area but that evidently these usually occurred when the Eckerlings were absent on marketing or provisioning trips, and their camp, except for one occasion when Indians stole some of their belongings, was usually left undisturbed. Complaints about the Eckerlings soon reached Virginia's capital at Williamsburg.

In this period the royal colony of Virginia claimed this entire frontier area, including what is now southwestern Pennsylvania up to the Forks of the Ohio and the Ohio country beyond. The claim was based on royal approval, and French claims to the same area set the stage for a bloody international confrontation. In the bitter winter of 1753–1754, George Washington, then a young major with some experience on the frontier, undertook his incredibly difficult and painful journey with Christopher Gist (and a few Indians of doubtful allegiance) into the heart of the French-claimed territory of what became western Pennsylvania to make clear to the French officers that this was English territory.[25] He could only report back to Governor Robert Dinwiddie in Williamsburg that the French were adamant and supported by a line of well-equipped forts.

Three months later he was on his way again to the Forks of the Ohio, the key to the whole territory, this time with a company of hardly 160 ill-equipped men, no match for the French and Indian forces. His defeat at Fort Necessity in July 1754 marked the beginning of what the historian Francis Parkman called "the war that set the world on fire." This disaster was followed the next summer by an even greater one — the ignominious defeat of the British-American army under General Braddock in the summer of 1755. The undisciplined Indian tribes (including the "friendly" Delawares), now mostly allied with the French, could now begin their vengeful assaults on English outlying settlements all the way to the edges of the settled East. The Cheat River territory was more perilous than ever.

The events that followed sounded the knell for Quaker government, and the old peace of William Penn was shattered. In the spring of 1756 Governor Robert Hunter Morris and his council declared war against the Delawares and Shawnees and offered rewards for Indian scalps, including those of women. A number of Quakers soon resigned from the assembly with the support and sympathy of the German peace sects and most German Separatists.[26]

The Eckerling camp, however, was by now well established, and for another two years after the Braddock disaster it apparently prospered. Gabriel continued his hunting, trapping, and trading activities — much to the disgust of the visiting Sangmeister, who, like Beissel, was adamantly opposed to "animal slavery" and the killing of God's creatures. The Eckerlings, moreover, are reputed to have had a number of horses to carry their loads of pelts and produce to market.

Perhaps because they found Virginia markets closer than those in eastern Pennsylvania, communications with Ephrata diminished. Back in 1750 Israel and Gabriel showed up at Ephrata for an extended visit. They were unprepared for the friendly welcome they received, and both expressed an interest in returning to embrace the cloistered life again, but nothing of the sort transpired. Israel, however, was soon back again from the frontier. Beissel placed no restrictions on him, but Israel started to make the same old mistakes again with endless sermons and ranting. It was all too evident that he did not fit in there anymore. At last he left in bitterness, and on his way back he cut off his two brothers, who were on their way to Ephrata, and dissuaded them from resuming the Ephrata life. Yet as late as November 1756, it is said, Israel sent a letter to Peter Miller at Ephrata of no less than 192 pages. One wonders whether the busy Peter Miller ever had the time and patience to read it all.[27]

Samuel Eckerling had his own troubles in these years of the gathering storm. Business affairs frequently called him to Winchester, then Virginia's principal western outpost. En route there in the spring of 1756, he was apprehended as a suspected spy for the French. The authorities even threatened to hang him, and it was not until he was taken to far-off Williamsburg that he finally won a reprieve. But Virginia military authorities became increasingly antagonistic toward Dunkers and other nonresisters. Samuel's activities were closely watched, and he was arrested again at Winchester in March 1757. He was nevertheless able to buy 140 acres on Sandy Hook, just in case the Cheat settlement became untenable. He then went to Williamsburg again and returned with a letter from Governor Dinwiddie to George Washington, now a colonel and Virginia's principal agent to the frontier, that granted Samuel permission to return to his brothers with the proviso that he be kept under surveillance until more evidence was gathered. He was sent off to Williamsburg again, however, and was examined by the governing council in October. The result was that Dinwiddie instructed Washington to send out a military detachment to round up the Eckerlings and bring them back to a settled area, with a promise that after "the present war" their Cheat River lands were to be restored to them.[28]

Under a Captain McKenzie a company of seventy armed men was promptly dispatched to the Cheat River, with Samuel in tow. Samuel, however, exhausted by his travels, became quite ill and returned to Sangmeister on Sandy Hook. When at last Captain McKenzie's company reached the Cheat River settlement, they were confronted by a grisly sight. The cabins of the Eckerlings and their Dunker associates were in ashes, still smoldering. Scattered around were the half-decayed, scalped bodies of everyone belonging to the settlement except Israel, Gabriel, and the Eckerlings' indentured servant, Johann Schilling. The evidence seemed to indicate that the latter three had been abducted and taken off as captives to Fort Duquesne, the recently reinforced French stronghold at the Forks of the Ohio. Later accounts explained that the perpetrators of this assault were a French-led band of either Ottawas or Mohawks (accounts differ). McKenzie doubtless realized that the abductors had a substantial head start, and it would be dangerous, perhaps fatal, to try to intercept them.

Later accounts of the fate of the captives rely largely on word of mouth, but a fairly clear story emerges. The war party with its prize went by canoe down the Monongahela, and it is said that the canoe carrying the Eckerlings and Schilling was pelted with rocks and stones as it approached the fort, an omen of more torture to come. While at the fort, Israel and Gabriel, half naked and ill-fed, were kept under heavy guard and frequently taunted by the Catholic French on account of their religion. Schilling, on the other hand, was given over to the Indians as a slave; being relatively unrestrained in his movements, he was able eventually to escape, but the circumstances remain a mystery.[29]

News of the abduction soon reached Samuel Eckerling, who was recovering from his illness at Sangmeister's on Sandy Hook. Hereafter Sandy Hook became his home, and he must have been thankful for his prescience in having purchased land there before the tragedy. In May 1757 he added his earlier purchase to 150 acres that he and Sangmeister jointly bought from one of the Funks, thus establishing a sizable communal holding. Here they built a communal house, a cabin for Sangmeister, and (some distance away) a house for Samuel, in which he established a pharmacy.

Evidently, however, Ezechiel, the independent mystic, and Samuel, the practical man of affairs, kept on their separate ways, and whether there was a real sharing between them is problematical. Sangmeister, who continued as an independent carpenter and expert cabinetmaker, does not seem to have appreciated the Eckerling mystique and had resisted the blandishments of the group on the Cheat River. Samuel, the first resident doctor-pharmacist in the region, also dabbled in all kinds of worldly matters, including the handling of wills and property titles for others, and in 1761 established a pottery that in years to come led to nearby Strasburg's reputation as a nationally known pottery center. But when Samuel, returning from a trip to Ephrata, brought back a female companion, Barbara Landes, and set up housekeeping with her, the celibate Sangmeister—indeed the entire neighborhood—was appalled. Sangmeister also noted with disgust that Samuel had adopted a "worldly" form of dress.[30]

Nevertheless, a loosely organized commune did take shape. In addition to Sangmeister, Eckerling, Barbara Landes, and of course Anthony Höllenthal, a few new recruits gradually appeared to adopt the "solitary" communal life. Martin Kroll had already arrived in 1756 and learned the tailor's trade—though it is said that he "suffered temptations" when fitting women's clothes. Then came two young Kelp (Kölb) brothers, and in 1762 their sister Catherina (to whom Sangmeister became quite attached, causing a good deal of local gossip) entered the commune as a celibate. Valentin Brückman, who arrived in 1761, was a weaver, and Barbara Landes made and sold willow baskets. To what extent earnings from such activities went into the communal treasury is not known, but the group as a whole kept milk cows and poultry and probably shared garden produce. The lifestyle of the commune, one supposes, was less disciplined and certainly less abstemious than Ephrata's.

Sangmeister, the acknowledged spiritual leader, refused any title or formal official status, just as he refused to baptize any of the others. He deliberately avoided any possible comparison with the "spiritual dictatorship" of Beissel, and it is likely that his rancor against Beissel—which may have been additionally stimulated by Israel Eckerling before the tragedy on the Cheat—grew increasingly psychotic even in absence. Yet he is said to have kept up an extensive correspondence with Ephrata, as well as with de Benneville and Christopher Sauer.

Ephrata was slow to learn the details of the abduction of Israel and Gabriel. Johann Schilling evidently made his escape from Indian captivity in 1761 and finally appeared in Germantown. Presumably the woeful tale he told there was then passed

on to Ephrata. Schilling went west again to Samuel Eckerling
at Sandy Hook, then took up residence on the New River,
where Samuel had promised him a tract of land. He was there
as late as 1773, but nothing is known of him thereafter.[31]

In the meantime, word must have reached Samuel that his
brothers had been sent under guard from Fort Duquesne all
the way to the headquarters of French power on this continent in Quebec and Montreal. It seems likely that this took
place in the spring of 1758, a year after their capture. It is probable that, considering the crude and hostile conditions of im-
prisonment, their health had already deteriorated, and the grueling seven-hundred-mile journey to Montreal could only have
weakened them more. Official French documents provide little
more than a bare record of the presence of the two brothers
in Montreal, where they were put under the supervision of
French Jesuits, but tales of their experience there somehow
reached the English frontier. Although evidently granted more
freedom than at Fort Duquesne, thanks to the care of the Jesuits,
they nearly starved under this "care" and were reduced to beg-
ging in the streets. It seems likely that they were able to communicate with their keepers, for they seem to have discussed
their religious convictions with them in a relatively amiable
manner. Perhaps they were able to remember their boyhood
French from bilingual Alsatia and Strasbourg.[32] At any rate,
it is said that they held fast to their religious views and that
the depth of their convictions won some sympathy from their
keepers.

We do not know how long they were kept in Montreal, but
there seems to be good reason to believe the tradition that eventually Israel and Gabriel were put onto a prison ship bound
for France. From here on their sad end is altogether unauthen-
ticated. It is supposed that the prison ship deposited its human
cargo at the medieval port of La Rochelle. In a letter dated
November 5, 1764, Samuel Eckerling, having heard that Benjamin Franklin was about to embark for England, asked him
to find out what he could about the fate of his brothers in
France. Franklin never seems to have replied, and for that matter he did not visit France until 1767. Eventually, Sangmeister
reported that he heard two different accounts of the deaths
of the brothers: "One says they died at sea, the other one that
they died there [at La Rochelle] in the hospital in great mis-

ery."[33] In recent years Klaus Wust has made inquiries of the archival authorities at La Rochelle but could get no confirmation of the two Eckerlings ever having been there.[34]

During these years, Ephrata itself was becoming a refugee camp. Depredations by Delawares and Shawnees had already reached the Paxton area near John Harris's Ferry (now Harrisburg) and spilled over Kittatinny Mountain into the Tulpehocken Valley a mere thirteen miles from Ephrata. In 1755 Indian marauders massacred their Christianized brothers at the Moravian mission post of Gnadenhütten (Tents of Grace), not many miles above Bethlehem in the Lehigh Valley.[35] Swinging eastward all along the line of less-settled areas, the Indian tide of destruction left no rural region secure. Fugitives streamed into both Bethlehem and Ephrata as their cabins were burned and their loved ones massacred. Both communities had good reason to fear for the future.

We have little knowledge of precisely what went on in Ephrata during these hard days.[36] It is apparent, though, that Beissel and the whole community conducted themselves with charitable distinction. All available space as well as the food reserves were applied for the use of the refugees. A company of infantry was dispatched from Philadelphia to protect the community, and they too needed food and supplies. When at last the turmoil was over, all that Ephrata received for its services was a pair of large glass communion goblets from the provincial government. But one thing was now painfully clear: Ephrata was essentially cut off from political and social events around it; in the tumult of those events it was becoming an anachronism.

Soon a chain of forts was constructed along the Alleghenies, the Indian stronghold at Kittanning was wiped out, and the Indian attacks slowly began to subside. But now Virginia, whose government had been better prepared and less ambivalent than Pennsylvania's in defending its frontiers, began to feel the full weight of the Indian terror. Sandy Hook was just emerging as a viable community, having recently acquired an additional tract of seventy-three acres at the foot of Massanutten Mountain, when Indian attacks exploded not far away in June 1764. Thereupon Sangmeister's commune also became a refugee camp, much like Ephrata. Samuel Eckerling was away in Germantown at the time, so Sangmeister took full charge. At the same time, George Adam Martin, an apostle of Beissel

and a wide-ranging evangelist, arrived with the intent of hold-
ing his wildly fervent camp meetings. Sangmeister tried to ignore him, and Martin soon left for Antietam Creek where he was to meet the seventy-four-year-old Beissel with the Brethren at what became Snow Hill.

The situation at Sandy Hook and Strasburg soon became untenable. With Sangmeister in charge, an organized withdrawal from the area was put in motion, and it is said that twenty-six people left the Shenandoah early in July 1764. Ezechiel himself and his friend Höllenthal, with a few others, headed directly east to Ephrata; others found their way to other, safer settlements, and a few headed for the well-established Moravian settlements in the Carolinas. Only Barbara Landes stayed behind, determined to take care of Samuel Eckerling's house and apothecary shop. But as the Indian raids continued, causing great damage, she moved in with Henry Funk and later took refuge in a nearby fort.[37]

The Indian incursions continued for years to come, despite the Peace at Paris in 1763 that had transferred all French claims east of the Mississippi to Great Britain. The central Pennsylvania frontier was still edgy, and Pennsylvania's Scotch-Irish frontiersmen were still furiously bitter about the province's attitude of protective custody toward the scattered Indian clans remaining behind in the area of settlement.

One such enclave existed hard by the growing town of Lancaster — a powerless and peaceful remnant of Conestoga Indians. For many years the citizens of Lancaster maintained useful and friendly relations with this harmless band, and both provincial and local authorities gave tacit approval to their tiny village. Hence the events that took place here in December 1763 defy all rational explanation. On the night of December 14 a mob of self-named "Paxton Boys," mostly parishioners of the Paxton church (near Harris's Ferry) with additions from Donegal, sneaked up on the Conestoga village and burned it to the ground. In cold blood they massacred the few Indians they could find — three old men, two women, and a little boy.

The citizens of Lancaster were horrified and gathered the scattered remaining individuals of the tribe for protection under guard in the Lancaster jail. But on December 27, when all Lancaster was at church and still in the Christmas spirit, the Paxton Boys raided the jail and put the last fourteen members of the tribe to the knife. Then they galloped on toward Philadelphia, intending vengeance on a protected band of Delawares. Finding the approaches to the town well guarded, they at last returned to their western homes. Not one of them was ever brought to justice.[38]

The Ephrata records do not mention these events. Perhaps the community was still too occupied with supporting its own refugees. The events of the French and Indian War, moreover, must have created a deep despondency in the Ephrata conscience, and its tales of terror from many quarters could have so blunted its sensitivities that yet another outrage could go unremarked. But the war as a whole, along with the change from a pacifist Quaker government protecting its own convictions to an agency of empire, meant that Ephrata's world was permanently changed. The only course left to it was to withdraw more and more into itself, knowing instinctively that its golden age could never return.

End of the Charisma

THE LAST YEARS OF

CONRAD BEISSEL, 1763–1768

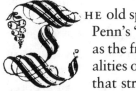 H E old spirit that suffused and enlivened William Penn's "holy experiment" was fast disappearing as the frontier moved farther west. The hard realities of empire and land greed intervened, and that struggle was followed by a movement for independence that buried the old aspirations for a higher consciousness and spiritual peace.

Religious aspiration was gradually displaced by searches for doctrinal and organizational security; revolutionary religious movements faded into "church religion" and quietism.[1] Movements became sects and sects became churches. Migration from the religious underground of Europe dried up, and the sons and grandsons of the seekers and mystics who had flocked to the province in response to Penn's vision lapsed into the quiet life with one eye on "the way to wealth" or hankered after new lands farther west. Germanic Pennsylvania began to take on the characteristics of stasis, turned conservative, sought security and a gentle, good life on its rich farms. The old spiritual excitement was gone, never to return.

Peter Becker, founder of the Church of the Brethren at Germantown, died in 1758. Christopher Sauer, Separatist and printer, passed away the following year. Conrad Weiser, who played a valiant but losing game to keep the frontier pacified, came to the end of life in 1760. Count Zinzendorf died in Europe the same year; August Spangenberg was recalled to the old country; and in 1762 the General Economy of the Moravians was abrogated for a system of exclusive Moravian private management of industries and farm leasing on shares. At Ephrata a large number who in the prime of youth sought out *145* the hermitage of Conrad Beissel in the Cocalico wilderness had been laid to rest. Some of their children were now mature Brothers and Sisters living a life of resigned quietism in the commune, but others had left the community never to return.

Beissel himself seems to have been drawn further and further into a psychic and spiritual shell. In the austerity of his hermit life at the very heart of the commune, he became increasingly inaccessible, even to close associates. The double effect of this removed him more and more from community management and heightened the inner trauma of his last years. Very likely he returned again to the practice of the Hermetic arts and Rosicrucian mysteries, and it is said that he often fasted and flagellated himself severely. Some who remembered his unique effect on women attributed this to a need to subdue the desires of the flesh, but that seems unlikely for a man in his seventies who had practiced a severe continence most of his life.

If in his advanced years Father Friedsam grew a bit bored and chagrined with Ephrata, he must have seen signs of the old excitement farther to the west. Perhaps he saw something of himself in George Adam Martin, who appeared in 1762.

Martin (whose personal history and confessional are included in the *Chronicon*) had once been a member of Peter Miller's former congregation at Tulpehocken, but he defected from the Reformed and in 1739 was ordained as a minister by Peter Becker, who assigned him to serve the Brethren's congregation on the Big Conewago in what became York County.[2] The area around the Conewago, then a beautiful, small river into which the Bermudian drained, was where the Gimbsheim settlers later gradually melded with the Becker Brethren. Although well trained in both German and Latin and equipped with a keen mind, Martin was impulsive, impatient, and averse to criticism. These characteristics evidently prompted a theological rift in the congregation, so Martin moved on to the Antietam Creek area in what is now Franklin County and organized a congregation there in 1752. But he also continued serving the Conewago and Bermudian groups occasionally—to no avail, for the rift continued to widen, and in 1760 the Germantown Dunkers excommunicated him.

When Martin came to Ephrata in 1762, he was so impressed with the saintly Beissel and the Ephrata life that he asked at once to join the community. Oddly enough, Beissel granted his wish without requiring him to undergo a novitiate or formally agree to the ordinances of the Brotherhood. Beissel raised him at once to the priestly office and assigned him as Ephrata's leader on the Bermudian. Thereafter, for a period at least, Ephrata and the Bermudian settlement were considered as one community.

But Adam Martin was a restless, independent man with a powerful gift for evangelization. In the same year as his Ephrata conversion, he pilgrimaged all the way to the edge of the frontier in what is now Somerset County, where he brought into being another congregation at Stony Creek. During the following two years he was busy in the Antietam region and also evangelized the backcountry of Maryland and Virginia. Singlehandedly he created a widespread backcountry religious "awakening."[3]

Beissel heard glowing reports of this revival and, in spite of his seventy-two years, made the first of three pilgrimages to the Antietam toward the end of July 1763. With him went an impressive delegation of Brothers, Sisters, and seculars alternately traveling on foot and by horse. The procession had all the earmarks of a state occasion, and the white-robed Ephrathites made a deep impression, we are told, on the susceptible minds of the frontier people.[4] While the group was at Antietam, one of the meetings was interrupted by the shocking news that, only a few miles away, schoolmaster Enoch Brown and six of his pupils had been massacred by an Indian party. The frontier was aflame again in the so-called Conspiracy of Pontiac. Apprehension, anger, and grief consumed the settlers, but Beissel stuck to his convictions and successfully counseled them not to take up arms.

The frontier, starved as it was for spiritual excitement, was subject to religious excess and visionary vagaries. It is not unreasonable to suppose that Ephrata's western pilgrimages were infected with this condition. At any rate, strange occurrences of spiritualism and clairvoyance soon transpired at the commune, although "the spirits" were said to have made their presence felt at Ephrata as early as 1759. The community, of course, was quite familiar with spiritual trances, visions, strange dreams, "signs," and other parapsychological phenomena. These were an integral part of the mystical experience. But now Ephrata was caught up in such phenomena as never before. The excessive excitement they produced may be regarded as a sign that Ephrata was beginning to lose its true spiritual focus.

For example, Jacob Martin, a recent recruit presumably from the Shenandoah and a friend of Sangmeister's, turned to the ancient forms of the arcane by dabbling in alchemy. He is said to have set up an alchemical laboratory at Ephrata in the vain hope that he could produce gold for establishing the New Jerusalem. Sangmeister himself seems to have claimed that the founder of Universalism, his friend George de Benneville, now of Oley, possessed a large supply of the gold tincture. Another Brother practiced astrology (a system of divination never far from the Ephrata consciousness), "divined" for ore in the nearby hills, and told fortunes. Yet another was suspected of being a sorcerer. Beissel himself was widely reputed to have direct command over evil spirits, and on one occasion is alleged to have disappeared into thin air to escape being served a warrant.[5]

Then too there was the complex case of Christopher Böhler (Beeler). When in 1740 or thereabouts his first wife, Catherina, became an Ephrata celibate named Sister Esther, Christopher took his three children and in a pique fled to the Shenandoah with a neighboring widow named Schüle. When Catherina died in 1741, Christopher married the widow, by whom he produced three more children. On the frontier he evidently accumulated a fortune, amassed large acreages in the Shenandoah country and farther west, and is even said to have owned a townhouse in Alexandria. When his second wife became seriously ill, he brought her back to Ephrata for medical treatment in 1757, but she died early the next year. Finally in 1760 he married his third wife, Henrietta Wilhelmina von Hönig, of allegedly noble birth. It was then that the "strange occurrences" began.

One winter night in 1761, so the story goes, the deceased second wife appeared to the third wife and revealed to her where she could locate a hidden cache of money. Sure enough, the next morning she and Christopher found it as instructed — money that the deceased had purloined from her husband. The eerie visitations continued, and whenever the spirit's instructions were not obeyed, it tore off the third wife's clothes — even in broad daylight in front of male observers. Several who were sent to investigate swore that the spirit dragged them around the room. Finally, the spirits of the first two wives appeared together before the Böhler couple and instructed them to go to Ephrata. There Beissel and some of the Solitary held

a midnight séance for the distraught couple to establish a reconciliation and give them peace. At last the spirit that appeared
directed that Christopher's two daughters, one by each of the
first two wives, should perform the act of exorcism. Thereafter, it is said, the spirits never reappeared. Beissel, and probably the whole community, was much affected by these events,
and indeed a thirty-nine-page "Relation" of the case of the
three wives and the spirits was soon issued by the Ephrata
press (1761). To this Beissel appended his own view of the
world of spirits.[6]

Beissel must have met the young clairvoyant Catherina Hum-
mer on the Bermudian in 1762, when she had already attained
fame in the backcountry. For two years, it is said, she had been
experiencing visions and angelic visitations, and the *Chronicon* glowingly records her lengthy confessional, of which the
following is an example:

> I lay in a trance for the greater part of seven days and
> seven nights, so that my spirit was separated from
> my body. In this state . . . I saw wonderful things
> that I greatly hesitate to reveal. After this it became
> quite customary for me to talk with good spirits and
> angels, and also to be transferred in spirit out of my
> visible body into heavenly principalities. . . . The Al-
> mighty God in his mercy also allowed me to translate
> myself in spirit into eternity as often as I wished . . .
> and there to see, hear and touch the divine wonders.
> My body was always as if asleep until my spirit re-
> turned. . . . There you feel a bliss that is inexpres-
> sible.[7]

Beissel hoped to woo this rare spirit to Ephrata, but Catherina's father, a wide-ranging Dunker preacher who used his
daughter's remarkable powers at revival meetings, strongly objected. Her fame as a spiritualist medium continued to spread,
and finally she and her sister visited Ephrata amid much excitement and rejoicing. It is disappointing to report that nothing came of the visit. Beissel warned her, in writing, against
marriage, but at last she took a husband and lost her virgin
estate. With that, it is said, the wondrous visions ceased.

In fact, the changing focus and shifting of events of the 1760s
were crowding out the mystical life, and Beissel knew it. By

then he must have known that creating a New Jerusalem in the New World was a lost cause and that the wave of the future was fast washing away the sand castle he had so laboriously built over a lifetime.

Moreover, internal tensions and disaffection surfaced again at Ephrata, and certainly the aging saint knew they were eroding his life work. An anti-Beissel faction was forming around the irascible Sangmeister, who, when he returned to Ephrata from the Shenandoah, remained outside the commune and formed his own "spiritual household" with the three Kelps — John Adam, Jonathan, and Catherina. The little establishment was in the Ephrata neighborhood, presumably in the settlement that eventually became a separate town also called Ephrata. Sangmeister's faithful friend, Anthony Höllenthal, however, was miffed by these developments, evidently fearing that he had lost his spiritual idol to the blandishments of Catherina. Brother Anthony made up his mind to revive the Sandy Hook community as soon as the Indian troubles subsided, and in 1766 he returned to the Shenandoah. There he, Barbara Landes, and the Christian Hackman family formed a tiny congregation that was soon visited by the roving de Benneville, whose preaching drew large crowds and augured a renewal of community goals. But in the spring of 1767, disastrous floods ravaged the Sandy Hook area. Then the unpredictable Barbara took a "vagabond doctor" into Samuel Eckerling's house. Höllenthal was outraged and soon moved away to the new town of Strasburg.[8]

Sangmeister himself hoped to return some day to the Shenandoah, but he never did. The only real home he had ever known was Ephrata, and in spite of his antagonism to Beissel he could not bring himself to leave its neighborhood. It was, after all, the home of the spirit life and of a few choice friends. His friendship with old Johannes Hildebrand, a mystic like himself and another petulant critic of Beissel, must have blossomed afresh. He too lived, at least much of the time, outside the pale of the commune. Christian Eckstein, the community doctor, shared their opinion of Beissel and seems to have become a part of the cabal.

Then too, Ezechiel's colleague on the Shenandoah, Samuel Eckerling, showed up at Ephrata again. He was much absent on business, but in the little town close by he set up shop as a physician and apothecary, perhaps under some understand-

ing with Eckstein. He had at last broken off his relationship
with Barbara Landes, even though she herself later returned to Ephrata, where she died in 1776. Samuel did not scruple to flaunt his possession of the title to 264 acres of Ephrata land, of which the commune claimed only 180. This he possessed as the sole surviving brother of Israel after Emanuel died in 1767, but just how he obtained the document is a mystery. Even before Emanuel's death, however, Samuel seems to have regarded the deed as his very own.

Title to the land was complicated by other claimants as well. Heinrich Müller, now the tavern keeper in Ephrata village, laid claim to 100 acres on the basis that the Brotherhood had assigned this amount of the land to him for his contribution to the building of Hebron. There was some precedent for this claim, since 84 acres—the difference between the 264 acres in the Eckerling title and the 180 claimed by the commune—seems to have been transferred already to John Sensemann, probably for another contribution to Hebron.

Samuel at first refused to have anything to do with Müller's claim, but in November 1764 Sangmeister finally persuaded him to issue a deed to the tavern keeper, without the concurrence of the remaining Solitary. Then Samuel proposed that the title to the remaining land be administered by trustees for the commune's use, the implication being that he, Hildebrand, Eckstein, and Sangmeister would be the trustees. It looked as though they were planning to cut the ground from under Beissel and the Brotherhood. No final action was taken on Samuel's proposal at this time, but as we shall see in the following chapter, the momentum of claims and counterclaims steadily mounted to a destructive climax.[9]

Father Friedsam, who had no mind for land titles and legalities, was probably confused and disheartened by these developments, but he was keenly aware that the "conspirators," who still claimed "membership" in the commune though they lived apart from it, were intent on limiting if not negating his central role in the community. What cut Beissel to the quick, however, was the defection of Mother Maria Eicher. It became known that she had secretly offered Samuel Eckerling two hundred pounds Sterling for the land title—a lot of money, which presumably would come from the separate treasury of the Sisterhood. She declared herself openly against Beissel and proposed that the Sisterhood become completely independent.

Beissel now intervened and, at the urging of Adam Martin from Antietam who was visiting him at the time, conducted an investigation. He called Maria to a trial before the older Sisters and, finding her still recalcitrant, deposed her. Barbara Meyer, once Conrad's star-struck pupil long years ago on the Mühlbach, was appointed prioress in Maria's place, though without the title of Mother. As for Maria, she wept bitterly and for a long time thereafter was said to be at the edge of hysteria.

It was obvious now that the internal structure of Ephrata was beginning to crumble. The land-title affair and the stresses in the Sisterhood, coupled with the increasingly strident gossip and criticism from the acidic Sangmeister, certainly contributed to Beissel's increasingly erratic behavior, petulance, and "dotage." Probably at Beissel's request, Peter Miller assumed most of the administrative duties, but the personnel available to him were scarcer now, aging fast and coming to the end of their days. Old Johannes Hildebrand died in 1765, some said of neglect in his final illness. It must have been a blow to the Sangmeister-Eckerling faction, for in spite of his association with the schismatics, the learned Johannes was one of the last to represent the legitimacy of Ephrata's theosophic tradition—excepting, of course, Sangmeister himself and the failing Beissel. Then Dr. Eckstein sold his house and apothecary in the village to make a fresh start in Germantown, though he continued his association with Samuel Eckerling. It is alleged that just as Eckstein was driving away to Germantown, he had a final confrontation with Beissel and Jan Meyle—and that the two old men were disgustingly drunk.[10] Potable spirits had become quite common in the community (after many years of abstinence), and the deterioration of Conrad's health along with his growing disappointments may well have driven him to drink. However, such lurid tales of Beissel's last years are traceable to the gossipy Sangmeister, who may have maliciously exaggerated the charge of alcoholism. Three years after his return to the Ephrata settlement, he had sent a vitriolic letter to Beissel, saying that his return was "against my own will . . . for I did not intend to ever settle here again." His extreme contempt for Beissel continued unabated.[11]

In Feburary 1765 Conrad fell down some stairs—gossips said he was drunk—and seriously injured his foot. It was excruciatingly painful and did not seem to heal. At last he sent for an old nemesis who was now considered a healer, Jean

François Régnier, the same who thirty years before left Ephrata in a state of mystic madness. He was now a married member of the Moravian community at Bethlehem. Surprisingly,
Régnier and his wife came at once and took up the single life
among the Brothers and Sisters. It proved to be another sad
mistake.

We do not know whether the healer's ministrations had any
success. Slowly the foot seems to have healed, but Beissel suffered increasingly from other infirmities. On what appears to
be insufficient evidence, one commentator diagnosed these as
membranous colitis, which may lead to cancer of the colon,
and neurasthenia, a weakness of the nerves or exhaustion of
nerve energy that leads to severe depression, sometimes to hysteria.[12] One could assume that these ailments exacerbated the
vagaries of a mystical mind grown old and forlorn, occasionally producing an appearance of drunkenness. In the *Chronicon* Peter Miller at least twice refers to the "seeming drunkenness" of the old man in his last years. There is also some room
for assuming, as Miller did, that putting on this appearance
could have been "a holy pretence."[13]

Gossip about his relations with some of the Sisters also took
a nasty turn. Before her demotion, Sister Maria had contributed to it. Perhaps the mental illness and death of her sister,
whom Beissel had rejected, unsettled her, and she herself may
have been fearful of his uncanny power over women. She was
certainly suspicious of his "intimacies" with some of the Sisters, and at one point frankly forbade him to visit the convent
anymore.

Added to this was the embarrassment caused by Régnier's
wife. She became unhappy in the convent; the conditions of
celibacy were not to her liking. She demanded the attentions
of her husband, who was apparently forced to yield against
his will. According to Sangmeister, she told her husband that
Beissel had appeared to her and caressed her during her sleeping hours, and that other Sisters had similar experiences. One
is alleged to have said, "Isn't it terrible that after working hard
all day, one must be subject to his *magia* all night!"[14] Evidently
Sangmeister insisted it was not a matter of *magia* but of real
sex. He may have so convinced Régnier, for the couple soon
left Ephrata, the husband fuming maledictions against the sick
old man's "whoremongering."

In spite of all these disturbing developments, the regular

economy and cultural life of the commune continued on an even keel. Farm, mill, and workshops of both celibate orders were busily productive; Ephrata's Latin Academy gained fame in the eastern cities; even the printing establishment continued sporadic but impressive production. And it may have been at this time that Peter Miller, who realized that Beissel's life was nearing an end, began to think about preparing a history of what he had wrought.

Peter probably made notes from his own memories, but a detailed record of Ephrata's internal events may have been available to him now — a long community "diary" said to have been faithfully kept over the years by Jacob Gast. Just when Gast (Brother Jethro) died, of apoplexy it is said, remains a mystery, for the recorded dates are conflicting, ranging from 1749 to 1764, and we are not even sure of his real identity, at least as diarist and thereby the alleged coauthor of the *Chronicon Ephratense*.[15] Brother Jethro had generally kept out of internal squabbles, though deeply aggrieved by his loss of the priorship. It is said that he was buried with high honors, which he richly deserved as a long and faithful member of the society. Sangmeister claimed, however, that some two hundred pages of the alleged six-hundred-page community diary were removed and burned because they were too critical of Ephrata and of its sainted father figure.[16] Whether true or not, Peter Miller apparently made a lengthy extract of the diary and sent it off to Germany for publication and some years later is said to have incorporated much of it in the *Chronicon*.[17]

The sporadic activities of the Ephrata press during this period give the impression that the creativeness of previous decades was fading fast. Nothing much of consequence was produced between 1754 and 1762. The *Neu-vermahrtes Gesäng* was published in the latter year, but the major piece of printing in 1762 was a substantial book called *M. Valentin Wudrians Seel* (Wudrian's Soul).[18] Little is known about Wudrian or his soul, but the book's theme emphasizes trust in the Cross as a support to the troubled and ill, a theme peculiarly appropriate to the current condition of Ephrata.

Another two-year gap intervened at the printery before the slender Gospel of Nicodemus was produced, an apocryphal work that scholars assign to the third or fourth century.[19] A more substantial book appeared in the same year (1764), *Von der Historia des Apostolischen Kampffs* (Of the History

of the Apostolic Struggle). This was an impressive work on
early Christian martyrology with a long lineage of translations.[20] It was brought out at the request of the Brethren "in Canegotshiken"—that is, Dunkers who had lately settled along the stream now called Conococheague in Franklin County. That area was again feeling the terror of Indian raids during Pontiac's War, so called, and the pacifist Dunkers felt the need for this kind of spiritual support, much as did the Skippack Mennonites almost two decades before when they convinced Ephrata to produce the *Martyrs' Mirror*.

In 1766 the last principal hymnbook of Ephrata was produced, the second to bear the opening title of *Paradisisches Wunder-spiel*. Its preface was undoubtedly written by Peter Miller, and it describes the Ephrata way of life and the merits of Father Friedsam, as if Miller were already beginning to memorialize the passing of the Ephrata dream and the accomplishments of his spiritual hero. Most of the 727 hymns had appeared in previous collections, of which it is said that 107 were written by Beissel. The production marks the end of Ephrata's poetic and musical genius.[21]

The community's physical prosperity was envied by many visitors who did not see the cancer of age breaking out below the surface. No new recruits entered the communal sanctuary now. Youth had turned away from spiritual "awakening," and the powerful personality of Father Friedsam had lost its magical magnetism. To the world around it, Ephrata had become an anachronism.

Increasing numbers of the congregation drifted away, some of them, it is said, making claims on the common property that the civil courts upheld.[22] Those who stayed behind were aging fast. Beissel must have been heartbroken by the communal deterioration; he must have known that the great hope, the great dream, was gone. So, too, were his days on earth. He knew when the end was near. He tried to make peace with those who had rejected or resented him and with those he himself had scorned or scolded. A few, perhaps—Maria Eicher among them—either remained unbending or could not put out their hand in peace to a dying man.[23] He told Peter Miller, feebly but with conviction, "I did not forsake my calling, because all carnal or world-minded people are still my enemies, just the same as at the time when I first entered upon this road." And he was loath to admit that he was sick; instead, he re-

ferred to his dying condition as the spiritual throes that preceded a new birth.

Even in his last few hours, when the Solitary had already
gathered at his cabin, he could not be prevailed upon to lie
down. He asked Prior Jaebez to anoint him, and the Brothers
paraded past to give him a last kiss of peace. Finally he lay
down and lapsed into an anguished lament that the conduct
of his office had come to nought. Before he lost speech, he
saw visions of the hereafter that brightened his final moments.
Thus it was that early in the afternoon of July 6, 1768, a great
and troubled heart stopped beating.

Notes were sent at once far and wide to places where there
were still remnants of the spiritual revolution inspired by Conrad Beissel. Two days after his death more than seven hundred people assembled at the cloisters for the burial service.
Even after his body was laid in the ground, his eagle spirit invaded the consciousness of others. He appeared, so it is said,
before one couple near midnight, and another swore they saw
him in broad daylight. An old Brother claimed to have had
direct conversation with him. It was claimed that he even appeared to Sangmeister, to Samuel Eckerling in Germantown,
to George de Benneville in Philadelphia.[24]

After more than two centuries, encased as we are in a world
that took a different turn, we still do not know how to evalu-
ate this pilgrim of God. Assessments of him in the principal
writings about Ephrata show a disconcerting range of opinion,
from devout to outraged and caustic. Small minds and narrow spirits have caviled about his sincerity and significance,
maligning his memory and criticizing his incorrigible and sometimes erratic devotion to a vision of life and an antique worldview about which they seem to know little and care less. De-
pending on whether we are able to penetrate beyond the heavy
layers of realism and rationalism that circumscribe our minds
today, our understanding of the man must remain partial and
limited. Yet the last historian of Ephrata, James Ernst, whose
posthumous work repeated the malicious Sangmeister slanders
and was sometimes punishingly critical of Ephrata's father figure, came to the following conclusion about him: "He yet remains one of the great wonders of the century . . . and he
may perhaps yet emerge as the profoundest spirit in Colonial
America."[25]

The magic and holiness with which his disciples endowed

him endured for many years, but most poignantly in the months
immediately following his demise. Some seven weeks thereafter a special *Liebesmahl* renewed his spirit among them. For it a certain Sister Athanasia (whose worldly name is not remembered but should not be confused with Anastasia) composed a loving and mystically evocative hymn-poem, "A Song of Praise," in Beissel's memory, which, with the *agapē* rite, must have produced an awesomely affectionate loneliness for that "wonder of the age."[26]

Beissel's devotees did not erect a memorial stone over his unmarked grave until 1775, seven years after his death. "Here rests an offspring of the Love of God," it proclaims, but even then there was renewed disagreement about the title of Father. The principal heading on the stone is simply "Friedsam"— seed of Peace. The seed may then have fallen on fallow ground for awhile, but, as we shall see, it has the potential for renewal. At least one thing is certain: whatever endures from the Ephrata mystique will ever be the kind of eagle spirit that graced the life of Conrad Beissel.

The Clouds of War

PETER MILLER'S EPHRATA IN THE

ERA OF REVOLUTION, 1768–1797

"EADERSHIP of the commune, after some misgivings and jostling from the Roses of Saron, fell into the deserving hands of Peter Miller, although he was not accorded the title of Father. Among his first acts was to invite those who had drifted away to rejoin the commune without being obliged to renounce and repent their separation. Evidently some took advantage of this "amnesty," but the effect was that of a truce rather than a unity of aspiration and outreach. No doubt Brother Jaebez understood this very well. In 1771 he wrote his friend Benjamin Franklin that hereafter while its visible congregation would be maintained, Ephrata "shall not propagate the monastic life upon the posterity; since we have no successors, and the genius of the Americans is bound another way."[1] With such resignation there was no real future for the commune, and the old spirit was quietly buried with the bones of Beissel.

Morgan Edwards, the learned pastor of the English Baptists in Philadelphia whose multivolume history of Baptist origins and development appeared in 1770, notes the character of the remaining Ephrathites at that time. He was impressed that "smiling innocence and meekness grace their countenances, and a softness of tone and accent adorn their conversation, and make their deportment gentle and obliging." Happily for the genealogist, he also recorded the names of the congregation members at the time. By his count only 14 Solitary Brothers remained, while the number of Roses of Saron was twice that many, for a total of 42. The secular congregation, counting baptized unmarried youths, numbered 99. The congrega-

tion as a whole thus totaled 141.[2] Most of the Solitary were
now aged or aging, and their once dominant position in the
community was disappearing. The lay congregation, of course,
included children not yet baptized.

A reshuffling of leadership also took place in the Sisterhood
after Beissel's death. Barbara Meyer was replaced as prioress
by Catherina Hagemann, but just what this meant, if anything,
has been befogged by time. Sister Maria Eicher, it should be
noted, continued as a faithful Sister in the convent until her
death in 1784 at the age of seventy-four.

The controversy over the Ephrata land title had continued
to simmer during Beissel's last years and was settled only in
1770. The matter had already been aired in the Lancaster court
when Peter Miller and the Solitary, in league with the tavern
keeper Heinrich Müller, whose claim of a hundred acres has
already been mentioned, petitioned against Samuel Eckerling's
claim. That court, however, declared in favor of Samuel's
title. Things then got a bit nasty, for it is said that the Solitary locked out Samuel and his adherents from the bakehouse
and granary, whereupon Samuel is alleged to have opened it
with a file!

Beissel was still alive during those years when the destiny
of Ephrata was in the balance, but his power had clearly ebbed,
for he was in no condition now to affect the outcome. He was
ill and doubtless distraught by the events around him; he withdrew more and more into his psychic shell. Quite understandably, he looked to Peter Miller, ever faithful to the Ephrata
ideal and a man who honored him and what he had wrought,
to stem the tide against communal disintegration.

In November 1764 Miller, armed with a plea from Beissel
and a signed petition from many of the Solitary, decided to
appeal the claims of Samuel Eckerling to the Provincial Assembly in Philadelphia. Heinrich Müller filed his own petition.
Eckerling, of course, did also. Finally, to the chagrin of Miller
and the Solitary, the assembly ruled that Samuel's title was valid
but that he was legally bound to vest the 180 acres claimed
by the Solitary in a trusteeship for the Brotherhood.[3] (In those
days women, meaning in this case the Sisterhood, had few if
any legal rights in regard to property claims.) It was probably
during the course of the assembly's consideration that Sangmeister convinced Eckerling to grant Heinrich Müller his 100
acres, thus eliminating him from the contest.

The assembly's decision, however, brought no peace to Ephrata; the quarrel continued unabated, even during Beissel's last tortured days and for two years after his death, while implementation of the "trusteeship" remained in limbo. Finally in 1770, Miller agreed to an accommodation, motivated, no doubt, by prudence and a weariness with the whole untidy business. For the "nominal sum of five shillings," it is said, Eckerling conveyed the communal tract "in trust" to "all members of the Christian Society of Ephrata." This body, however, was considered to include all "Virginians" from the Shenandoah who had found refuge in and around the village of Ephrata during the Indian troubles, even though they did not participate in the life of the cloister. Besides Eckerling and Sangmeister, they included John Adam Kelp, John Martin, Christian Luther, Martin Funk, Martin Kroll, as well as Catherina Kelp, Barbara Landes, and Christiane Luther.[4]

The settlement gave special recognition to Samuel Eckerling for "the Performance of his *benevolent* Grant and Privilege" (italics added). Since he was now reputed to be a wealthy man of much property, his "benevolence" is suspect. The arrangement divided the settling parties into three elements. Samuel Eckerling, M.D., of Ephrata village, was, of course, front and center. The second element was composed of five male trustees designated by Samuel — Sangmeister, of course, Christian Eckstein (presumably still resident in Germantown), Isaac Sensemann, John Adam Kelp, and John Martin. The deck, it may be said, was stacked. The third element of the settlement, considered the recipients of this "benevolence," now legally powerless, consisted of sixteen Brothers of Bethania, twenty Roses of Saron, and eight spinsters who apparently had left Saron but were living in the neighborhood.

It was a final victory for the divisive Eckerling spirit, but in the course of time it must have seemed an empty one. Their masterful antagonist was two years in his grave, and, with few exceptions, the Solitary who remained would give little thought to the land-title victory so long as they were not dispossessed in advancing age and were left in peace. To them, perhaps, it did not matter very much that the settlement essentially killed off the communal organization of the cloisters. The conveyance provided that each one living there be allotted a quarter acre for gardening and an equal share of any profits accruing from sales of products from fields and workshops. They had

to release to the trustees all interests in the estate but could
claim five pounds sterling when and if they left it. Ephrata
was no longer an economy in the image of the early Christians
but a mere association of individuals feebly sharing in a property contolled by those who had tried to bring the commune
to its knees in the first place. All in all, it was a tawdry settlement, the death knell of the commune and the Beisselian dream.

Whether or not the trustees expected to profit from it, any
such ideas were thwarted by the longevity of those remaining
and by further legacies to the "society." In 1772 it received a
bequest of two hundred acres from a certain Peter Shoemaker.
And ancient Jan Meyle left a bequest in 1783 of all his carpenter tools along with some money and property he had
somehow accumulated. Four years later Christian Eckstein,
the schismatic doctor, assigned the profits from a forty-acre
holding to the Ephrata survivors.[5]

This, then, was the enfeebled society that increasing numbers of visitors from "the world" observed. Some of them were
urbane and condescending in their comments and looked on
Ephrata as an antique curiosity. In 1771, the Reverend Jacob
Duché could not resist scorning the poor old souls in the cloister: "They should consider, in the first place, that they attempt
in vain to fly from their own evil dispositions, which will pur-
sue and torment them in their closest retreats; and in the second place, that by retiring from the world, they lose the only
opportunities they can possibly have of calling forth a thousand tender sensibilities, and exercising a thousand tender offices of sympathy, compassion, charity, and benevolence." He
missed the whole point, of course, but he did record a serviceable picture of the economy of Ephrata in its tired old age:
"They carry on several branches of business with great skill
and industry. They have a convenient oil-mill, paper-mill, and
printing press. They make parchment, tan leather, and manu-
facture linen and woolen cloth, more than sufficient to serve
their own society. The sisters are ingenious at making wax-
tapers, curious paper-lanthorns, and various kinds of paste-
board boxes, which they sell to strangers who come to visit
them. They likewise amuse themselves with writing favourite
texts of scripture in large letters curiously ornamented with
flowers and foliage. They seem to be rather works of patience
than of genius."[6]

Duché's good friend, the sophisticated Francis Hopkinson —

lawyer, musician, and later "poet of the Revolution"—saw Ephrata in much the same way. His versified "sentiment," which
was occasioned by a conversation with Peter Miller, contains
the following lines:

> Deep in Ephrata's gloom you fix your seat,
> And seek religion in the dark retreat;
> In sable weeds you dress the heav'n-born maid,
> And place her pensive in the lonely shade:
> Recluse, unsocial, you your hours employ,
> And fearful, banish ev'ry harmless joy.[7]

The "heav'n-born maids," one is constrained to add, were
growing old by now, and as for Peter Miller, he was by no
means that remote from the world around him. For much of
the rest of the century he carried on extensive correspondence
with some of the most prominent leaders of the revolutionary
era. His learning and linguistic abilities were widely valued,
and in 1768 his name was proposed for membership in the
prestigious American Philosophical Society by Charles Thom-
son, who would soon be serving as secretary to the Continental and Revolutionary congresses. The paper he presented for
this honor explained scientific observations on destruction
wrought by the Hessian fly, experiments on preventing insect
ravages on peas and lentils, and referred to his specifications
for a new earth-boring screw auger.[8]

Prior Jaebez was also heavily occupied with editorial and
publishing duties and supervising the Ephrata press. After yet
another interim, the press was busy in 1769–1770 producing
two more books for the Mennonites—a question-and-answer
catechetical tract for youths, and a book of prayers and "com-
mandments."[9] Meanwhile, the *Vorsteher* was collecting and
editing a substantial sheaf of Beissel's spiritual discourses, using
accumulated notes taken when they were delivered and written manuscripts. These issued from the press in 1773 as *Deliciae Ephratenses, Pars I,* and to it Miller added, as a footnoted
introduction, the original German of Beissel's *Mystiche Abhandlung* on the Fall of Man.[10] Miller's old friend and former
Ephrata agent, Christopher Marshall, was at the same time
engaged in making an English translation of the work; his letter to Miller of August 1773 indicates that the translation was
nearly completed.[11] It never appeared in print and presumably
has been lost.

Clouds of war were now once again darkening the land as the colonists girded for the drive to independence and the birth of a new nation. Ephrata, though considerably overage for involvement in the struggle, was again suspect as a haven for pacifists — and that was tantamount, in the eyes of many local people, to flaunting sympathy for the Tory cause. There was, of course, plenty of cause to worry. The revolutionary Committee of Safety had issued strict regulations against suspected Tories; even "nonassociators" were hounded and harassed.

James Reed, one of the revolutionary leaders, had evidently written a letter of inquiry (or warning) to Ephrata, and on October 10, 1776, three months after independence was declared, Peter Miller answered him with a straightforward reply, embellished with Latin quotations from the ancients about Christian responsibility to a "higher magistracy" than the State. "We ought to abhor all War," he wrote without reservation, "for to subject all Men without Distinction to the Civil Law, is injurious to the Christian Cause, as some may be under a higher Magistrate, and also consequently emancipated from the civil Government. . . . In the present struggle there is a third Party, who observe a strict Neutrality."[12] By the "third Party" he meant, of course, not only Ephrata but Quakers, Dunkers, Mennonites, Schwenkfelders, Moravians, and a host of other Pietists and Separatists who had come to the province to escape the persecution of the state for following the Way of Peace. As a whole, the third party may have constituted a quarter or more of the total population of Pennsylvania. And Prior Jaebez was not going to mince words about their convictions vis-à-vis the state, regardless of his amiable, friendly relations with some of its officers. As for Ephrata, it was bound and determined to remain its own *imperium in imperio,* even in its tired old age.

There is no question that Peter Miller tried to maintain amicable relations with all sides in an era when that was suspect. As late as 1774 he was in correspondence with Lady Juliana Penn in England, wife of the conservative Thomas Penn. In a letter to her he refers to Ephrata as "a small republic" and adds, "I am persuaded that many of the British dominions have favored our institution, being well adapted to raise the spirit of ancient Christianity, and I humbly think that your Ladyship is among that number."[13]

As evidence that he was highly trusted by revolutionary leaders also, the revolutionary Provincial Council contracted with

Miller and the Ephrata press on December 4, 1775, to translate into German and produce four hundred copies of "Rules and Regulations and Articles of Association" for the German sector of the bilingual province.[14] There is also a strong tradition that in 1776 the Second Continental Congress pressed him into translating the Declaration of Independence into seven different languages, though this is not verifiable.[15] He did, however, translate some of the official diplomatic correspondence of the new government.

His high standing with the leadership in Philadelphia enabled Miller to intercede on behalf of peace-church conscientious objectors, including several Mennonites who were heavily fined for not apprehending some Britishers (who may have been in the process of deserting anyway). In fact, his role as a man of mercy came to be recognized, even honored in some quarters, throughout the war.

Events of the war now moved closer to Ephrata. On September 11, 1777, the Battle of the Brandywine, in the Quaker countryside around Chadd's Ford and Birmingham Meeting seventy miles to the southeast, cost the continental army three hundred lives, six hundred wounded, and about four hundred taken prisoner. The stout resistance of the army did not stop General Howe and the British troops from taking over Philadelphia for comfortable winter quarters. The Continentals retreated upcountry, were defeated in another fierce contest at Germantown, and finally took up winter quarters in a desperate condition at Valley Forge. It was the darkest hour of the American Revolution.

After the Brandywine encounter, by orders of General Washington, about five hundred of the wounded were dispatched in wagons and carts from the battlefield to Ephrata. It was a gruesome trek over rutted roads. Many wounds turned gangrenous; cries of excruciating pain could be heard from the column day and night, until after three days the blood-stained wagons arrived at the cloisters.[16]

Ephrata, of course, had no choice in the matter, and the Brothers and Sisters immediately mobilized into round-the-clock action as nurses, orderlies, and provisioners. All the reduced resources of Ephrata's granary, almonry, workshops, and mills were allocated to the task. Kedar and Zion were turned into crowded hospitals; other available space was commandeered for the harsh winter to come. (Christopher Marshall's diary noted that 247 were still hospitalized at Ephrata at the end of December.)[17]

Five days after Brandywine the Continental Congress convened in Lancaster's courthouse on the square (as did the Pennsylvania legislature, which stayed until June 1778). But the Continental Congress held only one session in Lancaster; its sole action was to pass a resolution to put the Susquehanna between it and the British and to reconvene in York. There it finally adopted the Articles of Confederation and stayed until the end of June 1778, when it was safe to return to Philadelphia.[18]

During the winter of 1777–1778 at Ephrata, pain, death, and epidemic took an incredible toll, not only among the wounded but among those who nursed them as well. It is estimated that about one hundred fifty soldiers died at the cloisters.[19] They were given military burials at first, but as the death rate increased they were simply interred in trenches, and ceremony was forgotten. There simply was no time or energy to do otherwise. All too soon the dreaded "camp fever" raged through Kedar and Zion, along with typhus and scarlet fever. Ten of the aging Ephrathites (about 28 percent of the estimated thirty-six members) lost their lives in the epidemic and were buried in God's Acre. Others who came to help, like the neighboring Mennonite John Baer and his wife, succumbed also. By the time the crisis had passed, not much remained of the real life of the cloister.

As the recovering wounded were able to wander back to their homes or rejoin Washington's resurgent army, the pall of disease still lingered behind. Ephrata had to cleanse itself completely, and in the process was forced to destroy its finest buildings, Kedar and Zion. The reserves of foodstuffs, medicines, blankets, and cloth were used up, and those who survived faced a bleak and disheartening future. Once again Ephrata's acts of mercy remained unrewarded, except, we are told, for General Washington's presentation of a pair of "exquisitely wrought" wooden communion goblets.[20]

One of the wounded later inscribed his grateful memory of Ephrata's loving care. His identity is unknown, for the original source has since been lost, but a Sabbatarian historian printed it in 1851. The unnamed American officer who wrote his account was deeply moved: "I came among this people by accident, but I left them with regret. . . . They all acted the part of the Good Samaritan to me, for which I hope to be ever grateful; and while experiencing the benefits of their kindnesses and attentions . . . and listening to the words of hope and pity with which they consoled the poor sufferers, is it strange that . . . their uncouth garments appeared more beautiful in my eyes than ever did the richest robes of fashion . . .? Until I entered the walls of Ephrata, I had no idea of pure and practical Christianity. Not that I was ignorant of the forms, or even the doctrines of religion. I knew it in theory before; I saw it in practice then."[21]

For Ephrata, healing and care and death were not the end of the matter. When Washington, whose army was short of paper for shot wadding, learned of the existence of a large paper supply at Ephrata, a captain and some aides were dispatched to confiscate it. Captain Henderson arrived with two wagons while the work of caring for the wounded was still going on. The rest is best told by Peter Miller: "As, at that time, the English army was in our vicinity, we remonstrated and told the captain, that, as this would hurt our [neutral] character, we would not consent, unless he should take them by force, for which we should have a certificate; to which he consented. Accordingly he ordered six men, with fixed bayonets, from the hospital . . . and they loaded two waggons full. The captain afterwards settled with us, paying us honestly, and we parted in peace; though we never asked from him a certificate, but trusted to providence."[22]

In the eyes of the German sectarians, the most direful effect of this event was the confiscation of the unsold copies and unbound printed sheets of the *Martyrs' Mirror*. To those who prized their Anabaptist heritage, this work was sacrosanct, and to Ephrata it represented an enormous sacrifice and one of the commune's greatest achievements. Its destruction for the purposes of war, therefore, appeared as a bad omen for the rebellion and the new nation it created. Later, however, a number of the bound copies were returned.

That Peter Miller was a forgiving man is demonstrated by the story of one of his appeals for clemency. Michael Widman, then tavern keeper at what later became the famous Eagle Hotel in Ephrata village, had on several occasions bedeviled the nonresistant prior, hitting him soundly on one occasion and spitting in his face on another. Michael was alleged to be one of the richest Tories in Lancaster County. He got caught expressing his political opinions, was arrested for treason, escaped through a window of his tavern, and fled to Bethania in Ephrata, where he hid. He was soon captured again and was sentenced to be hanged. Miller at once started off on foot to see his friend General Washington at Valley Forge, a grueling journey. The General at first refused to intercede, but when he discovered that his friend had walked sixty miles through snow on behalf of his worst enemy, he relented and granted a pardon. Miller then walked another fifteen miles with the pardon note to West Chester, arriving, it is said, just in time to see Widman being led to the scaffold. The Tory allegedly saw the prior arrive and, insensible to the ways of the non-resistant Christian, assumed he had come from Ephrata to gloat. The pardon was produced in the nick of time, and Widman was released. It is said that the two men walked back to Ephrata together, Widman no doubt a chastened man. All of the Tory's property was confiscated and sold at auction by orders of the new government. Widman's political views did not change; he was jailed again, won a release, and thereafter disappeared into the west.[23]

Even in the difficult war years, Peter Miller kept part of his mind focused on preserving the history of the commune. He looked back on its rich but troubled past and the memory of Conrad Beissel with longing and heartache. A note of August 1777 in the diary of Christopher Marshall (who was living in Lancaster between 1777 and 1781) indicates that Miller and old Ludwig Höcker, the former schoolmaster, brought him a manuscript titled "Annals of the Brethren at Ephrata," consisting of 488 quarto pages.[24] They asked Marshall to edit it, but this version also seems to have disappeared; another nine years would go by before the original German *Chronicon* was printed (and 112 years before J. Max Hark's English translation).

The prior looked with some yearning in these years to the little congregation on the Antietam, a hundred miles to the west. During the war he kept up a steady correspondence with Andrew Snowberger and his wife, Barbara, a devout convert of Beissel when she was but eighteen. In 1776 the Ephrata press printed a couple of touching poems by Andrew and Barbara that signaled the transference of the spirit of the older Ephrata to the community that became Snow Hill.

Miller himself was acutely aware of the decay of Ephrata and the impossible burdens the war had placed upon it. Fi-

nally, in May 1782, after receiving more hymn-poems from
the Snowbergers and no doubt wearied to exhaustion by the
hard times that had come upon Ephrata, he bared his heart
to them in his most poignant lines: "We here find ourselves
at a strange place of entertainment, in the land of our enemies,
where our poor spirit with respect to conscience, must experience so many a hard trial, as I distinctly notice in the hymns
you sent us. In the meantime let the goodness of God be praised,
which in so many distresses, untill the present has so firmly
protected us, that we have not yet been brought to disgrace
in the presence of our enemies."[25] But for all the hard trials
borne without "disgrace," the gentle and scholarly Peter Miller
must have been wondering how Ephrata survived the revolutionary era at all.

Not enough strength remained in Ephrata after the trials
of war to mount a recovery. Some of the shops and mills continued to produce, but levels of production dropped off significantly. The cloistered Solitary who survived the war were
too old and feeble to renew the Ephrata aspiration, and the
stern regimen of former times was sacrificed for their comfort.
About twenty Sisters still inhabited Saron in the mid-1780s,
but most of them were in their sixties or seventies. Even fewer
Brothers remained in the cloister; though some were more active than the Sisters, they too were elderly. A few young people
were admitted to membership, but most of them, finding the
outside world beckoning, left in their mid-twenties or earlier.[26]

Under the circumstances, it is quite astonishing that the
Ephrata press produced so many books and pamphlets in the
1785–1795 decade. There could have been only a handful of
relatively able-bodied Brothers capable of setting type, press-
ing sheets, and making paper and bindings, and the workmanship was no longer up to the old standards. In 1782 the press
had issued a thin sheaf of eight spiritual poems written by four
women of the Antietam congregation under the title of *Ausbund geistlicher Lieder.* A second *Ausbund,* a sheaf of sixteen
pages with a slightly altered title, appeared in 1785. One of
its contributors was Barbara Snowberger. In the latter year also
the *Ernsthaffte Christenpflicht,* the prayerbook of the Mennonites, was reissued for the third time, probably at their request.

The following year was busier. Perhaps out of concern for
preserving the nonresistant convictions of Ephrata-sponsored
frontier congregations where Indian troubles still flared up,

the press now issued Anthony Benezet's principal work in de-
fense of the aborigines. Benezet, a Quaker of Huguenot background, had probably attended as many conferences with the
Indians as any man living. He was a tireless pamphleteer for
many good causes; as a matter of fact, back in 1763 Ephrata
also published one of his antislavery tracts in a German translation. The shorter work on the Indian character, however,
was his last work, and his modern biographer calls it "the
greatest written testimony to the kindness, hospitality, and
generosity of the Indians ever offered."[27]

Also in 1786 Ludwig Höcker's short school primer was published. He was not teaching any more, but his heart was still
in it. For some time he had been kept busy at the printery,
and according to the primer's title page the little book was
printed and "put together by the schoolmaster, printer and
bookbinder," meaning Brother Obed himself. He was now approaching the end of his life (he died in 1792), and this was
a labor of genuine love and devotion.[28]

The climax of the year, however, was the publication of
the long-awaited original German version of the *Chronicon
Ephratense*. It is the foundation for all later historical study
of Ephrata, and in spite of the now-fashionable criticism of
its natural biases and subterfuges, the book still has its charms
as a unique chronicle. There is nothing quite like it in American literature. The late Paul Wallace, a sensitive observer of
the history of that era, admitted its "allegorical, ambiguous
style" that nevertheless displayed "a healthy humor," adding
that it was "somewhat in the vein of *The Pilgrim's Progress*."[29]
It has a direct, naive simplicity that gives even its occasional
drifts into the arcane a certain charm. As for its supposed lack
of candor, that characteristic is shared with other works of
history written at the time. Best of all, it tells a story that is
unique in our annals — and tells it well.

In 1787 the press was busy producing a version of the New
Testament, which its colophon states proudly was published
"at the expense of the Brothers." Like the *Chronicon* the year
before, it illustrates the decline of the printer's art, but producing its 792 cramped pages must have been a heavy burden
on the old men in the printery.[30]

Two productions of 1788–1789 are also worth recalling. The
Apologie of Alexander Mack, Jr., demonstrates that the loose
ties between Ephrata and the Germantown Dunkers were never

fully severed. Mack, the former Brother Theophilus, who had been lured away to the camp of the Eckerlings and found that unsatisfactory too, was now the aged bishop of the Dunkers at Germantown. Brumbaugh, the scholarly governor of Pennsylvania early in our own century as well as Brethren historian, called Mack's *Apologie* "the most important defense of the Church of the Brethren in the 18th century."[31] Yet as if to balance the Ephrata-Dunker scale, the Ephrata press in the next year republished Beissel's dissertation on Man's Fall and Redemption, as the *Göttliche Wunderschrift,* and, several years later, a small sheaf of his letters called the *Geistliche Briefe.*[32] Although grown old and weak, Ephrata was still the child of Father Friedsam.

With three exceptions, productions of the 1790s were short, ephemeral pieces: a pamphlet on physic for "man and beast" (in which beasts took precedence); the story of a man who sold his soul to Satan and was redeemed; a little work prophesying the end of the world; a short, allegorical travel account; a pamphlet on Universalism; a booklet of prayers; and a smattering of broadsides.[33] The three other productions are more memorable. The first, the *Christliche Bibliothek* (1792), was evidently the work of George Adam Martin, the irrepressible schismatic who, having sold his farm and left the Antietam in 1772, had long since gone off to the Alleghenies to gather souls.[34] The work, which may have been guided or edited by Peter Miller, deserves more study than it has been given; it discusses the spiritual development of man, the ordinances of primitive Christianity, the decay of the church, and the views of sectarians. The second was the elaborate defense of Christian A. Roemeling, who early in the century was ousted as minister by German Lutherans and joined the Mennonites in Holland. It is a theosophical, mystical work showing kinship to the thought processes of Ephrata in its golden age, with appended writings of Gottfried Arnold and Gerhard Tersteegen. The third, a separate work of Tersteegen, also issued in 1792, "on the Christian use of songs and singing," reminded the Ephrathites how central their own choral music had once been to the mystical fervor of their lives.[35]

Peter Miller had now grown old and somewhat garrulous, a condition he probably shared with the rest of the Solitary who still remained on earth. By the time a fascinating Frenchman, Théophile Cazenove, visited the place in 1794, only thirteen Sisters and six Brothers remained.[36] In the following year his noble countryman, the duc de la Rouchefoucauld-Liancourt, also paid Ephrata a visit and recorded his comments. Those on Peter Miller, who was "not far from eighty years of age" (actually he was eighty-five), reveal the aristocrat's anticlerical bias:

> His eyes still sparkle with a degree of fire, and his imagination is still lively. Our curiosity led us to inquire after the institution of the house, and the doctrines of the order. Father Miller satisfied this curiosity in a manner the most tediously diffuse, by giving us a minute account of every point, however trifling, of the doctrines and history of the *Dunkers*. This history is a tissue of absurdities, like that of all monks. A ridiculous compound of ambition, and of a desire of insulating themselves apart from the state, is common to them all.

The duke also talked at length with a younger "monk" (perhaps a hireling). One wishes he had recorded the name of the man: "He was a printer, a man of thirty years of age, who had lived thirteen years in this house. He told me that the discipline of the order is by no means so strict, as the old monk pretended; that they divide their earnings only if they choose; that they live just as they please, and drink coffee and tea. He did not appear so enthusiastic a friend of the vow of chastity as Father Miller . . . 'for,' said he, 'are not women truly charming?'" Particular about his own comforts, the nobleman had only scorn for what he regarded as the hypocrisy of the place, "displaying everywhere an ostentatious poverty by half-hidden beds of down." He refused to visit the "nunnery," for "the nuns, being old, could not in the least interest our curiosity." And his conclusion is condescending: "They are a good-natured sort of people, they live upon the produce of an estate of three hundred acres, injure nobody, are laughed at in the country, and yet tolerably well beloved."[37]

Had he heard the duke's comments in person, the old *Vorsteher* would now probably have ignored them with his knowing, gentle smile, but he was not always so tolerant. Only a few years before he had taken some pains to refute the numerous inaccuracies in a long article written by a British officer who visited Ephrata some time after the Revolution, which was widely circulated in England and America. Peter Miller called the article "scurrilous and sordid" and thought the officer must have been an atheist or near to it and that he must have composed the account "in liquor," though the piece hardly deserves such biting comments. The editor of the *American Museum,* which reprinted the article from the *Edinburgh Magazine,* appended a note quoting Miller's letter to the distinguished William Barton wishing that "such greedy vultures, as he [the British officer] and his companions were, may never more come to America."[38]

Brother Jaebez was doubtless fed up with worldly, sophisticated Europeans who, merely out of a perverse curiosity, came around to poke into the lives of the old folks and the decaying fabric of Ephrata. As a matter of fact, one of the best travel accounts of Ephrata was written by a distinguished German who was prevented from visiting by bad roads and weather. Dr. Johann David Schöpf's account in his *Travels in the Confederation* is based simply on careful and judicious inquiry, and it assesses the Ephrata character and ethic with understanding honesty.[39]

As with Father Friedsam, Brother Jaebez's last years were also befogged by infirmities and pangs of regret that the once-great aspirations of Ephrata had quite vanished. Little was recorded of Peter Miller's last days or even of his funeral—who was left to record?[40] The old scholar passed on to his final rest September 25, 1796. Prioress Christina Hagemann died only a few weeks afterward.

Their positions as such were not refilled, for there was little left to lead or direct.[41] Christoph Daniel Ebeling, then continental Europe's leading authority on American affairs, reported from Germany in 1797 that "now at least every brother works for himself, but some shops are operated by the community, as a whole."[42] The lay congregation was taking over, and the demise of the Solitary orders as operating organisms was in reality (if not officially) an accomplished fact.

Snow Hill Afterglow

THE EPHRATA IMAGE IN ITS

OFFSPRING ON THE ANTIETAM, 1796–1889

ITH one pallid exception, what had made Ephrata unique as a socioreligious organism simply did not take firm root in other settings. That had little to do with geography, nor was it a matter of too much inwardness at Ephrata, for its missionizing outreach had been forceful and persistent. Yet it had little success in replicating itself. The climate of the times militated against its extension, and the soil wherein it tried to transplant its scions proved to be too thin or rocky for so rare a plant. Its communal mysticism was too exotic for a young America moving into a different orbit.

Ephrata did play a not inconsiderable role in the development of Sabbatarian and Baptist Brethren communions in the Pennsylvania and Virginia backcountry, but the peculiar Ephrata formula did not take root in them, except temporarily. Falckner's Swamp, Nantmill, Coventry, and Amwell never attained the Zion-citadel of Ephrata; the Shenandoah settlements and the Bermudian and Stony Creek congregations went down a different road.

Snow Hill is something of an exception to that failure, but compared with the vibrancy of Ephrata in the 1735–1765 period it was only a pale reflection. Yet the Ephrata story would be incomplete without at least a postscript about it.

Until the publication of Charles M. Treher's study in 1968, relatively little was known about Snow Hill.[1] Most surveys of American communal experiments ignored it altogether; even the contemporary nineteenth-century religious communes, such as the Shakers and the Harmonists, do not seem to have known *173* it existed. For that matter, Snow Hill made little effort to reach out beyond itself, except backward in time and direction to Ephrata. Moreover, it was remote from the main arteries of population movement.

One can visit the site in the eastern portion of Pennsylvania's Franklin County by driving north on Route 997 from Waynesboro toward the village of Quincy. What local folks vaguely refer to as "the old nunnery" is on the east side of the road in a charming but remote cove surrounded by foothills at the base of South Mountain. Through the cove runs a branch of the historic Antietam, narrow, clear, and deep at this point as it tumbles onto the fertile flatland of the Great Valley. In the distant hazy west the first ridge of the Alleghenies, massive barrier to the westward movement of young America, rises above the plain below. Even today it is a handsome landscape.

The physical remains of Snow Hill—a great, double-winged brick common house, a huge latter-day barn, and across the stream a plastered stone meetinghouse with handsome curved benches inside—remind us little of Ephrata. The place is quiet and solemn enough, but we are in another age here. It has a different kind of harmony.

The Antietam congregation originated in 1752 when the impulsive George Adam Martin formed a scattered group of settlers as a unity of German Baptist Brethren.[2] After Martin was excommunicated by the Germantown church for unorthodoxy stimulated by Beissel, he had a difficult time overcoming the counterstrokes of Germantown delegations. The *coup de grace* was really administered by Beissel and the Ephrata pilgrimage of 1764, which were followed by two more Beissel visits in close succession. But it remained for Peter Miller to found a regular Sabbatarian congregation there around 1775.[3]

Snow Hill took its name from the Schneeberger family (anglicized to Snowberger; *Schneeburg* means Snow Hill). They had arrived in the area in 1750 from the Canton of Berne in Switzerland. Two decades later the son of the head of the household, Andreas (Andrew), married a remarkable woman, Barbara Karper or Karber, who at a young age had been deeply stirred by the Beissel *magia* during one of his visits. The Snowberger family, however, remained faithful to the convictions of the Germantown Brethren, and Barbara's Beisselian bias caused some internal conflict. At last she could stand it no longer; one night, with a young child in her arms, she started

off alone for Ephrata. Andrew was chastened, overtook her,
and promised to adopt at least her Sabbatarian convictions. Thereafter their log house, only a stone's throw from the later cloister, became the rallying place for the Sabbath-keepers in the whole area, from the Bermudian in the east to the Conococheague (now with Dunkers settling in) to the west.

In 1772, Adam Martin grew restless again and moved on to Stony Creek, far to the west.[4] That prompted the aging Peter Miller to visit the Antietam and, by letters, maintain a pastoral continuity there. Eventually he ordained Andrew Snowberger to the ministry and in so doing perpetuated the Ephrata priesthood into the next century. Andrew is remembered, however, as a strong, silent frontiersman who never had much to say, a doer rather than an evangelist, even though, like his wife Barbara, a thoughtful hymn writer. Barbara was the one who kept the little congregation together. Andrew must have breathed a sigh of relief when Peter Lehman arrived from the Alleghenies and took up the pastoral role.

Lehman is said to have been a hermit in the western mountains. He was of Amish or Mennonite background, young, tall, and of a commanding presence. He had heard of Peter Miller's Ephrata and was intrigued with the Ephrata ideal. Miller had also heard of him and wrote him in 1788, apparently hoping that this uneducated but dynamic eremite would either found a community of like-minded recluses in the Allegheny Mountains to the west or even come to revitalize Ephrata itself.[5] Finally Miller asked him at least to visit the Antietam, and curiously, a mountain prophetess named Hannah thrice dreamed that a spiritual flock had need of him and told Lehman her mystic message.

Barbara Snowberger apparently had no knowledge of these developments, but so sensitive was she to "the mystic voices" that she too had a dream. In it she was walking in a large open space, perhaps seeking spiritual help, when she perceived a man in the same area wearing a long coat. She was acutely aware that the vision forecast an important development. As she remembered it, the dream became a reality when Peter Lehman approached the community. Not long thereafter, old Peter Miller confirmed young Peter Lehman as spiritual leader of the Antietam flock.

By the year of Peter Miller's death, Peter Lehman was urging his parishioners to take up the monastic life in the image

of Ephrata. The idea was at first repugnant to Andrew Snowberger, and even his wife seemed reluctant to take that step,
but Lehman was very convincing to their three unmarried children, who were all over twenty. They in turn convinced their
mother, who finally got Andrew's reluctant agreement. The
Snow Hill celibate commune thus came into being in 1798 with
the establishment of a communal dining room in the stone house
Andrew had built in 1793.

Daughters Barbara and Elizabeth Snowberger became the
first single Sisters; son John Snowberger and Peter Lehman took
the celibate and communal vows soon thereafter. Additions
to this little nucleus came slowly, but a communal dam and
gristmill were erected in the meadow in 1807, and with reluctance Andrew Snowberger agreed to become the first prior of
the little Order of the Solitary. His mystical wife, Barbara, the
real founder of Snow Hill, died in 1810, just as the formative
phase of the commune was ending.[6]

Membership in the Order followed the general Ephrata
pattern, but its discipline was more relaxed and its organization simpler. Charler Treher summed up the arrangement between members: "If they had been married before, this did
not bar them from the society. Neither did they have to promise continued celibacy. Persons entering the cloister could
have no independent estate or personal property. Possessions
were to be turned over to the communal order. However, this
property was accurately appraised and a certificate given,
and if a member wished to leave, he was returned his possessions. If he died in the cloister, the property accrued permanently to the establishment."[7] This appears to be a more
businesslike arrangement than Ephrata's, at least in the post-
Eckerling period. One has the impression that Snow Hill was
much more exacting in and concerned with its economy than
Beissel's Ephrata, though it never took on the harsh requirements of the Eckerling work ethic. Moreover, Snow Hill did
without the hierarchic trappings and fanciful names of the
Ephrata orders and did not divide or separate the male and
female contingents. It was and remained a simple brotherhood
of all. Its policies were guided by a governing body of five
trustees regularly elected for four-year terms by an assembly
of both cloister members and the lay congregation. The trustees
not only had defined responsibilities for the economy of the
commune but also assessed applications for membership and

judged whether postulants properly carried out their six-month novitiates.

The Snow Hill commune made a much clearer demarcation between spiritual and temporal leadership than that at Ephrata, where these functions were often confusingly interlinked. Peter Lehman, however, was something of an exception and hence a leader in the Beisselian tradition. But after his death in 1823, the *Lehrer* (teacher-pastor) kept to his spiritual and pastoral roles while economic management devolved onto the prior and trustees.

The new *Lehrer,* Andrew Fahnestock, was a remarkable man and came to be regarded throughout the region as something of a "character." The home communion's attitude toward him was ambivalent. The trouble with Andrew Fahnestock was that he like to travel, which he did on foot, in flowing beard, long, drab coat, broad-brimmed hat, and carrying a pilgrim staff. When the opportunity came to combine his Snow Hill pastorate with ministering to the remaining lay congregation at Ephrata, he was away much of the time, and he seems to have been more enamoured of the Ephrata memory than of current opportunities at Snow Hill. For several periods between 1840 and 1855 (the year he baptized the only black person of the denomination), the congregation on the Antietam was moved to designate others to serve in his place; only one of three so appointed was a member of the commune.[8]

Temporal management of affairs at Snow Hill passed, in 1825, from Andrew Snowberger to his grandson Samuel. Except for a one-year interlude, Samuel maintained a deft and steady control of the commune's economic affairs until his death in 1883. Treher's researches revealed that Samuel "kept what amounts to a diary of poems, all in German, reflecting his spiritual musing as well as life in the cloister."[9] The manuscript of 309 pieces deserves further study, which may yet reveal Samuel Snowberger as the dominant genius of Snow Hill's history.

Snow Hill seems to have remained remote from the larger world around it, a condition favored by the geography of the place. Even some of the relatively close neighbors thought of it, if they gave it any attention at all, as a quiet Catholic nunnery. The commune's only confrontation with "the world" was on the issue of Sabbatarianism and working on Sunday. State law specifically forbade Sunday labor and enforced it with more rigor than in colonial times. Local informers saw to it that fines were levied, and the cloister members, unlike the Ephrata Brothers a century earlier, dutifully paid them for some time. Finally in 1846 the congregation appealed to the state legislature, but in vain. That same year Jacob Specht refused to pay his fine; the "great defender," Thaddeus Stevens, represented his case before the state supreme court—also in vain. In 1848 several of the congregation lost property and several others were thrown in jail. But after that, public opinion seems to have influenced the law to overlook the continued infractions.

What is more perplexing about the community's remoteness from the world around it is the evident lack of recorded response to the dramatic events of the Civil War. There is little evidence about Snow Hill's "peace witness," unlike Ephrata's, although the Brethren were professed nonresistant Christians. Yet the war broke out all around them. Presumably the men of the congregation paid the heavy levies required by the Union for the hiring of "substitutes."

Lee's first attempt to invade the North was halted not far away on the Antietam in Maryland in September 1862, and in the next month the Confederates under Jeb Stuart raided Chambersburg and the rich lands of Franklin County with startling success. Early in July of the following year, the greatest battle in American history raged for three fateful days at Gettysburg, hardly thirty miles away from Snow Hill. We simply do not know how or whether these critical events affected life at Snow Hill, though their impact must have been substantial.

The economy of the cloister was effectively administered and prosperous in this era, thanks to the careful stewardship of Samuel Snowberger. Although few if any observers from the outside world left a record of penetrating the Snow Hill sanctum, a visitor at midcentury would have been awed by what so small a collectivity had accomplished. In 1830 the commune numbered only five Brothers and ten Sisters, and the number was barely doubled in the following fifteen years, but the productivity of the enterprise far exceeded the size of the membership. Its industrial establishment combined agriculture, milling, and a variety of workshops. Grain from its gristmill gained fame in eastern cities for its excellence. Its textiles, woven of home-produced linen and wool and purchased cotton, were

used both internally and for sale. At its peak of activity the
commune also conducted a cooper shop for barrel making,
a tin and copper shop, a blacksmith enterprise, a cabinet shop,
a broom shop, and a brick kiln.

A comely, gentle place, remote but busy. Snow Hill never
seemed to have suffered the internal tensions and turmoil of
Ephrata. Stresses of celibacy were minimal, perhaps because
the male and female members were not divided into separate,
sometimes competitive orders as at Ephrata. Out of a total of
forty-three listed as members during the course of its existence,
only two — Lydia Snowberger and Jacob Specht — withdrew in
favor of wedlock. And the Snow Hill celibates lived long lives.[10]

The midcentury visitor would have found a society very much
at peace with itself. There had been no straining after growth
and expansion, and the erection of buildings was less a matter
of societal ambition than of simple necessity. The first portion of the great common house had been built in 1814 over
a bubbling spring in the meadow. The spring, which still flows
generously, was a boon not only as a built-in water supply
but also as a cooler for storage of food products. Three large
additions to the common house were built only as needed, between 1835 and 1843. The whole commune was housed and
fed here. The structure reached a total length of 150 feet with
more than fifty rooms (not cells as at Ephrata), nine larger
"community rooms," a refectory, kitchen, and other facilities.
This is a plain, almost styleless structure, purely utilitarian
and without the evocative panache of Ephrata architecture.
Yet it was a good place to live, and comfortable.

Snow Hill did not reject physical comforts, as did Ephrata
to sharpen the life of the spirit. One finds no evidence here
of the extremely abstemious Ephrata diet, the narrow, board
benches for sleeping, or the square wooden blocks for pillows.
Nor did Snow Hill practice the chill night watches or limit its
sleeping hours so drastically. It was a regimen of moderation
rather than abstention.

Knights of the road, of which there were many in the nineteenth century, appreciated that. Hospitality, whether for traveler or tramp, was generous at Snow Hill; good meals and warm
beds were always available, and no one needed an introduction. It perpetuated the Ephrata tradition of charity, but it did
not extend far beyond the neighborhood. An exception was
Snow Hill's response to the Irish famine of 1845–1847, when

Illumination created at Snow Hill.
Courtesy The Pennsylvania German Society and Charles M.
Treher.

it shipped both money and flour to the sufferers, though it had
no connections with Ireland whatsoever.

Unlike Ephrata's, Snow Hill's outreach to the world beyond
it was very limited. Its religious pilgrimages may have been
reminiscent of Ephrata's only in form; they seem to have been
confined to little formative congregations of German Baptist
Brethren and "Seven-dayers" to the west, to Morrison's Cove
across the Great Valley, and to Stony Creek in Somerset
County. No one confronted the citadels of power like Michael
Wohlfahrt did in colonial Philadelphia.

Snow Hill was in no hurry to establish itself in the eyes of
the state. Actually, the "Monastical Society" (as it was officially dubbed by the state) was not formally incorporated until
1834. The next year the state legislature passed an act vesting
the commune's accumulated real estate in the society, property that heretofore had technically remained in individual or
family deeds.

There is, indeed, some justification for hesitating to call Snow
Hill a commune at all. The flour mill, for example, was not
strictly a communal enterprise, for the miller paid a rent to
the society and received so much per barrel for grinding the
grain. Under the direction of Samuel Snowberger, the society's
economy, as Charles Treher noted, "was partially communal,
and partially capitalistic, and partially a bartering of goods
and services."[11] But whatever the formula, it seemed to work —
and it worked as a collectivity.

Economic production was not the only sign of its collective

character. Its *Fraktur* is in the collective *Volk* tradition, yet
has a style of its own that is delicate and precise. If less inspired and less imaginative than that of the Sisters of Ephrata, it has a rewarding simplicity that echoes the Snow Hill way of life.[12] Just as Snow Hill borrowed its *Fraktur* art from Ephrata, so too did it borrow its music. This was based entirely on Beissel's musical system and objectives, and some of the Ephrata manuscripts and hymnals were simply transferred to Snow Hill until the Sisters there began to make their own copies. Peter Lehman tried to transfer the special angelic quality of Ephrata choral music, but there was no Conrad Beissel charisma to inspire it. Nevertheless, it was beautiful singing. Dr. William M. Fahnestock, who wandered far afield from Snow Hill and became something of an opera-goer abroad, used to return there in summers to hear the choir on Friday evenings, the commencement of the Sabbath, and on the following holy day. As a child he had heard Ephrata singing and never got over it. Though a sophisticated man of the world, and knowing that Snow Hill's music was "weak in comparison with the old Ephrata choir," he would invariably burst into "tears of ecstatic rapture" when hearing Snow Hill's "strains of celestial melody." Those emotions were recorded in 1835; the last of the Snow Hill leaders, Obed Snowberger, said that Snow Hill singing "ceased to be heard about 1880–85" when the voices were too old and feeble.[13]

Obed Snowberger was the last personification of the Beissel tradition. He was devoted to what he called "the Old School" of the Seventh Day Baptists who adhered to the mysticism of Ephrata. By midcentury most of the Snow Hill monastics were growing old. Their numbers had decreased steadily, and they had had little success in attracting the youth of the lay congregation. America had clearly turned away from mysticism, and the "Sevendayer" young bloods, as in so many denominations, opted for the security of Bible literalism, the word rather than the spirit. Obed remembered—with pangs of deep regret—the division that occurred within his own congregation:

> The real cause of the division of 1850–55, existed
> under the surface, at that time. We distinctly heard
> and saw, that grave differences of opinion, were en
> tertained, on the interpretation of the Scriptures. . . .
> The Old School party, could be said to be intense

readers of the Ephrata books. The New School party, were not intense readers of the Ephrata books. The Old School party, censured the New School party for setting aside some of the first principles of the Ephrata church. The Old School party, contended for the authority of the church—the New School party, for the authority of the scriptures. The Old School party, contended for the government of the Spirit. The New School party, for the government of the letter.[14]

By 1872 the Snow Hill cloister had dwindled to eight Sisters and eight Brothers, and the society itself came to an end toward the last of March 1889, when the common dining room was closed and Brother Obed moved to a small house nearby. The last of the Sisters, Senopie (Zenobia), whose worldly name was Elizabeth Fyock, died in 1894 at the age of eighty-three. A year later Obed Snowberger, the last of the Brothers, died at the age of seventy-two.

Although he never made perceptible waves in the world around him, the last spiritual heir of Conrad Beissel was a lovable and remarkable man. He was an inveterate reader, an affable philosopher, foot pilgrim to the western congregations, a poet, hymnist and musician, mechanic and clock repairman, and a printer on the old press that had been brought from Ephrata. Obed felt especially close to the Dunker settlement at Morrison's Cove across the Great Valley in eastern Bedford County. The congregation there had suffered grievously during the revolutionary era; in 1777 thirty of its settlers are said to have been massacred in an Indian uprising. Thereafter, however, the congregation seems to have survived and prospered. And Brother Obed was good tonic.[15]

With Obed more than a century and a half of spiritual history that began with Conrad Beissel's *Wanderjahre* in the Rhine country came to a gentle end. Heirs, congregation, and the Commonwealth of Pennsylvania contended for the physical remains of the "Monastical Society" on the headwaters of the Antietam. At last it was dissolved into a society of the lay congregation, which appointed trustees to care for the property. So it remains to this day, in spite of efforts by the Pennsylvania Historical and Museum Commission in 1966 and 1968 to purchase it for preservation as a historic site for the general public.

Much remains to be rediscovered there, but decay is slowly taking its toll. Treher notes that the old artifacts are being depleted, perhaps by not-too-scrupulous collectors hankering after the *Frakturschriften,* music manuscripts and hymnals, Ephrata imprints and antique Bibles. Pleaders for public preservation of them (including the present writer) have met with little success. At the very least, what remains deserves a careful archival recording. And the arts, poetry, and journals of Snow Hill have yet to be studied in depth, before it is too late.

The Later History of Ephrata

HAT happened to the trusteeship established as a result of Samuel Eckerling's land settlement remains obscure. Very likely its supervision devolved upon the lay congregation, which as time went on at least acted in that capacity. The remnant in the cloister can only be referred to as an unorganized "society" cared for in part, one supposes, by the congregation. Some of the land previously willed to the Solitary by Peter Shoemaker, and thus held jointly apart from the trusteeship, was now considered a cashable resource, and the Brotherhood sold 150 of the 200 Shoemaker acres. The main part of this tract was sold in 1809 to the land-hungry Robert Coleman, the great ironmaster who lived like a baron of old on his huge estate at Elizabeth Furnace not many miles from Ephrata.[1]

A faint semblance of cloister life continued for another two decades. Sir Augustus J. Foster, a British diplomat, visited Ephrata about 1810 and found only a shadow of life there: "At the Time of my visit to Ephrata there existed but two Brothers, only one of whom inhabited the great House, and he, as I learned from an old Sister, was a scandalous fellow: He wore a beard which the other did not: the latter, however, had been converted but eleven years previously and resided in a house in the Meadow, where he followed the occupation of Clock Maker. There were still 8 Sisters remaining of whom five lived in the Cloisters and 3 without them. The oldest of the 5 was 80 years old and the youngest 65."[2]

During the first quarter of the nineteenth century even the memory of Ephrata seems to have been erased from the consciousness of young America and the world beyond its cloistered compound. Not that the Ephrata ideal itself was dead. Religious communism with its countercultural implications was reborn in America in this quarter-century. The Shakers now

reached their apogee; having spread their communitarian settlements throughout New England in the last decade of the
previous century, they were now developing seven new towns
in Ohio, Kentucky, and Indiana. George Rapp's Harmonists
migrated to America from Württemberg in 1803–1805 and in
the next two decades built three beautiful towns, models of
communitarian planning, in western Pennsylvania and Indiana. Yet Rapp, who had visited friends in Lancaster County
to seek support, seems never to have heard of Ephrata, a spiritual commune very like his own—a sad commentary on the
depths of obscurity into which Ephrata had fallen. Rapp, indeed, became the Beissel of the new era.

Even the Sabbatarian lay congregation of Ephrata seems
to have lost membership and lapsed into a stasis, this in spite
of the fact that a general conference of American Sabbatarian
churches was held at Ephrata in August 1823. The Ephrata
church at that time had only fifty members, and its young people
were drifting away on the westward movement.[3]

A glimmer of historical interest in the earlier Ephrata did
not appear until 1827, when the accounts of Redmond Conyngham and Christian Endress were published together in the
Memoirs of the Historical Society of Pennsylvania. Although
based on some first-hand observation, they provide very thin
gruel for the modern scholar and suffer from errors of both
omission and commission. In the following decade Samuel
Hazard reprinted them and some other items about Ephrata
in his Register of Pennsylvania, the most important of which
was William Fahnestock's "Historical Sketch of Ephrata."
This article marked the real beginning of historical writing on
the subject.[4]

The cloister was now a ghostly place, and indeed the ghost
of Brother Ezechiel Sangmeister, in his grave for four decades,
seems to have been glowering over it. In the years 1825–1827
the four pamphlets of the Leben und Wandel (Life and Conduct), posthumously attributed to him, greatly shocked most
of the remaining Sabbatarians at Ephrata with its fulminations
against Beissel and those who remained faithful to him. Aside
from its autobiographical content, the work was deliberately
calculated to provide a harsh antidote to the official history
of the commune, the Chronicon Ephratense. But to put the
Sangmeister Leben und Wandel into perspective, it is important to bear in mind not only the history and character of the

author but also the mysterious circumstances under which the work was produced.⁵

Sangmeister's life, which began in Lower Saxony in 1723, was never serene. When Sangmeister was nine years old his father died, and at the age of thirteen he had to leave school to earn his way. He learned the joiners' trade, and after three years' apprenticeship set out on his journeyman wanderings. While he was in Württemberg his master determined to emigrate to America, and the journeyman went with him. But for four years after his arrival Ezechiel had to bear the indignities of indentured service to pay for his ocean passage. Thereafter he settled down in Germantown as a joiner, but, to borrow the words of Klaus Wust, "despite an active and at times quite boisterous life, he was haunted by an inner loneliness, and in the fall of 1747 he booked a passage for Europe."⁶ Just at that time, however, his friend Anthony Höllenthal introduced him to Wilhelm Jung, the former agent for the Eckerlings and now the suspect recruiter for Beissel and the Brotherhood. Jung convinced them both to join the Ephrathites.

For four and a half years Sangmeister, with increasing resentment toward the strict communal regimen, grew steadily more unhappy and bitter under its "spiritual dictatorship." At the same time, it must have been during these years that he became an unusually sensitive and knowledgeable mystic, doubtless under the influence — resent it as he might — of Beissel himself. His mounting bitterness, however, took over, and one night in October 1752 he and Höllenthal slipped away on their trek to the Shenandoah. The rest of his story has already been told.

To explain the story behind the *Leben und Wandel* itself, one must begin by noting the sale of a part of Ephrata's communal printery to Johann Baumann of nearby Ephrata village in 1799. During the next decade, several books of home remedies and religion for the German-reading market appeared under his imprint. Then his son Joseph Bauman (without the double *n*) took over and produced a curious melange of Pietist and theosophic works (including two of Boehme's) and some items calculated to appeal to the folk beliefs and *Hexerei* tradition of backcountry Germans, such as John George Hohman's famous "pow-wow" book, *Der lange verborgene Freund* (The Long-secret Friend, 1828).

In 1825 a mysterious incident was alleged to have taken place

that had serious implications for later historical study of Ephrata. The younger Bauman claimed to have discovered a manuscript of over a thousand pages written by Sangmeister that
had been hidden behind some wainscoting for forty years or
more, presumably in what had been the Sangmeister-Kelp cot-
tage, although the place was not clearly specified except as a
"Brother house." Bauman's prompt publication of it, as the
Leben und Wandel, prefaced with his own bitter criticism of
the *Chronicon,* caused a great stir, and evidently, because it
contained lurid and salacious allegations against Beissel and
his followers, copies of the booklets were bought up by Ephrata's lay congregation with the intent to destroy them.

The few copies that survived became a gaudy hunting ground
for later historical writers, some of whom showed little sensitivity to the real character of Ephrata and the Beisselian mystique. Oswald Seidensticker, the pioneer of later historical study
of Ephrata, thought it "the most serviceable material" on the
"inner condition" of Ephrata, but added, "They are the confessions of an unbeautiful soul . . . dissatisfied with himself
and the whole world; he was an intolerable wrong head . . .
always on the lookout for vileness."[7] Sachse seems to have
ignored the *Leben und Wandel* for the most part as a scurrilous work, but the late James Ernst cited it frequently and
abstracted from it at length.

It was not until 1944, when the scholar Felix Reichmann
published his findings and assessment of the *Leben und Wandel,* that the authenticity of Bauman's tale of its discovery and
of the work itself were called into question.[8] Reichmann could
find no evidence of any wainscoting behind which a huge manuscript could have been hidden; even if it had been (near a window as alleged), it would have deteriorated irrecoverably over
the course of more than forty years while the structure itself
must have been falling apart. Nor was there any evidence that
Sangmeister left hints of the work's existence with the anti-
Beissel faction. Moreover, if there really had been a manuscript of over a thousand quarto pages as alleged, how could
they have been fitted into six pamphlets as Bauman said he
planned, no matter how tightly the type was set? After part 4
was published, Bauman announced that further publication
was suspended for lack of demand. Suspiciously enough, thereafter he claimed that the manuscript had been "lost" in a fire.
Reichmann concluded that the work was "a compilation made

by Mr. Bauman from the *Chronicon Ephratense* (perhaps from an unabridged manuscript) and from several letters of Sangmeister"—that it was, in effect, at least partially, a literary forgery.

These findings went unchallenged until 1977 (Ernst's history, published in 1963, does not discuss them), when the study by Klaus Wust, who generally disagreed with the "late attempt to discredit the work altogether," was published. As evidence for a more judicious view, he quotes the anonymous author of the *Heutiges Signal* of 1812 to the effect that Sangmeister's writings were then "still preserved in manuscript form."[9] If true, Sangmeister before his death, or someone thereafter, could have placed them in the hands of the Baumans for safekeeping, and the younger Bauman could simply have manufactured the tale of the manscript discovery out of whole cloth as an opportunistic sales pitch. We may never know.

We must assume, however, that Joseph Bauman did have access to Sangmeister manuscript materials, for in 1819–1820 Bauman published a little-known but significant work of Sangmeister, the *Mystische Theologie,* and there is no known reason to doubt his authorship of it.[10] That work deepens and enlarges our view of Sangmeister, the shining philosophic side of him in contrast to the dark, petulant, acerbic, embittered nature of the man. His mystical work explores the misleading ways of "well-meaning devoutness," discourses on the apocalyptic chapter 24 of the Gospel of Matthew about false prophets and on wars and world destruction, and concludes with thoughts on the mystical implications of Sabbatarianism. To it is appended the *Kurze Lebensbeschreibung* (Short Life Description), adjudged by Wust to be "most eloquent in the long self-assessment of his ascetic life," which he wrote to his fellow mystic, the alchemist Jacob Martin, shortly before his death.[11] And yet there was some strange chemistry in the man, provoked by the painful dichotomy between bitter critic and far-seeing mystic, that made him a perpetual misfit.

The printer of the two Sangmeister works, Joseph Bauman, left Ephrata and moved westward with his printing equipment to a farm near Shepherdstown in Cumberland County in 1830 or 1831. Whether he was impelled to move as a result of continued dismay over the *Leben und Wandel* is not known. At any rate, he took along his Ephrata press, and it is said that his son continued using it until 1900.[12]

Most sources allude to only two presses once owned and
operated by the Ephrata commune, and their subsequent history is murky and confusing. One of these is generally identified as having come into the possession of the Historical Society of Pennsylvania (displayed for some time at the Franklin Institute and now on indefinite loan to the Ephrata Cloisters); the other is identified as the one now in the hands of the Ford Museum in Dearborn, Michigan. There is clear evidence that one such press was sent by the Brotherhood to the formative commune at Snow Hill, perhaps around the turn of the century, and various efforts have been made to trace it. However, Betty Jean Martin, who made a careful study of the alleged Ephrata presses in connection with her study of Ephrata music, claims that there must have been "six or eight" presses used by the Brotherhood over the years, and cites evidence that the Bauman-Ephrata press was made after 1786. "No press in existence today," she claims, "dates to the early years of Ephrata printing, despite claims to the contrary. The six or eight presses used at the Cloister . . . have disappeared."[13]

The independence of the fading cloister came to an end in 1814, when Pennsylvania's General Assembly incorporated "The Society of Seventh Day Baptists of Ephrata." The act assigned the administration of cloister lands and buildings to trustees appointed by the lay congregation. At the time only four — Catherina, Johann and Jonathan Kelp, and Christian Luther — were living there, and their occupancy rights were confirmed for the rest of their lives. Nevertheless, the arrangement produced a good deal of litigation in the years to come.[14]

By 1835 William Fahnestock reported that some of the buildings were "crumbling to pieces" and that only "several single sisters" remained in the "convent." Five years later he wrote despairingly, "Ephrata has fallen — degenerated beyond all conception. It is now spiritually dead. Ichabod is written upon the walls of this branch of our Zion."[15]

Advanced decay of Ephrata continued through the rest of the century and well beyond. Few came to see the place, though several prominent artists were among them. The first to catch the harmonics of the ruins was Isaac L. Williams, once a student of the distinguished Philadelphia portrait painter John Neagle. Williams had a studio in Lancaster in the years 1854–1855, and it was probably in this period that he painted a memorable watercolor panorama of the cloister buildings from across the Cocalico, an exceptionally fine landscape with the still-standing Brother's house of Bethania most prominent.[16] The evocative 1881 drawing of the famous etcher Joseph Pennell suggests the mystical quality that still lingered in the forms of the nearly abandoned cloister. It is a vision by which one would like to remember Ephrata—the steeply rising medieval roof lines of the Saal and Saron and the solid Pennsylvania German stone corner of the Almonry.[17]

The popular illustrator Howard Pyle visited Ephrata in the late 1880s, when, according to him, four celibate Sisters were still inhabiting the cloister, and apparently a congregation of Dunkers, established in 1864, was replacing the Seventh Day communion. Pyle wrote an affectionate article for *Harper's* about the scene and accompanied it with his own illustrations, among them an interior of the chapel and an imaginary evocation of revolutionary soldiers awaiting the help of a Sister. He noted that Beissel was very fond of the Aeolian harp, "one of which," he claimed, "he had in his cell"—perhaps a touch of poetic license.[18]

Thereafter artists seemed to ignore the lingering beauties of Ephrata until the 1930s, when a major American painter, Charles Sheeler, recorded on canvas the architectonic harmony of what remained. Two Sheeler paintings (at the Springfield Museum of Art) reduce the central cloister architecture to the clean, bare essentials, and in spite of some liberties with the subject evoke their harmonies through his unique *Urform* style.[19]

In the latter part of the nineteenth century, antiquarian and historical interest in Ephrata, some of it tinged with the romanticism of the era, blossomed afresh in the work of Oswald Seidensticker, J. Max Hark's English translation of the *Chronicon,* the masterful (if erratic and confusing) work of Julius Friedrich Sachse, and the probity of two fine historical scholars who became governors of Pennsylvania, Samuel W. Pennypacker and Martin G. Brumbaugh. Both Sachse and Pennypacker were collectors of Ephrata artifacts, manuscripts, and imprints—at a time when prices for them had not yet soared beyond reason. But this did little for the cause of cloister preservation; sometime between 1910 and 1912 Bethania, the Brothers' house, was torn down as unsafe.

For all its drama and psychological color, the story of Ephrata has been little used in creative literature. Only a few story tellers have given it any attention, and that without notable success. Edward Eggleston temporarily turned away from his midwest scenes to write a story in the 1890s called "Sister Tabea," based on an episode in the life of Sister Anastasia.[20] Ulysses S. Koons, under the pseudonym of Brother Jabez, published a novel called *A Tale of the Kloster* in 1904, but it failed to elicit any attention from critics and literary historians. It remained for a great German writer of our century, Thomas Mann, to write a masterful novel in the 1940s in which a quite subsidiary but important theme related to the old Ephrata music and the Beissel mystique. But that will be considered more fully in the next chapter.

Meanwhile, the cloister property continued to deteriorate until early in the 1940s. In 1939 the state government had finally authorized state acquisition of the property. Henceforth known as Ephrata Cloisters Park, the site was put under the management of the Pennsylvania Historical Commission.[21] Then in 1941 G. Edwin Brumbaugh, a noted specialist on rehabilitation of historic properties, was appointed restoration architect. His was a long and painstaking task carried out with sensitivity and careful regard for the methods and materials used by the original builders. (The restoration was completed in 1968.) Thanks to him and his colleagues, the Ephrata Cloisters today present a partial but striking resemblance to the physical character of the old commune. Meanwhile, occasional archaeological investigations of the cloister grounds have been undertaken.[22]

Back in the days when Ephrata was still a vibrant social organism, the Baptist historian Morgan Edwards remarked about the Ephrathites to Elhanan Winchester, friend and Universalist disciple of de Benneville: "God will always have a visible people on earth, and these are his people at present, above any other in the world."[23] When and as God's visible people appear again, they will do well to remember what happened on the Cocalico—and how time erodes great spiritual aspirations.

Postlude

THE EPHRATA MOTIF IN THE

NINETEENTH AND TWENTIETH CENTURIES

AND IN THOMAS MANN'S *DOCTOR FAUSTUS*

ION in its Ephrata meaning, as a metaphor suggesting the attainment of God-consciousness in a collective unity, was relatively short-lived. Its syndromatic power was at work in the commune for little more than a third of a century. Its brief life does not diminish its importance, for actual attainment of the citadel of Zion-consciousness is a rarity. The earth-bound realities of "the world," the pressure of events alien to the unity over which it has no control, militate against a collective endurance on the Hill of the Lord.

At Ephrata the full power of Zion-consciousness prevailed for only a generation — from the formulation of communal unity about 1733, let us say, to the beginning of Conrad Beissel's physical decline about 1766. Even so, it was not always pure and unalloyed, for during that period the unity of purpose was roiled by numerous distractions and misdirections, both internal and external. It is remarkable, really, that it prevailed as long as it did. Although it continued as a living memory for another generation — in the spirit of Peter Miller, for example — only from 1733 to 1766 can Ephrata be said to have made its mark as a unique countercultural example in colonial America. Thereafter it was only a curious anachronism, buffeted by the world around it.

In the ensuing century, except in the little enclave at Snow Hill, Ephrata was virtually forgotten. At the same time, the spiritual revolution that had powered the migrations from the German world to Pennsylvania faded to a provincial sec-

tarianism, and the old forms of mutual aid mellowed into the
Gemütlichkeit of a quiet agrarian prosperity. The rich accomplishments of Ephrata's golden years—the poetry, music, *Fraktur,* book production—were silently interred until late in the century a handful of antiquarians began recovering the remains.

Yet in the nineteenth century, communalism flourished in backcountry America from coast to coast, as evidenced by the two dozen enterprises listed in table 3. The "successful" communes of that era, in terms of endurance and economic vitality, were religiously inspired by the "primitive" Christian model and by much the same kind of Zion-aspiration that had once prevailed at Ephrata. (Icaria, which might be added to the successful list, was an exception.) Although unaware of the Ephrata history, the Harmony Society, Zoar, Amana, Bethel and Aurora, Oneida, Saint Nazianz, and the Hutterites all had some similarity to Ephrata. Moreover, nearly all of the successful communes (except Oneida and Icaria) were ethnically and linguistically Germanic (as were some unsuccessful ones also).

On the other hand, the nineteenth-century secular communes fared poorly. Their highly intellectualized character and emphasis on political and economic theory failed dismally to produce internal unity. The socialist Owenite and Fourierist colonies, for all their idealistic humanist pretensions that were much in the public eye, were generally short-lived failures. (Nevertheless, one is constrained to add that they had a remarkable impact on the political climate of the era.) It has yet to be proved that a utopian community can survive for long without a central spiritual commitment and a "father figure" to personalize the spiritual goal, around which a committed membership can instrumentalize a disciplined and psychically rewarding unity of effort. This kind of communal lifestyle, obviously, is not for everybody.

Eventually, the rising tide of materialism and laissez-faire economics beclouded the original inspiration of even the successful communes, subtly altered their objectives, and at last fragmented their unity. A perceptive study of them came to this conclusion: "To the degree that the successful nineteenth century groups began to develop efficient systems for production and management of external relations, they also began to undermine community, weakening commitment, and making the group vulnerable to the forces that finally dissolved it."[1]

Critics of the communal system are quick to point out its internal "dictatorial" structure, its suppression of individuality, its isolation from the outside world, its Spartan and sometimes drab lifestyle, and the "neurotic" effects of the self-imposed constraints of its members.[2] The criticisms, however, seem to emerge from a worldly sophistication that, by its very nature, misreads the goals of communality, the necessarily "exclusive" character of the Zion-aspiration, and the small-scaled, localized, and internalized nature of its societal or religious revolution. As a result, the critics tend to overstate the negative case without providing sufficient solid evidence. In their defense, however, and given their vantage point, the "excesses" of some modern experiments justify their words of caution.

Communalism experienced a long dry spell during America's laissez-faire Gilded Age, when the accumulation of wealth became the desideratum at the expense of ethical values. Curiously, the only memorable commune to develop in that period was The Woman's Commonwealth in Texas, a successful enterprise and a harbinger of modern feminism. Considering its remarkable achievement (see Appendix, table 3), its history has been undeservedly ignored.[3]

With two notable exceptions, the communal drought continued through the first half of the present century. The dislocations resulting from two world wars combined with rapid urbanization and a money-oriented work ethic produced a climate of individualism that inhibited communal experimentation and altered older community values. Even the Great Depression, with conditions that might have prompted communal development, failed to do so; socioeconomic experimentation was taken over by government.

One exception to the dry spell was the development of the Bruderhof or Society of Brothers, which in some respects was our century's version of the Ephrata motif. Formed in Germany in the aftermath of World War I by its charismatic leader, Eberhard Arnold, it found its inspiration in Apostolic Christianity. The Brothers studied the writings of the sixteenth-century Anabaptists, and this in turn led to a transatlantic union with the Hutterites from 1931 to 1950. The Bruderhof was expelled from Germany by the Nazis in 1937, regrouped in England where it gained many new members, then established a large settlement in Paraguay. Finally, having rejected the "pa-

triarchal authoritarianism" of the Hutterites, it established
headquarters in 1954 at Woodcrest in New York State, with two other branch communes. Its notable economic success arose mainly from developing a nationwide business producing high-quality children's toys, but it wisely feared the consequences of growing too rich and periodically cut back sales.[4]

Another exception was Koinonia, a unique interracial commune founded in rural Georgia in 1942 by Clarence Jordan. It too bears witness to the historical tradition of radical and practical Christianity, with a strong service outreach to the rural poor of the area. Having survived severe harassment from those opposed to integration, it is today an economically successful enterprise with several businesses ranging from pecan culture to recordings, but these are kept fully consonant with its service motivation.[5]

It is not possible in so short a compass, nor is it the purpose of this chronicle, to review the multitude of communal experiments in America that have taken shape since midcentury. Since the 1958 founding of Synanon in California, a center for "unorthodox" treatment of drug and alcohol addiction that took a communal form, hundreds of communes have appeared in America.[6] Many of them were only temporary havens for young people who no longer believed in the old value systems and were seeking a different rationale and purpose in their lives.

As a whole, the new wave of communalism in the late 1960s and the 1970s lacked historical perspective or even an awareness of communal counterculture movements of past ages. With few exceptions, the Zion-aspiration, the Ephrata motif, and the spiritual discipline it requires were not a part of the communal epidemic. Lacking that kind of discipline and perspective, some (as is alleged of Synanon) seemed to have become excessively dictatorial with "brain-washing" techniques, while others simply disintegrated. Too often, bizarre patterns of behavior antagonized the world around them. One has the impression that the new communal movement lacked a unifying "theology," that its perspective was more directed toward external conditions than toward the development of internal unity.

That is not without its perils. The central issue, posed by the noted German sociologist Ferdinand Toennies, is the conflict between *Gemeinschaft*—the integrative principle, affective, nonrational, clan-building, and unifying—and *Gesellschaft,* the practical, task-oriented application of community resources and impulses.[7] To the end of its days, except during the Eckerling interlude, Ephrata opted for the former, though it could not recover from changing external conditions over which it had no control. Most of the nineteenth-century communes, on the other hand, came to their end in the snares of economic ambition and externalization of resources. In the twentieth century, with its high degree of urbanization and the fading of community consciousness, the *Gemeinschaft* principle seems to have lost its relevance to the communal movement. Moreover, since "there arose that notorious rift between faith and knowledge," as C. G. Jung phrased it, our scientific view of life overlooked "the *psyche,* the very thing that the scientists knew the least about," and we no longer appreciate (or remember) the ancient archetypes and symbols of spiritual aspiration that for many centuries nourished the countermovements in western civilization.[8] Our cybernetic age cuts us off from that tradition.

Yet partly because of the accumulated effects of two world wars, Korea, and especially Vietnam, the search for different value systems and lifestyles appears again. Though the search often lacks focus, it goes beyond rationalism and the kind of scientific "objectivity" out of which man has created heretofore unimagined technologies and agencies of destruction. There is something familiar about this phenomenon if we look to the past. One is reminded of the change brought on by the penetration of early Christianity into the fabric of the Roman superstate, by the assault of the Radical Reformation on the medieval establishment, by the migrations to early North America caused by the interminable war-anguish and pauperization of Europe.

The youth revolution of the 1960s and 1970s was a frontal assault on our normative ways of thinking and feeling. It spawned innumerable communal cells that often lacked centrality of purpose and discipline, but it did help to reanimate the ideas of brotherhood and mutual aid in an increasingly predatory society and the potentials of "the simple life" in an era of rampant materialism.[9] It asked fundamental questions about the norms that could trap us in the painful pointlessness of the Vietnam war.

Perhaps this revolution has run its course. Many who participated have rejoined the "me generation." Others have taken up more specialized causes such as ecology; the perils of atomic

power and the Bomb; and problems arising from multination-
widens the gap between the haves and the have-nots, and
from the imbalances created by the continued fattening of the
military-industrial complex. Still others refuse to participate
in society; the power systems governing our world seem too
impervious and complex, too dense and intransigent, to confront, and they prefer to build a life outside them.

Many are tempted to look back on the 1960s revolution
as a psychedelic side show with disturbing aberrations in
lifestyle and conduct compounded by new vulgarities and
hallucinogens. Yet the aberrations were only a part of the spectrum of change; the revolution did alter our perspectives
and plant unsettling doubts about norms we had taken for
granted. The revolution, however, was essentially secular, and
it lacked the peculiar adhesive power of anything akin to a
Zion-consciousness.

Curiously, the secular revolution has been superseded in
some measure by what one might call a pentecostal counterculture. The term is used here with some misgivings, but essentially it suggests a religious revivalism composed of many
disparate strands and sources, with a wide variety of cult leaders and preachers and gurus, sometimes inspired in ways reminiscent of the Inspirationists of Conrad Beissel's youth. It is
a phenomenon of many unrelated forms and styles — from the
born-again "Jesus movement" to Islam, which spread through
black communities; from the Reverend Sung Myung Moon's
Unification church, around which so much controversy has
surged, to a wide assortment of Bible pentecostal cults, and
highly personalized, messianic "churches" (such as the one that
led to the tragedy at Jonestown, Guyana); from Buddhist and
Hindu cult centers to the Christian-Hindic Self-Realization
Fellowship.

Generalizing about this current phenomenon is perilous except as a way of noting a new dimension, a reaction against
the spiritual dryness that most of us inherited from the era of
rationalism. Just as in the seventeenth and early eighteenth centuries the dry formularies of established Christendom produced
a reaction of Pietism and mysticism in many forms, so now
again people reach out for spiritual enlivenment. In this sense,
the Ephrata motif has reappeared.[10]

As early as 1922 (the year the second volume of *The De-*

cline of the West appeared) Oswald Spengler forecast an inevitable alteration in our worldview, a "second religiousness" to replace the time-worn political-economic "Caesarism" of the superstate:

> It appears in all Civilizations as soon as they have fully formed themselves as such and are beginning to pass, slowly and imperceptibly, into the non-historical state in which time periods cease to mean anything. . . . The Second Religiousness is the necessary counterpart of Caesarism. . . . But both have their greatness nevertheless. That of the Second Religiousness consists in a deep piety that fills the waking-consciousness . . . and that of Caesarism consists in its unchained might of colossal facts. . . . The material of the Second Religiousness is simply that of the first, genuine, young religiousness—only otherwise experienced and expressed. It starts with Rationalism's fading out in helplessness, then the forms of the Springtime become visible, and finally the whole world of primitive religion . . . returns to the foreground, powerful, in the guise of the popular syncretism that is to be found in every Culture at this phase.

Noting that "it begins with the State-destroying wish for universal reconciliation," in another passage Spengler comes to a memorable conclusion:

> And while in high places there is eternal alternance of victory and defeat, those in the depths pray, pray with that mighty piety of the Second Religiousness that overcomes all doubts forever. There, in the souls, world-peace, the peace of God . . . is become actual—and there alone. It has awakened that depth in the endurance of suffering which the historical man in the thousand years of his development has never known. Only with the end of grand History does holy, still Being reappear. It is a drama noble in its aimlessness, noble and aimless as the course of the stars. . . . We may marvel at it or we may lament it—but it is there.[11]

This is not to suggest that that time is upon us. Caesarism has yet to run its course, and one does not yet sense a real epidemic of desire to cut all ties with the world as we know it. The new pentecostalism still seems disjointed and unevolved. It is a sign nevertheless. And as to Caesarism, it is a fearful thing that we no longer dismiss the possibility of resorting to the apocalytic Bomb.

What worries most of us about the pentecostal impulse (in whatever guise) is its strong proselytizing tendency, carrying with it a conviction that the particular cult and its guru-hierarchy embody all "truth," a kind of closed circuit of belief. Proselytizing in this context, sometimes shallow and impermanent, can lead to spiritual empire-building and a temptation to enrich the founding organization. It is significant that Beissel, on the other hand, never formulated an unalterable creed and, with a policy of intentional poverty, never presumed that his New World Jerusalem was more than a tiny model and a "prevision." His beliefs were not calculated for mass appeal.

The universalizing tendency in the new religious counterculture is more particularly apparent in what may be called its yoga phase, in which Eastern, especially Indic, thought forms replace Western religious traditions. To Jung, the yoga phase presents an unresolvable problem: "The historical development of our Western mentality cannot be compared in any way with the Indian. Anyone who believes that he can simply take over Eastern forms of thought is uprooting himself, for they do not express our Western past, but remain bloodless intellectual concepts that strike no chord in our inmost being. We are rooted in Christian soil."[12] Or are we? Have we drained out the last spiritual sustenance of the West? Are we now entering a period of history analogous to the springtime of Christianity when Tertullian could say to the Roman superstate: "We recognize but one commonwealth, the world"?

The yoga phase of contemporary counterculture is characterized by a universalizing impulse, a nurturing of brotherhood within and beyond itself, a fusing (perhaps still incomplete) of Indic and Christian components, a strong sense of inner discipline and commitment. A notable example is the movement launched by Paramhansa Yogananda, which evolved after he came to America and settled in California in 1936, and is now called the Self-Realization Fellowship. Its cellular structure and guru system of reinforcement (not unlike Beissel's role at Ephrata) suggest that its future may evolve in some communal form, and there are already evidences to that effect.[13]

The rejection of the world we have known and the seeking for a different range of consciousness have too much momentum now to dismiss them lightly. In one of the *Don Juan* books of Carlos Castaneda, a Mexican Indian sorceress remarks, "If I don't focus my attention on the world, the world collapses"— meaning the constraining surface world of affairs, perhaps too the world of "grand History" in Spengler's meaning.[14] This rejection and seeking experience, in other words, is personal and inward, with no preconceived design of social consequences. And yet the new alternations in psychic awareness also have an important corollary: a rejection of statism in whatever guise with "the State-destroying wish for universal reconciliation." As once at Ephrata.

It is only right that we return to the German world again at the end of this chronicle. Perhaps no one dissected the deterioration of the German spirit with greater sensitivity than Thomas Mann, who escaped from the cataclysm that destroyed it. Indeed, he wrote his great if difficult novel about it, *Doctor Faustus,* in California in the 1940s.[15] At that time the war in Germany was coming to its catastrophic conclusion, and Mann, who had so deeply loved the old Germany that was no more, ends his book with a wrenching lament for it: "Today, clung round by demons, a hand over one eye, with the other staring into horrors, down she flings from despair to despair. When will she reach the bottom of the abyss? When, out of uttermost hopelessness—a miracle beyond the power of belief— will the light of hope dawn? A lonely man folds his hands and speaks: 'God be merciful to thy poor soul, my friend, my Fatherland!'"

It is appropriate to discuss *Doctor Faustus* at the end of the Ephrata saga because here we meet again Conrad Beissel and his most original accomplishment, the Ephrata music—yet this in so subsidiary a way that it is difficult at first to understand Mann's purpose with it in the enormous canvas of the whole. Yet there is a logic to it, an aesthetic requirement central to the novel's overall design.

The novel is the story of a fictional German composer, Adrian Leverkühn, as told by his lifelong friend, Serenus Zeitblom, a classicist and rationalist in whom we may read some-

thing of Mann himself. The two grew up together in the early
part of our century, attending first a school founded in the fifteenth century by the Brothers of the Common Life, then the University of Halle, the fountainhead of Pietism. When Adrian turned from theological studies to a life of music, his principal mentor in the new career was a strange character named Wendell Kretschmar, a stuttering but accomplished musician and an émigré from Germanic Pennsylvania with a background traceable to Snow Hill and Ephrata. Kretschmar had heard about the Ephrata music from his father and never got over it: "His own father, Kretschmar said, had often heard these sounds as a young man, and in his old age, when he talked to his family about it, his eyes had always filled with tears. . . . He had, so the elder Kretschmar had said, sat in English, French, and Italian opera houses; that had been music for the ear, but Beissel's rang deep down into the soul and was nothing more nor less than a foretaste of heaven."[16] The words have a familiar ring. They are a rephrasing of a passage in "An Historical Sketch of Ephrata," and Kretschmar's father can be none other than a recalling of William M. Fahnestock, who wrote the "Sketch" in 1835.[17]

Mann himself was an accomplished and devoted student of music. Perhaps he was speaking for himself in the person of Zeitblom, who, in contrast to Leverkühn, belittled the naiveté of Beissel's musical system of "master" and "servant" notes and irregular rhythms to fit the words. Yet Leverkühn, like his teacher, must have sensed the "foretaste of heaven" in the peculiar but magical Ephrata music.

But heaven was not to be the destiny of Leverkühn. Mann seems to have patterned his character's inner life on that of the philosopher Nietzsche, whose work was a major influence on Mann's own career.[18] Demonic by nature, having rejected Christian theology and the traditional moral standards of his youth, Adrian, like the philosopher, grew increasingly bitter toward the world around him—lonely, despondent, less and less accessible even to his friends, even ascetic. In his one fall from grace he contracted a debilitating venereal disease that slowly, painfully eroded his health (a fate attributed to the philosopher himself). Hoping for a prolongation of his life to fulfill himself in his musical compositions, Leverkühn makes a compact with the devil.[19] The long scene is deliberately written in archaic language with difficult obscurantist allusions, reminding us less of Goethe's *Faust* than of the medieval German origins of the Faust legend.

What follows after this life-prolonging bargain is the evolution of Leverkühn's masterworks. In the difficult task of conceiving these, Mann carefully studied the musical ideas of Schönberg, "in order to portray the whole cultural crisis in addition to the crisis of music . . . the fundamental motif of my book: the closeness of sterility, the innate despair that prepares the ground for a pact with the devil."[20] Yet in contrast to Adrian's extreme musical sophistication, Kretschmar sees the faint echo of Ephrata music: "the Elemental in Music," a sign of "the primitive, the primeval beginning" — a characteristic on which Leverkühn was to build his greatest compositions. Toward the latter part of the composer's painful life, as he completes his monumental *Apocalypse* oratorio, a "herald of barbarism," Zeitblom is moved to see the Beissel shadow in it:

> There are impressions which, unimportant as they
> seem to the reason, work on in the subconscious
> mind and there exercise a decisive influence. So it
> was now: the figure of that queer fish across the
> ocean and his arbitrary, ingenuous musical activity,
> of whom another queer fish, Adrian's teacher, had
> told us in our youth, and about whom my companion
> expressed himself with such spirited approval . . . :
> the figure and the history of Johann Conrad Beissel
> was such an impression. . . . A whole world lies be-
> tween his naive unabashed theory and the work of
> Leverkühn, pushed to the very limits of musical
> erudition, technique, intellectuality. And yet for me,
> the understanding friend, the spirit of the inventor of
> the "master" and "servant" notes and of musical
> hymn-recitation moves ghostlike in it.[21]

Leverkühn was now inexorably lapsing into madness but was still capable of producing one last masterpiece: the *Faust* cantata, a "giant 'lamento'," at the very opposite pole to the exaltation in the finale of Beethoven's Ninth Symphony. It expressed "the substantial identity of the most blest with the most accurst. . . . a Utopia in form, of terrifying ingenuity, . . . completely swallowed up by thematic thinking." Substance,

life itself, is drowned in form, emptied of aspiration. There-
through its last wrenching events, and at last the composer
dies, his mind totally gone, obscure and unsung.

Thomas Mann conceived his novel as a paradigm of the decline and death of what was once great in the civilization of
Germany. Adrian's life, after a decade of irreversible insanity,
came to an end in 1940. Decay of the old German spirit was
already far advanced, and at the very end of the novel, Mann,
in the person of Zeitblom, foresees the cataclysm to come in
the Nazi insanity.

Mann's masterwork haltingly took shape in the years 1941
to 1947, the fateful time when the survival of Western civilization was in the balance. At first, the Germanic world, "the
hectic on her cheek, was reeling then at the height of her dis-
solute triumphs," and then inexorably the enormous wave of
blood and destruction swept back upon it.[22] Germany too had
made a Faustian pact with the devil, and what had been great
in its long-evolved civilization came to a painful end, like Adrian
Leverkühn's.

During the writing of *Doctor Faustus,* Mann was far removed from the ordeal of the battle for Europe, living in Pa-
cific Palisades, California, but in constant touch with prominent German and other European émigrés in the United States.
Even when he finished his novel, and the battle for the world
he knew no longer raged, he felt impelled to reconstruct the
many facets of his personal and intellectual life during 1941–
1947 from which the novel emerged. *The Story of a Novel:
The Genesis of Doctor Faustus,* based on his diaries of those
years, was issued in its original German in Amsterdam in 1949.

Mann's genius may have been exhausted by this time, for
though it is autobiographically fascinating, *The Story of a Novel*
is a disappointing work. All he tells us about his discovery of
the Beissel theme is this: "I stumbled across some curious information, in some magazine, concerning spiritual music among
the Seventh-Day Baptists of Pennsylvania, with emphasis on
the strange figure of Johann Conrad Beissel," whom he calls
"the buffoon 'systematician' and schoolmaster whose memory
haunts the whole novel." Later, presumably in 1945, he visited
the Library of Congress, where Luther Evans, then chief librarian, showed him "the actual manuscripts" of Beissel, "and

I saw with my own almost incredulous eyes the actual productions of this naive and dogmatic innovator in music whom I had used so slyly in my novel."[23]

The evidence indicates that Mann had seen "Hymns and Music of the Pennsylvania Seventh Day Baptists," by Hans T. David, in the June 1943 issue of *The American-German Review,* published in Philadelphia. (It is possible, of course, that Mann also read David's article on "Musical Composition at Ephrata" published a year later in the same journal.) There is virtually no evidence that Mann searched any further in the extensive Ephrata literature of earlier years to learn more about Beissel—a surprising fact in view of his uncannily perceptive use of him. Moreover, he was interested in Beissel only in a musicological sense; the total Ephrata experience in its historical and countercultural dimensions was not to his purpose. In 1968 the German scholar Theodor Karst, who studied all the available literature about Ephrata and Thomas Mann, wrote a masterful, definitive paper on the Beissel-Ephrata aspects in the novel. Among other things, on facing pages he matched paragraph for paragraph David's article with the German text of *Doktor Faustus* relating to Beissel and Ephrata, showing Mann's almost literal use of the article.[24]

Admittedly, the correspondences between the "angelic" music of Beissel and the wild musical laments of Leverkühn must remain obscure and deeply buried, a hidden mystical counterpoint. One bespeaks the dying, chilly autumn of the German spirit; the other echoes its springtime in medieval mysticism, the recovery of primitive Christianity in Radical Reformation and Pietism, the dawntime of spiritual renewal. "A whole world lies between" Beissel and Leverkühn, yet the springtime "moves ghostlike" through the expanse. Something Faustian can be found at both ends of the spectrum.

In one of his discourses to his followers, Beissel made this remarkable revelation: "I have had great difficulties with myself so that my own conscience has often sent me to the lowest regions of hell—and that for forty-seven years."[25] One may suppose that he was referring to the call of the flesh, for his attraction of and to the female nature pursued him throughout life, and one remembers that his hymn-poetry was frequently cast in erotic imagery.[26] With the weight of guilt upon him, he often flagellated himself severely to drive out the demons. His innate and uncontrollable charisma tempted him

in other ways, too—into messianic delusions, flirtations with
strange doctrines and rituals that did not befit his psyche, and
at times into vain dreams of spiritual empire that were not
consonant with his true purpose in life. He was only true to
himself, really, as Brother Conrad, not as Father Friedsam.
A Faustian dichotomy.

As a dying man he lamented that his great dream for Ephrata as a "prevision" of a New World had come to nought.
Yet he could say with honest conviction, "I did not forsake
my calling." In spite of all the temptation, Satan had not con-
quered, and though his vision of a New Jerusalem was dying
out in a changing world—and he knew it—there is a timeless
quality to it. A probing scholar of the Ephrata milieu concluded
that Brother Conrad was "deeply learned in the labyrinth of
the human soul . . . a mystic of rank equal to Boehme, Tauler
and Eckhart."[27] The ensuing age forgot the man for awhile,
but, given the signs of spiritual renewal in our time, the Beissel
vision may yet be born again. In the words of Oswald Spengler:
"We may marvel at it or we may lament it—but it is there."

Appendix
Notes
Bibliography
Index

Appendix

TABLE I.

Religious and Communal Countercultures
Prior to the Reformation

Group	Place of Origin	Century of Origin	Founder	Characteristics	History
Essenes	Palestine	2d B.C.	—	Practiced community of goods in small, diverse units; generally celibate, highly ascetic; rejected institution of oaths, slavery.	Faded out soon after the beginning of the Christian era.
Therapeutae	Egypt	1st B.C.	—	Much like Essenes; Greek Jews of Alexandria.	—
Apostolici	Near East	1st A.D.	—	Obscure communal unities in image of first church; celibate.	Faded in 3d C.; revived in 13th C. as Order of the Apostles (see below).
Marcionites	Rome	2d	Marcion of Pontus	Church communities on basis of complete equality; rejected Romanization; ascetic dualism.	Faded in West in 4th C., survived in East to 7th; absorbed by Manichaeans.
Montanists	Phrygia	2d	Montanus	Developed communal monasticism; mystical, ascetic; revolted against secular tendencies.	Spread to Rome, Gaul, N. Africa; reduced to sect in 3d C., faded back into the church.

Group	Place of Origin	Century of Origin	Founder	Characteristics	History
Mandaeans	Asia Minor	2d–3d	—	Mystical dualism, rejected materialism of post-Nicene church; repetitive baptism.	Flourished in parts of Mideast; first heard of in Europe in 1622.
Manichaeans	Babylonia	3d–4th	Mani of Ctesiphon	Abstemious, pacifist, Pauline; absorbed elements of various religions.	Gained wide appeal in Roman world; persisted under severe repression till 13th C.
Basilians	Asia Minor	4th	Basil the Great, bishop of Caesarea	Propagated communal monasticism within the church; emphasized hard labor, charity; preserved old writings.	Spread throughout Eastern Empire and to Russia, where it set monastic standards, and to Italy.
Paulicians	Asia Minor, Armenia	4th	Constantine of Mananali	Rejected Catholicism, monasticism, water baptism; refused to consider marriage a sacrament; dualistic, Pauline in outlook.	In conflict with Byzantine Empire; spread to Bulgaria then to much of Europe; widespread during Crusades.
Bogomils	Bulgaria	10th	—	Regarded "church" as spiritual union in which all held equal share; practiced adult baptism, rejected Catholic doctrine.	Spread to Serbia, Bosnia, then to Italy, where movement influenced Albigenses and was thereby absorbed.
Albigenses	N. Italy, S. France	11th	—	Honored for charity, good works; divided into *perfecti* (mystical leaders) and laic *credentes;* antisacerdotal, protested corruption of clergy.	Thrived till 1209 when pope ordered crusade against them; extinguished by Inquisition in 13th and 14th C.

Group	Place of Origin	Century of Origin	Founder	Characteristics	History
Cathari	—	—	—	Essentially the same as the Albigenses but more widespread.	Spread through much of Europe and the East.
Waldenses	N. Italy, S. France	12th	Peter Waldo of Lyons	Encouraged life of voluntary poverty and sharing of all wealth; opposed capital punishment, oaths, priesthood, asceticism.	Severely persecuted, driven into remote Alpine valleys. Pope decreed their extermination but they survived to join Radical Reformation.
Order of the Apostles	Italy	13th	Gerard Segarelli	Practiced communal life of povery and chastity, existed by begging; aimed to establish communistic millennial kingdom.	Spread to Germany and England, lingered to early 15th C. under severe church persecution.
Brothers of the Common Life	Holland	14th	Gerhard Groote	Practiced communalism in small units, chastity, poverty, but took no vows; first to establish integrated lay communes.	Thomas à Kempis lived in first commune in 1390s; spread through Low Countries and Germany; faded out in early 16th C.

Note: The table does not pretend to completeness. Alfred Firmin Loisy's *The Birth of the Christian Religion* (New York: University Books, 1962) presents a Catholic view of Marcion, Montanus, and the Mandaeans; but Spengler's *Decline of the West,* II, 213–14, 225–28, 251–54, is more insightful on the same groups, and his chap. 8 on "The Magian Soul" is of great philosophic value. On Basil: Hans Lietzmann, *A History of the Early Church* (Cleveland: Meridian Books, 1961), IV, 197–202. Gibbon's *Decline and Fall,* VII, 47–58, is useful on the Paulicians. On the Albigenses and Waldenses, see Comba, *History of the Waldenses,* Warner, *Albigensian Heresy,* and Watts, *The Waldenses.* Scholarly treatment of the Brothers of the Common Life is provided by Jacobs, *Essays in the Conciliar Epoch.* Numerous religious countercultures and communal sects or experiments emerged from the Anabaptist "left wing" of the Reformation and its various offshoots up to the nineteenth century; a number of these are referred to in the text. Several heretical groups are described in Umberto Eco's novel, *The Name of the Rose* (New York: Harcourt Brace Jovanovich, 1983).

TABLE 2.
Religious Communes in America, 1662–1800

Effective Dates	Principal Community	Location	Ethnic Origin	Principal Leader(s)	Religious and Social Character
1662–1664	Hoorn Kill	Delaware Bay near Lewes, Del.	Dutch	Peter Plockhoy	Mennonite; liberal Socinian socialism, noncelibate
1684–ca. 1730	Bohemia Manor	Upper Chesapeake Bay, Md.	Dutch	Petrus Sluyter	Labadist (and Mennonite); ascetic communism, celibate
1694–1708	Wissahickon	Near Germantown, N. of Philadelphia	German	Johannes Kelpius	Lutheran Pietist; highly mystical, celebate
1733–1796	Ephrata	Lancaster County, Pa.	German	Conrad Beissel	Seventh Day German Baptist Brethren; highly mystical, ascetic communism, celibate
1742–1762	Bethlehem	Northampton & Lancaster counties, Pa.; N. Carolina	German, Czech, English	Count Zinzendorf, A. Spangenberg	Unitas Fratrum (Moravian Brethren); communal "choir" system, community controlled marriage
1787–ca. 1930	New Lebanon, New York	Spread throughout New England, later to Midwest	English	Ann Lee (d. 1784), Joseph Meacham, Lucy Wright	Shakers; market-oriented communism, highly organized social order, celibate
1788–1821	New Jerusalem	Genesee County, N.Y.	English	Jemima Wilkinson	Society of the Universal Friend (Shaker and Quaker influences); millennialist communism, celibate
1798–ca. 1880	Snow Hill	Franklin County, Pa.	German-Swiss	Barbara Snowberger, Peter Lehman	Offshoot of Ephrata; semicommunal, mainly celibate

Note: The Shakers and "New Jerusalem" are outside the purview of this study, but see especially Edward Deming Andrews, *The People Called Shakers* (Oxford, 1953; rpt. New York: Dover, 1963); Don Yoder, "The Spiritual Lineage of Shakerism"; and Herbert A. Wisbey, *Pioneer Prophetess: Jemima Wilkinson* (Cornell University Press, 1964).

TABLE 3.
Nineteenth-Century Communes in America

Common Name	Location(s)	Ethnic Origin	Principal Leader(s)	Max. Number	Comments and Characteristics
Harmony Society[a] (1805–1905)	Western Pa. & Indiana	German	George & Frederick Rapp	900	Combined agricultural and industrial production with far-flung trade system, later heavy external investments. Independent Pietism: adopted celibacy and mixed households 1807.
Zoar (1817–1898)	Eastern Ohio	German	Joseph Bäumeler	50	Agriculture with small industries and regional trade. Pietistic Separatists; adopted celibacy 1822, discontinued 1830. Later external investments lost money and contributed to decline.
New Harmony[b] (1825–1827)	Indiana	English & Scottish	Robert Owen & sons	1,000	Failed to develop economic base, but carried on important educational and intellectual activities. Rapidly disintegrated and dispersed. Secular and noncelibate.
Order of Enoch (1831–1834)	Missouri	English	—	—	First United Order of the Mormons and their first totally communal experiment. Pressure from neighboring areas forced its early dissolution.
New Philadelphia (1833–1834)	Western Pa. & Louisiana	German	Count de Leon (B. Müller)	80 (est.)	Schismatic group of Harmonists. Millennialists, noncelibate. Faction under Leon migrated to Louisiana; others later joined Bethel commune.
Oberlin (1833–1841)	Northern Ohio	English	John Shiphard	50 (est.)	Based on Christian evangelism. Failed to develop effective economic program, but Oberlin College (founded 1833) developed from its activities.

Common Name	Location(s)	Ethnic Origin	Principal Leader(s)	Max. Number	Comments and Characteristics
Brook Farm (1841–1847)	Near Boston, Mass.	English	George Ripley	100	Transcendentalist and Unitarian origins, later Swedenborg influence, then became Fourierist phalanx. Attempted to combine unstructured manual work with intellectual and educational activities. Noncelibate and loosely organized.
Hopedale (1841–1856)	Near Milford, Mass.	English	Adin Ballou	200	Universalist inspiration, highly moral "practical Christianity." Joint stock proprietorship with fixed wage scale but failed to reconcile individual and communal interests.
Northampton Association (1842–1846)	Mass.	English	—	180	Decentralized and diffuse internal direction; lacked clear economic rationale. Nonreligious. Emphasized education and industry.
Amana (1843–1933)	Iowa — 7 villages	German	—	1,800	Efficient agriculture-industry combination with dual leadership system. Called Society of True Inspiration, from German Inspirationist origins. Required 1 year of premarriage separation. Industrial sector transformed to a corporation.
North American Phalanx[c] (ca. 1843–1856)	Red Bank, New Jersey	English	—	112	Economic system developed on socialist theory of Charles Fourier in France, popularized in U.S. by Arthur Brisbane and Horace Greeley. Agriculture, milling, and a few small industries; varied wage scale, monthly payroll. Nonreligious.
Skaneateles (1843–1846)	New York State	English	John Collins	90	Functioned on anarchist theory, experienced tension between anarchists and less radical group. Doubled assets in 2½ years, but economic system not well developed.

Common Name	Location(s)	Ethnic Origin	Principal Leader(s)	Max. Number	Comments and Characteristics
Fruitlands (1843)	Mass.	English	Bronson Alcott & Charles Lane	13–15	Transcendentalist in outlook, somewhat like Brook Farm in objectives. Schism between the two leaders prevented full development.
Bethel and Aurora (1844–1880)	Missouri & Oregon	German	William Keil	700–1,000	Original revivalist inspiration, modified by former schismatic Harmonists; essential Harmonist features but noncelibate. Successful agricultural and artisan enterprises, but dissolved year after Keil's death in 1879.
Bishop Hill (1846–1860)	Illinois	Swedish	Eric Janson	1,500	Volatile messianic leadership; millennialists. Two abortive attempts to establish celibacy. Janson murdered 1850. Prosperity vanished in financial speculation and crash of 1857.
Icaria (1848–1895)	Texas, Illinois, & Iowa	French	Etienne Cabet	600 (est.)	Strong benevolent dictatorship under Cabet, who died 1856. First settlement in Texas (1848–1849) a failure, then bought deserted Mormon town of Nauvoo, Ill., and prospered, with branch in Iowa, which after dissension and hard times became their final home.
Utopia (1847–1851) Modern Times (1851–1866)	Ohio & Long Island	English	Josiah Warren	45 (est.)	Anarchism as economic reform on communal base. Work system based on exchange of "labor notes" substituting for money. Permitted "free love" as anarchistic response to family-property ties.
Communia (1847–1855)	Iowa	German	Wilhelm Weitling	79	Marxist experiment. Reimbursed defectors for services rendered. Internal dissension and a charge of embezzlement led to dissolution.

Common Name	Location(s)	Ethnic Origin	Principal Leader(s)	Max. Number	Comments and Characteristics
Oneida (1848–1881)	Upstate New York	English	John Humphrey Noyes	288	"Bible communism" imitating primitive Christianity. Called themselves the Perfectionists. Tightly controlled practice of "free love" for breeding, punished "exclusive" relationships. Concentrated on industrial production, employing many outsiders. Transformed into joint stock company 1881, but retained some communal characteristics thereafter.
Jasper Colony (1851–1853)	Iowa	German	Hermann Diekhoner	40 (est.)	Small sectarian group about which little is known. Family arrangement. Internal schism presumably led to dissolution.
Preparation 1853–1855)	Iowa	English	Charles Thompson	200 (est.)	Group of schismatic Mormons. Abstemious, forbade personal adornment. Dissolved in a revolt against the leader and subsequent law suit.
Saint Nazianz (1854–1896)	Wisconsin	German	Fr. Ambrose Ochswald	450	Catholic commune of German immigrants. Principally agricultural production and processing. Development impeded by lack of incorporation and death of leader, producing dissension under dual leadership. Transformed into joint stock company.
Hutterites (in N. America since 1874)	Colonies throughout northern plains, U.S., & Canada	German	–	15,000	Organized in cluster-type agricultural colonies. Sect dates back to 16th century. Patriarchal leadership, preserving Anabaptist views. Extremely prolific family structure. About 150 colonies, all property under common ownership.

Common Name	Location(s)	Ethnic Origin	Principal Leader(s)	Max. Number	Comments and Characteristics
The Woman's Commonwealth (ca. 1883–ca. 1904)	Belton, Tex., to 1899, then Mt. Pleasant, near Washington, D.C.	English	Martha McWhirter	50	Feminist and celibate, though a few men were admitted. Called the Sanctified Sisters; pentecostal, Pietistic, believed in direct individual communication with God. Early extreme persecution, but became economically successful operating a dairy and a hotel that became famous in Texas. Mt. Pleasant center primarily a communal residency rather than an economy.

Note: The list does not pretend to be all-inclusive. Literature on specific nineteenth-century communes is extensive and uneven, and is not included in the Bibliography, but basic data on most of the groups can be garnered from Kanter, *Commitment and Community*, and, for the first half of the century, from Tyler, *Freedom's Ferment*. See also works listed in the Bibliography by Albertson, Bestor, Hinds, Holloway, Nordhoff, and Noyes.

a. The Harmonists built three model towns: Harmonie in Butler county, Pennsylvania (1805–15); Harmony on the Wabash in southern Indiana (1815–25); and Economy on the Ohio below Pittsburgh, now within the borough of Ambridge (1825–1905).

b. New Harmony, Indiana, was purchased by Robert Owen in its entirety from the Harmonists. Smaller Owenite communes, also of very short duration, were started in Ohio, Indiana, and Tennessee.

c. More than forty Fourierist "phalanxes" are said to have been started in eastern states, Ohio, and the upper Midwest, but few, except the Wisconsin Phalanx (1844–50), lasted more than a year.

Notes

Works listed in the Bibliography are cited in the Notes by author and title only.

CHAPTER I: PRELUDE

1. Thomas Mann, in *Doctor Faustus*. See chap. 15 below.
2. Hollyday and Schweitzer, "The Present Status of Conrad Beissel/Ephrata Research," 176.
3. Greek utopian ideas owed much to Pythagoras and Plato and to the legend of Atlantis (e.g., in Plato's *Critias* and *Timaeus*). Ancient Greek ideals of the harmonic community faded under Rome, as described by Fustel de Coulange, *The Ancient City* (New York: Doubleday, 1956). On the Essenes: descriptions and comment by ancient writers are appended to A. Powell Davies, *The Meaning of the Dead Sea Scrolls* (New York: New American Library, 1956); Millar Burrows, *The Dead Sea Scrolls* (New York: Viking, 1955), 279–94, describes the character of the sect.
4. Elaine Pagels, *The Gnostic Gospels* (New York: Random House, 1979). C. G. Jung provides a penetrating analysis of Gnostic symbolism in chap. 13 of *Aion* (New York: Pantheon, 1959).
5. Quoted by Walter Woodburn Hyde, *Paganism to Christianity in the Roman Empire* (University of Pennsylvania Press, 1946), 120, from the 1905 Fowler edition of Lucian's *Works,* IV, 82–83.
6. Ibid., 225, quoted from the *Apologeticus*. On Tertullian's pacifist and antistate beliefs, see Heering, *The Fall of Christianity,* 28–30.
7. Gibbon, *Decline and Fall of the Roman Empire* (London, 1862), VI, 1; and Burckhardt, *The Age of Constantine* (New York: Doubleday, 1956), 308.
8. Chap. 4 of P. D. Ouspensky's *A New Model of the Universe,* 2d ed. (New York: Knopf, 1969) presents a provocative analysis of the primitive Christian "hidden wisdom" and its burial at the hands of "church Christianity"—a view that would have been echoed at Ephrata.
9. On municipal communes of the late medieval period, see chap. 5 of Prince Peter Kropotkin's *Mutual Aid* (New York, 1925). See also Kautsky's *Communism in Central Europe in the Time of the Reformation.*
10. Erasmus's plea was put forward in his *Enchiridion Militis Christiani* of 1504. On his writings and critical views: José Chapiro, *Erasmus and Our Struggle for Peace* (Boston: Beacon, 1950), 28–68; and Heering, *The Fall of Christianity,* 60–64.

11. Münzer (or Müntzer) was both an Anabaptist *and* a revolutionary, a combination not accepted by later Anabaptists. On his life and apocalyptic communism: Abraham Friesen and Hans Jürgen Goertz, eds., *Thomas Müntzer* (Darmstadt, 1978).

12. Hostetler's *Hutterite Society*, 6–118, reviews the sect's origins and migrations.

13. The Preface to the "Frame of Government" is reproduced with commentary in Tolles and Alderfer, *The Witness of William Penn*, 106–112.

14. See Seidensticker, "William Penn's Travels in Holland and Germany in 1677"; Sachse, *The Fatherland*, 117–21, 127–34; and Penn's journal of the 1677 journey in vol. 1 of *The Papers of William Penn*.

15. Spengler, *Decline of the West*, II, 310–14. The theme is further discussed in chap. 15.

CHAPTER II: THE MAKING OF A MYSTIC

1. Full bibliographic commentary on both German and English versions of the *Chronicon* is given in the valuable work of Doll and Funke, "Ephrata Bibliography," nos. 184, 185, 427. Subsequent references are to the English version. On authorship of the *Chronicon* see chap. 11, esp. n. 15.

2. See Karst, "Beissel in 'Doktor Faustus'," 562*n*, referring to recent findings in Germany.

3. Sachse (*The Fatherland*, 95) alleges that in Württemberg alone "from 1634 to 1641 over 345,000 human beings perished by sword, famine and pestilence, and at the end of the war the Duchy had but 48,000 inhabitants."

4. Quoted by Durant, *The Age of Louis XIV*, 692. For the effect of French incursions on stimulating German migration to America: Sachse, *The Fatherland*, 113–14, 139–42, and Klein, *Beissel*, 7–14.

5. Although some Pietistic ideas are traceable to pre-Reformation sources (e.g., in the formative years of the Franciscan and Dominican orders), Pietism as we know it is a Protestant phenomenon. It deeply influenced early Pennsylvania settlers; see Stoeffler, *Mysticism in the German Devotional Literature*, 32–42; Seidensticker, *Ephrata: Klostergeschichte*, 9–17; also Durnbaugh, *The Believers' Church*.

6. Sachse, *Pietists*, 49–51. The central role of Spener (1635–1705) tends to obscure the importance of the Reformed communions in the Rhine corridor in spreading the movement.

7. On Francke (1663–1727): Stoeffler, *Mysticism in the German Devotional Literature*, 34–35.

8. On Beissel's *Wanderjahre*: Seidensticker, *Ephrata: Klostergeschichte*, 31–37; Sachse, *Sectarians*, I, 36–40; Klein, *Beissel*, 21–35; Ernst, *Ephrata*, 13–36.

9. The version of the *Chronicon* (4) is hard to believe, and Sachse wisely modified it (*Sectarians*, I, 36–37).

10. On Boehme see Jones, *Spiritual Reformers*, 151–235; Underhill's

brilliant introduction to *The Confessions of Jacob Boehme;* and Stoudt, *Sunrise to Eternity.* Jane Leade (1623–1704) wrote an influential diary, *A Fountain of Gardens,* 4 vols. (London, 1696–1701), which, translated into Dutch, helped spread the movement on the Continent.

11. Stoudt's note in Ernst, *Ephrata,* 14n.

12. On the elder Eckerling in Strasbourg and Schwarzenau, see Durnbaugh, *European Origins of the Brethren,* 79–80, and Wust, *Saint-Adventurers,* 9–14.

13. Banished from Germany, Gichtel (1638–1710) published a 2-volume edition of Boehme's collected works in Amsterdam (1682) and formed a mystical commune, the Engelsbrüder, a name later adopted for the first Ephrata brotherhood. Arnold (1666–1714), whose writings were popular among early Pennsylvania Germans, published Gichtel's correspondence. See Jacoby, *Two Mystic Communities,* 39–42; Sachse, *Pietists,* 47–48.

14. The "left wing" Reformation extended beyond Anabaptism as such. Goertz, *Radikale Reformatoren,* includes Paracelsus (ca. 1490–1541), for example, in the broader European underground that nourished utopian ideas.

15. *Chronicon,* 4–5.

16. The Beissel 1755 Letter Book, evidently copied by Peter Miller, is written in a discouragingly small German script, but deserves much more intensive study. It is preserved in the Cassell Collection at the Historical Society of Pennsylvania. Several of the letters are dated 1756.

17. Sachse, *Pietists,* 37–38, 62. It is probable that some Rosicrucian ideas and rituals were first introduced in America about 1694 by the Kelpius commune on the Wissahickon, but see note 29 below.

18. The translation is by Walter C. Klein (*Beissel,* 28–29). The *Theosophischen Lectionen* were not printed until 1752 (see chap. 10, n. 6).

19. On German Baptist origins: Brumbaugh, *German Baptist Brethren,* 29–44; pt. 1 of Gillin's *The Dunkers;* and throughout Durnbaugh's *European Origins of the Brethren.* L. Schultz's *Schwarzenau* has a good map of the area and many attractive photos.

20. Chap. 13 of Renkewitz, *Hochmann von Hohenau,* sums up his credo, which had a marked effect on Beissel. See also Brumbaugh, *German Baptist Brethren,* 16–24, 72–88; and Flory, *Literary Activity of the German Baptist Brethren,* 3–13.

21. The life and ideas of the elder Mack (1679–1735) are well summarized by Falkenstein, *German Baptist Brethren,* 58–67. See also the cited works of Brumbaugh, Durnbaugh, Flory, and Gillin.

22. Krefeld was a center for both Dunker and Mennonite migration to Pennsylvania; both groups helped develop the great textile industry there, skills they transferred to Germantown. See Pennypacker, *Settlement of Germantown,* 1–20; Hubben, "Pilgrims from Krefeld"; and Smith, *Mennonite Immigration,* 34–35, 83–88.

23. *Chronicon,* 248. On Becker: Brumbaugh, *German Baptist Brethren,* 191–208.

24. The Berleberg Bible was issued in eight large volumes (later

bound in four). Though said to have had great influence on Pennsylvania German sectarians, it was probably inaccessible to most because of its cost and size. See Bell, *Life and Times of de Benneville,* 18–21; and Stoudt, *Pennsylvania Folk-Art,* 92–94.

25. Quoted from Ernst, *Ephrata,* 34, but see also *Chronicon,* 11. On Rock (1678–1749) and the Inspired: Renkewitz, *Hochmann von Hohenau,* 289–94; Ernst, *Ephrata,* 32–35.

26. *Chronicon,* 12.

27. Sachse, *Sectarians,* I, 42.

28. On Kelpius and the Wissahickon hermitage: Seidensticker's essay on Kelpius in *Bilder aus der Deutsch-Pennsylvanischen Geschichte;* Pennypacker, *Settlement of Germantown,* 212–33; Sachse, *Pietists,* 13–27, 131–36; Randolph "German Seventh Day Baptists," 944–68; and my own introduction to *Johannes Kelpius: A Method of Prayer.* Willard Martin, "Mystics and Hymnists," argues against identifying the Wissahickon mystics as Rosicrucians.

29. Sachse, *Sectarians,* I, 42.

CHAPTER III: THE SEARCH FOR SOLITUDE

1. This first of Penn's three promotional tracts appears with commentary in Tolles and Alderfer, *The Witness of William Penn,* 113–22.

2. On the Frankfurt Company: Sachse, *The Fatherland,* 123–25.

3. Germantown origins are described at length in Pennypacker, *Settlement of Germantown;* and Learned, *Life of Pastorius.* See also Kuhns, *German and Swiss Settlements;* and Hocker, *Germantown.*

4. Jackson, *Encyclopedia of Philadelphia,* IV, 1204–05.

5. Falkenstein, *German Baptist Brethren,* 29; Ernst, *Ephrata,* 39.

6. See entries on "Conestoga" and "Pequea" in Donehoo's *Indian Villages.*

7. Kuhns, *German and Swiss Settlements,* 46–47. The Hans Herr House was recently rehabilitated as an historic property.

8. Falkenstein (*German Baptist Brethren,* 57) identified the "exact" location of the Mill Creek camp at half a mile north of the railroad station in the village of Bird-in-Hand.

9. On the important Van Bebber family: Pennypacker, *Settlement of Germantown,* 142–43; and Sachse, *Sectarians,* I, 57–58.

10. Plockhoy outlined his design for a socialistic community in a tract issued in London, 1659; an undated reprint was recently issued by the British Cooperative Union. The principal modern source on him is Harder and Harder, *Plockhoy from Zurick-Zee.* His utopian ideas are reviewed by Bernstein, *Cromwell and Communism,* 213–24; Durnbaugh, *Every Need Supplied,* 143–55; and Pennypacker, *Settlement of Germantown,* 177–211.

11. Bartlett B. James, *The Labadist Colony in Maryland* (Baltimore, 1899; rpt. New York: Johnson Reprint, 1973). *Journal of a Voyage . . . 1679–80* (Brooklyn, 1867) by Jasper Danckärts and Petrus Sluyter described the Labadist search for land in America. See also Sachse, *Sectarians,* I, 59–62.

12. *Chronicon,* 16–20.

13. Ibid.

14. Sachse, *Sectarians,* I, 78.

15. See esp. Maxson, *The Great Awakening in the Middle Colonies,* for fuller background on the related movements.

16. The perceptive essay on Jonathan Edwards in Vernon Louis Parrington, *The Colonial Mind, 1620–1800* (New York, 1927), 148–63, leads one inevitably to contrast the severity of New England Calvinism with the relatively mild religious spirit in Germanic Pennsylvania.

17. A. S. Brendle, *A Brief History of Schaefferstown* (Schaefferstown, 1979), 10, alleges that German Jews were there "as early as 1705." But see Day, *Historical Collections,* 420–21; and Sachse, *Sectarians,* I, 116–18.

18. On Bauman and the Newborn: Sachse, *Sectarians,* I, 73–74; Klein, *Beissel,* 47–48; Ernst, *Ephrata,* 48–49; and esp. Heinrich Rembe on "Emigration Materials from Lambsheim" in Yoder, *Rhineland Emigrants.*

19. It is not certain, though it is probable, that Beissel claimed to have originated the backcountry awakening; but see Stoudt's note in Ernst, *Ephrata,* 45n.

20. Sachse, *Sectarians,* I, 80–82.

21. *Chronicon,* 18.

CHAPTER IV: BIRTH OF A SPIRITUAL COMMUNITY

1. *The Autobiography of Benjamin Franklin* (New York: Random House, 1944), 130–31. His *Pennsylvania Gazette* no. 303 (Sept. 25, 1734) also contains a notice of Wohlfahrt's preaching.

2. Sachse, *Sectarians,* I, 83, but we know very little more about him.

3. Martin Urner (sr.) is identified by Brumbaugh, *German Baptist Brethren,* xi, as the first Elder of the Brethren in America. On the Coventry congregation, "the second in America" after Germantown, see pp. 289–96.

4. The principal source book on the sect's colonial period is Durnbaugh's valuable *Brethren in Colonial America.*

5. A balanced account is given by Falkenstein, *German Baptist Brethren,* 42–43.

6. *Chronicon,* 27–28; Sachse, *Sectarians,* I, 100–03; Ernst, *Ephrata,* 51–53.

7. The Germantown view of relationships with Beissel is amply explored by Brumbaugh, *German Baptist Brethren,* 298–317, 438–70; Gillin, *The Dunkers,* 116–24, 142–43; and Falkenstein, *German Baptist Brethren,* 49–57.

8. Sachse, *Sectarians,* I, 120. Both Sachse and Seidensticker spell the name Gass, but I use Hark's *Chronicon* spelling. There is still uncertainty about Gast's real identity: see chap. 11, n. 15.

9. Sachse, *Sectarians,* I, 125–27, but quotation from II, 18n. For

more on Hildebrand, see Flory, *Literary Activity of the German Baptist Brethren,* 220–28.

10. Sauer (sometimes Saur, anglicized Sower) spent his early years in a village near Berleberg; he did not arrive in America until he was 31. See Durnbaugh, "Christopher Sauer"; Reichmann, *Christopher Sower Bibliography,* 1–11; Brandt, *Christopher Sower and Son;* and Brumbaugh, *German Baptist Brethen,* 338–400.

11. On the origins of Ephrata hymnody, see especially B. Martin, "Ephrata and Its Music," 154–61, 164–65.

12. Quoted in Sachse, *Sectarians,* I, 136. See also Rothermund, "The German Problem of Colonial Pennsylvania." According to Arthur Graeff (in Wood, ed., *The Pennsylvania Germans,* 8) Franklin characterized the German immigrants as "Palatine Boors." Hocker, *The Sower Printing House,* 1, quotes from a Franklin letter (May 9, 1753) objecting to the German influx on the basis of "intermeddling in our elections" and dominating the press. Gipson, "The New World Paradise," estimates that Germans constituted half the population of Pennsylvania as late as 1755.

13. Sachse (*A Unique Manuscript,* 6–7) notes that Franklin's business journal was not begun until July 1730, hence omits recording his earlier Ephrata printing. Yet it seems unconscionable that, for example, the Franklin biographies by Carl Van Doren (New York: Viking, 1938) and Bernard Fäy (Boston: Little Brown, 1929) make no mention whatever of Ephrata.

14. Doll and Funke, "Ephrata Bibliography," gives bibliographic data on these works (nos. 165, 169–71, 175, 203); see also C. William Miller, *Benjamin Franklin's Philadelphia Printing,* nos. 14–16. The so-called *Ehebüchlein* against matrimony no longer seems to be extant.

15. Falckner's Swamp, a dispersed German settlement in what became upper Montgomery County, was a large area granted by Penn to the Frankfurt Company. It later came under the control of John Henry Sprogell, who was accused of land speculation and fraud. See Pennypacker, *Settlement of Germantown,* 21–50; and E. G. Alderfer, *The Montgomery County Story* (Norristown, 1951), 56–57.

16. See Falkenstein, *German Baptist Brethren,* 48, on the migration.

17. The London Company was established by royal charter in 1606 to procure immigrants and manage land transactions: Lyon Gardiner Tyler, *England in America, 1580–1652* (New York, 1904), 36–38, 59–61, 86–88. See also Diffenderfer, "The Early Settlement of Lancaster County"; and Eshleman, "Birth of Lancaster County," and "Political History."

18. Sachse, *Sectarians,* I, 174–75; Ernst, *Ephrata,* 79.

19. *Chronicon,* 54.

20. *Chronicon,* 56. Ernst (*Ephrata,* 80) says, "She left him in 1730, in which Jacob Weiss, 'her second lover', was helpful," but no supportive evidence is cited.

21. Abel Noble of Upper Providence was the first Sabbatarian preacher in Pennsylvania, having defected from the Quakers in the Keithian schism. Beissel's conversion to Sabbatarianism has been

credited to Thomas Rutter, the great ironmaster, but this lacks documentation.

22. *Chronicon,* 59–60; Ernst, *Ephrata,* 84–85.

23. According to Donehoo (*Indian Villages,* 31) an Indian village existed on the Cocalico "before 1724." John Taylor made the first land surveys in 1733–1734 (maps at the Historical Society of Pennsylvania). Williams (in Klein, *Lancaster County,* I, 395) translates a letter of Beissel about his going into the wilderness "with several others."

24. As given in Sachse, *Sectarians,* I, 184–85. A larger portion of the lyric is translated differently by Ernst, *Ephrata,* 89–90.

25. The *Vorspiel* contains all the hymns of the *Göttliche Liebes* plus a number of new ones as well as a mystical ABC. Franklin gave the *Vorspiel* a cramped and ill-styled production. On the three hymnbooks printed by him, see Stoudt, *Pennsylvania Folk-Art,* 84–87.

26. First published in 1702 as *Das eheliche und unveheliche Leben der ersten Christen,* the book was treasured by early Pennsylvania German sectarians.

27. Loose, "Two Distinct Periods of Ephrata Cloister History," and Sachse, *Sectarians,* I, 191. The biblical names had symbolic significance for the Ephrathites: Kadesh was a stopping place for the wandering Israelites and southern gateway to "the promised land"; Zoar was one of "the cities of the plain" saved by Lot's prayer; Hebron, where Sarah was buried, was long a residence of Abraham and was David's capital before Jerusalem; Massa refers to a tribe descending from Ishmael who was driven into the wilderness and saved by divine intervention.

CHAPTER V: METAMORPHOSIS FROM CAMP TO COMMUNE

1. Ernst, *Ephrata,* 96, without citation. But there seem to be no records of evictions or prosecutions.

2. Thomas Penn came to Pennsylvania in 1732, having assumed proprietary responsibilities with his two older brothers, John and Richard, as early as 1718. It is said that Thomas was cold and calculating, viewing the province as a private estate to produce profit. He was not popular in the province nor sympathetic to the Indians, unlike his father.

3. *Chronicon,* 66; Sachse, *Sectarians,* I, 92.

4. Sachse, *Sectarians,* I, 253–54.

5. Zerfass (*Souvenir Book,* 10) alleges that the still-standing stone "Almonry" was built as early as 1730, but this must be an error; more likely it was built in 1732–1733, the earliest of the communal buildings. It has a distinctly different style from the later buildings.

6. Sachse, *Sectarians,* I, 248–49. Ephrata architecture deserves more intensive study, but see G. Edwin Brumbaugh (later director of the Ephrata restoration), *Colonial Architecture,* with plates showing prerestoration conditions.

7. Sachse, *Sectarians,* I, 273–78.

8. Kriebel, *The Schwenkfelders,* 26–54. On their founder, Kaspar Schwenkfeld (1490–1561), see Jones, *Spiritual Reformers,* 64–87.

9. Ernst, *Ephrata,* 98. Maria Heidt became one of the four original members of Ephrata's Order of Spiritual Virgins.

10. Mattice ("The Palatine Emigration") includes a map of the route taken and notes that the Iroquois aided them. See also Kuhns, *German and Swiss Settlements,* 48–51.

11. The most extensive biography is Wallace's *Conrad Weiser,* but see also those by Graeff and C. Z. Weiser, and Sachse, *Sectarians,* II, 274–95.

12. Sachse, *Sectarians,* I, 231, quoting church records. Miller was born 1710 in the Palatinate, studied at Halle and Heidelberg, and arrived in Philadelphia in August 1730. Zerfass (*Souvenir Book,* 11) described him as "tall in stature, with a kindly face and friendly manner," a contrast to Beissel whom he eventually succeeded. He richly deserves a definitive biography, but see, e.g., Sachse, *Sectarians,* I, 229–47; Gibbons, *"Pennsylvania Dutch,"* 145–54, 160–63; and *Dictionary of American Biography,* XII, 632.

13. *Chronicon,* 70, 71; Ernst, *Ephrata,* 102–03.

14. This according to Ernst, *Ephrata,* 104–05.

15. See Sachse, *Sectarians,* I, 247.

16. B. Martin, "Ephrata and Its Music," 77–79. The only known (and probably later) copy is in the Cassel Collection, Historical Society of Pennsylvania. Surprisingly, it is in Roman script; it includes 233 hymns, a number of European origin.

17. *Chronicon,* 77–78; Sachse, *Sectarians,* I, 252–53.

18. *Chronicon,* 76–77; Sachse, *Sectarians,* I, 249, 252. For the biblical name Kedar, Genesis 25:13. No iron was used in this and later Ephrata buildings, for the mystics believed that iron had evil connotations.

19. *Chronicon,* 67–68. Régnier's own *Lebens-Beschreibung* appeared in Fresenius, *Bewährte Nachrichten,* I, 327–479; a translation of the portion dealing with his 1734 madness is in Reichmann and Doll, *Ephrata As Seen by Contemporaries,* 9–12.

20. B. Martin, "Ephrata and Its Music," 75–77. *Jacobs Kampff* is a slight production of fifty-two pages with thirty-two new hymn-poems, probably all by Beissel. It is really just a supplement to the *Vorspiel.*

21. Sachse, *Sectarians,* I, 258–59. The Hebrew meaning of Ephrata is "fruitful," that of Bethlehem "house of bread."

CHAPTER VI: BACKCOUNTRY ZION

1. Sachse, *Sectarians,* I, 256. The claim that the Saal was the largest of its kind in the province seems open to question.

2. *Chronicon,* 79–80.

3. Ernst, *Ephrata,* 115–16. The last sentence is misleading, for the *Episteln* (first printed in 1745) are quite different from the *Lectionen* of 1752.

4. *Chronicon*, 122; Sachse, *Sectarians,* I, 262–63. Mallott (*Studies in Brethren History,* 75–76) says the Amwell church was founded in 1733. Amwell was a dispersed settlement, actually the name of a township. Pictures of church and cemetery are in [Falkenstein and Reber], *History of the Brethren of the Eastern District.*

5. *Chronicon,* 145; Sessler, *Communal Pietism,* 22–24; and on Schwenkfelders vs. Moravians, Kriebel, *The Schwenkfelders,* 103–19.

6. The *Chronicon,* 145–56, devotes a full chapter to its interpretation of Moravian-Ephrata affairs.

7. *Chronicon,* 86–87. The accounts of Sachse and Ernst seem embellished.

8. Sachse, *Sectarians,* I, 270–71. Thomas was the Penn sons' lieutenant-governor from 1739 to 1747; because he tried to promote military defenses in the Quaker province, his tenure was stormy.

9. Ibid., 298.

10. B. Martin, "Ephrata and Its Music," 79–80, 340*n.*

11. Durnbaugh ("Christopher Sauer") contends that Sauer built his own press and used type sent him by Christopher Schütz, a German Inspirationist. See also Hocker, *The Sower Printing House,* 14–16. Ernst (*Ephrata,* 149) supposed that the press was sent by the Berleberg Pietists.

12. B. Martin, "Ephrata and Its Music," 82; Sachse, *Sectarians,* I, 319–20; Ernst, *Ephrata,* 150–51. Franklin's effort to corner the paper market is not mentioned in the cited Franklin biographies.

13. Pennypacker, "The Quarrel." Sauer published his side of the story in *Ein abgenöthigter Bericht* (1739) which includes an accusatory astrological assessment of Beissel. Pennypacker's translation of the Sauer publication and of Beissel's petulant unsigned reply appears in Reichmann and Doll, *Ephrata As Seen by Contemporaries,* 13–27. For more detail, see Ernst, *Ephrata,* 151–61.

14. B. Martin's detailed description ("Ephrata and Its Music," 81–84) of the *Weyrauchs Hügel* is especially valuable. This hymnbook is considered the first book printed with German type in America. Most of the hymns appeared previously in the Franklin imprints, and a large number are from European sources.

15. Ibid. The Ephrata Codex at the Library of Congress has sometimes been mistaken for a manuscript of the *Turtel-Taube* music. Guy T. Hollyday's "The Ephrata Codex" is valuable and effectively illustrated. See also Stoudt, *Pennsylvania Folk-Art,* 87–90.

16. *Chronicon,* 106–08. The account includes an interesting note on Jüchly, on whom see also Sachse, "Registers of the Ephrata Community."

17. Sachse, *Sectarians,* I, 357–58.

18. Sachse, (*Sectarians,* I, 354 f.) was apparently much influenced by Freemasonry and may have exaggerated its influence on the Brotherhood.

19. Jacoby, *Two Mystic Communities,* 44–45; Sachse, *Sectarians,* I, 359–61.

20. Sachse, *Sectarians,* I, 352. The burial ground that visitors see today was not laid out until ca. 1750.

21. Sachse, *Sectarians,* I, 273; *Chronicon,* 95–101. On Koch's life and ideas: Brumbaugh, *German Baptist Brethren,* 133–43; and Flory, *Literary Activity of the German Baptist Brethren,* 228–33.

22. Randolph ("German Seventh Day Baptists," II, 1081–82) points out that the Sunday School was held both on Saturdays (for Ephrata children) and Sundays (for neighboring "church" children). This pre-dates most claims for the "first" Sunday School, but it is said that John Wesley held such sessions in Georgia in 1737, though probably not on a permanent basis.

23. On Anastasia's art: Stoudt, *Early Pennsylvania Arts and Crafts,* 282–90, and Weiser and Heaney's splendid *Pennsylvania German Fraktur.* Seidensticker, "A Colonial Monastery," tells the story of her being renamed by Beissel.

24. *Chronicon,* 160; Sachse, *Sectarians,* I, 352, and II, 137. B. Martin, "Ephrata and Its Music," 363*n,* notes that "for over seventy years writers have been repeating Sachse's error in naming Ludwig Blum as an Englishman. . . . That Blum was German would seem somewhat certain." She suggests that he was a Moravian.

25. Estimating Ephrata's population at any one period is hazardous because of name changes, overlaps, and lack of a Householder's registry. In 1736 Spangenberg (see Kieffer, "An Early Visit to Ephrata") numbered the "completely cloistered" at 20 and Householders at 150. The *Chronicon* (120–21) lists the Solitary of 1740 at 69, not including Beissel, 35 Brothers and 34 Sisters. Sachse admits that the Ephrata registers he issued were not systematically maintained; he probably relied on the manuscript "Death Register . . . 1728–1921" now held by the Cassel Collection at the Historical Society of Pennsylvania.

26. *Chronicon,* 123-25; Sachse, *Sectarians,* I, 368–69.

27. Sachse, *Sectarians,* I, 373–74.

28. *Chronicon,* 113–18. Ernst (*Ephrata,* 137) is unduly caustic about this, but the centrality of Beissel's role makes the Father title seem altogether natural.

CHAPTER VII: THE COUNT VERSUS THE PEASANT

1. Literature on Moravians in colonial America is substantial; in this chapter I have relied heavily on Sessler, *Communal Pietism,* which also lists the many published writings of Count Zinzendorf (248–50).

2. Spangenberg wrote an 8-volume biography of Zinzendorf (published in Germany 1773–1775); it was translated and abridged into one volume by Samuel Jackson (London 1836).

3. The first Georgia settlement (1734) was along the Savannah on land provided by English trustees. According to Gollin (*Moravians in Two Worlds,* 155) thirty-one "Herrnhut missionaries" were located there by 1736.

4. The Moravian Archives at Bethlehem, Pa., constitute a rich resource for scholars of colonial America; for summaries of the Archives,

see K. Hamilton, "The Resources of the Moravian Church Archives,"
Pennsylvania History 27 (1960), 263–72; and E. G. Alderfer, *Northampton Heritage* (Easton, Pa., 1953), 287–89, 295–97.

5. Antes eventually joined the Moravians. After becoming "business manager" at Bethlehem, he left them in 1750, but two years later
helped Spangenberg lay out the Moravian settlement in North Carolina.
See McMinn, *A German Hero.*

6. Sachse, *Sectarians*, I, 425–34.

7. Hildebrand, a learned but contentious man, was deeply influenced by Boehme's works; he was a critic of both Beissel and the
Moravians. Both he and Kalkglässer, who died at Ephrata in 1748, had
been members of the "mother church" at Schwarzenau.

8. *Chronicon,* 149–50.

9. "Minutes" of the synods were printed in five parts by Franklin
in 1742 (Doll and Funke, "Ephrata Bibliography," nos. 222–26, 228),
for the Moravians had little use for Sauer and the feeling was mutual.
The reports are reviewed in Sessler, *Communal Pietism,* 31–60, and
translated portions are reprinted in Reichmann and Doll, *Ephrata As
Seen by Contemporaries,* 27–33.

10. Excerpts of Beissel's letter appear in Sessler, *Communal Pietism,*
42–43.

11. Ibid., 43, 56. Zinzendorf's presumption as "Reformer" of the
Schwenkfelders had evidently been expressed some years before in Europe: Kriebel, *The Schwenkfelders,* 27.

12. Sessler, *Communal Pietism,* 57–59.

13. Sauer printed three of the Ephrata treatises in 1743; detailed list-
ings are given in Doll and Funke, "Ephrata Bibliography," nos. 174,
179, 195; see also no. 239 for reprints in Fresenius, *Bewährte Nachrichten,* III.

14. "Countess" Benigna's Ephrata gossip prompted a rebuttal letter
to the *Bewährte Nachrichten* (III, 718–22) by an unnamed Ephrata
Sister in 1748, who said that Benigna was regarded "as an innocent
child, who knows neither good nor evil." It is translated in Reichmann
and Doll, *Ephrata As Seen by Contemporaries,* 187–89.

15. After the synods, Zinzendorf made mission journeys to Indian
villages which are said to have been rash and ill-advised. Kelley (*Pennsylvania The Colonial Years,* 225–27) gives an excellent account of
them. Graeff (*Conrad Weiser,* 88–90) indicates that Weiser, now drawn
to the Moravians, accompanied Zinzendorf as interpreter. The count
returned to Europe permanently in January 1743.

16. See Armstrong, *Organs for America,* on the life and work of
Tannenberg, with an appreciative foreword by E. Power Biggs. On the
full range of Moravian musical composition, see Albert G. Rau and
Hans T. David, eds. *A Catalogue of Music by American Moravians,
1742–1842* (Bethlehem, 1938). Except for one hymnbook printed by
Sauer in 1742, the Moravian hymnals were produced in London and
Europe.

17. Murtagh, *Moravian Architecture and Town Planning,* is rich
with illustrations and old prints.

18. This account is based on Sachse, *Sectarians*, I, 435–38, but Hardie remains a shadowy figure.

19. On his life and achievements: Ledderhose, *Life of Spangenberg*. He was "highly skilled in the delegation of power to others" (Gollin, *Moravians in Two Worlds*, 43), hence his administration in America was considerably more decentralized and democratic than what prevailed under the autocratic administration of Zinzendorf in Europe.

CHAPTER VIII: THE FALL OF THE ECKERLINGS

1. Sachse (*Sectarians*, I, 416–19) indicates that the later account of the 1742 comet was based on an "old tradition"; it is thus possible that in time it was confused with Grischow's comet of 1743. Records of short-period comets do not predate 1819.

2. *Chronicon*, 134; Sachse, *Sectarians*, II, 88–93. The comet(s) prompted Beissel to write a mystical *Cometen-Buch*, discussed below in chapter 9.

3. As translated by Sachse, *Sectarians*, II, 93.

4. Ibid., I, 401; Ernst, *Ephrata*, 190–92. The construction of Peniel began in October 1741.

5. The symbolic priesthood of Melchizedek is elucidated in Hebrews 7:1–4 and 21–28; the symbolism was very important to Ephrata.

6. Mack and Riesmann may have been the first to explore the Bermudian creek area (York County) where in 1758 Ephrata established an offshoot colony. The claim of Ernst (*Ephrata*, 190) that they headed for "a Dunker settlement at Conocoschick" farther west is questionable, for Dunker penetration there did not occur till later. Jüchley also left Ephrata about this time to claim his patrimony in Europe, but died enroute in Philadelphia after willing his funds to Ephrata.

7. *Chronicon*, 136.

8. Ernst (*Ephrata*, 325–26) avers that Meyle "never owned the land which he sold twice."

9. An excellent review of the Ephrata mills, with schematic drawings, is given by Loose, "Two Distinct Periods of Ephrata History."

10. Wohlfahrt died on May 20, 1741. A long, affectionate summary of his life and death is in the *Chronicon*, 140–43*n*.

11. On the Sauer Bibles: Reichmann, *Sower Bibliography*, 4–6 and nos. 42–43; Hocker, *The Sower Printing House*, 37–44; Flory, *Literary Activity of the German Baptist Brethren*, 68–112. Two "states" of the 1743 Bible are preserved at the Pennsylvania State Library.

12. Muhlenberg (1711–1787) had just come to America in 1742 after studies at Göttingen and Halle and a deaconship. He is regarded as the "father" of American Lutheranism and organized its first synod 1748. He married Weiser's daughter Anna Maria and lured Weiser back to the Lutheran fold. His *Journals* provide the richest personal account of Pennsylvania colonial life.

13. As in Ernst, *Ephrata*, 188, copied from the *Chronicon*, 139.

14. Ernst, *Ephrata*, 187: "The Brethren bought a mill seat at the

foot of Zion hill from Andreas Kropf consisting of 24 acres of land, a house and grist mill. It was paid for by the money willed to Ephrata by Benedict Yüchley." I have not found the corroborating evidence.

15. Heretofore Ephrata's ink (Sachse, *Sectarians,* I, 409) was "a decoction of gall apples [presumably acorns] and copperas," the latter causing "irretrievable damage" to the earlier *Frakturschriften.*

16. Hebron was built late in 1743 at close right angles to Peniel. See *Chronicon,* 142–44; and Sachse, *Sectarians,* I, 468–72.

17. Wallace (*Conrad Weiser,* 61–64, 102–11) is not very explicit on the Anna Eicher affair; see Sachse, *Sectarians,* I, 174–75. The *Chronicon* (280–84*n*) includes a long and gentle note on the Eicher sisters.

18. *Chronicon,* 85.

19. The letter, in Sachse's translation, is reproduced by Reichmann and Doll, *Ephrata As Seen by Contemporaries,* 35–37. Randolph ("German Seventh Day Baptists," 1142–45) reviews the Weiser affair and notes that he and Beissel were later fully reconciled.

20. *Chronicon,* 174; Sachse, *Sectarians,* II, 119–20.

21. De Benneville (1703–1793) was a wide-ranging, unallied preacher and herbal physician who built a large mansion in the Oley valley. Son of a persecuted French Huguenot nobleman and a godson of Queen Anne, and, according to Rothermund (*Layman's Progress,* 10*n*), once an editor of the Berleberg Bible, in America he was first befriended by Sauer and was highly respected by the Schwenkfelders. Most of his papers are preserved in the Schwenkfelder Library. His remarkable life merits a full biography, for Bell, *Life and Times of de Benneville,* and Winchester, *Some Remarkable Passages,* do not do him full justice.

22. On the New England pilgrimage: *Chronicon,* 175–78; Sachse, *Sectarians,* II, 95–113; Randolph, "German Seventh Day Baptists," 1043–47.

23. There are two *Fraktur* mss of *Die Rose,* the house book of Saron, preserved in the Cassell Collection of the Historical Society of Pennsylvania. Both are dated 13 May 1745, but are quite different in styling and length. Ernst (*Ephrata,* 250–63) provides a valuable extended abstract of the regulations, etc. On the daily routine of Saron, see B. Martin, "Ephrata and Its Music," 35–36.

24. The *Chronicon* (136) indicates that some of his writings "were kept hidden by his admirers long after his death." A few ephemeral pieces survived: Doll and Funke, "Ephrata Bibliography," nos. 174, 366, 367.

25. On the Eckerlings in the West, see Wust, *Saint-Adventurers,* and chap. 10 below.

26. As late as 1759 Andrew Burnaby turned back from this area "as the Cherokees had been scalping in those parts only a few days before." See *Travels through the Middle Settlements in North-America* (rpt.: Cornell University Press, 1960), 41–42.

27. *Hoch-Deutsch Pennsylvanische Bericht,* no. 70, May 16, 1746, as translated by Sachse, *Sectarians,* II, 220.

28. It is unlikely that Emanuel stayed in Zoar for long. Wust (*Saint-Adventurers,* 55–56) claims that he tried to be accepted by the German-

town Dunkers, later spent some time with his brothers at New River, then "established a large congregation of First Day Dunkers in South Carolina. He died in Philadelphia County in 1767."

29. Durnbaugh (*The Brethren in Colonial America,* 152–54) locates Mahanaim "between Christiansburg and Newbern at the junction of Montgomery and Pulaski counties," but in 1939, according to Wust (*Saint-Adventurers,* 59), the site was immersed under Claytor Lake.

CHAPTER IX: RECOVERY OF EDEN

1. "The Way to Wealth" was Franklin's preface to *Poor Richard Improved,* 1758. It gained fame on both sides of the Atlantic.

2. The Comet Book, *Ernstliche Erweckungs-Stimm in ein Lied verfasst* (Earnest Awakening Voice Composed in a Song), if it survives at all, must be in private hands. Sachse (*Sectarians,* II, 87–91) reports that the only copy known in 1900, dated 1745, was then in Pennypacker's collection.

3. On the origins of the printery: Sachse, *Sectarians,* II, 222–28; and Seidensticker, *Ephrata: Kloster-geschichte,* 124–28.

4. The Doll and Funke "Ephrata Bibliography" (no. 407) indicates that the original German version did not appear in print until included in the *Deliciae Ephratenses* of 1773 and a separate issue of 1789. Sachse reprinted Miller's translation in *A Unique Manuscript* (1912). Miller noted that "The Father would never publish any creed, and was not pleas'd with the many we have now."

5. The original preface by Israel Eckerling was removed and burned. The volume was reissued the same year with the title *Urständliche und Erfahrungsvolle Hohe Zeugnüsse.* It is said that the Beissel work corresponds closely to the ideas of Gottfried Arnold. See also Jacoby, *Two Mystic Communities,* 28.

6. The pre-Constantine debate as to whether Sophia (i.e., the Logos) should be regarded as an independent personality is discussed by Hans Lietzmann, *History of the Early Church* (New York: Meridian, 1961), II, 101–02. Origen's Neo-Platonic emphasis on the Logos was later labeled heretical.

7. The most detailed analysis of Ephrata music is B. Martin's "Ephrata and Its Music," based on the most thorough research to date. It includes many valuable illustrative transcriptions. See also Sachse's *The Music of Ephrata Cloister,* and Hans T. David's articles on Ephrata music.

8. From Fahnestock's "Historical Sketch of Ephrata," reprinted by Reichmann and Doll, *Ephrata As Seen by Contemporaries,* 164–86.

9. Sachse, *Sectarians,* II, 132–33.

10. Duché, *Caspipina's Letters* (London, 1777), reprinted by Reichmann and Doll, *Ephrata As Seen by Contemporaries,* 101–02.

11. The *Turtel-Taube* contains a *Vorbericht* and a *Vorrede* which together constitute Beissel's remarkable treatise on music, later translated by Sachse in *Music of the Ephrata Cloister.* Blakely's translation

of the second part, in "Beissel and Music," is regarded as a more accurate version. The 1747 hymnbook was followed by later variant editions: see B. Martin, "Ephrata and Its Music," 87–95, 297–310.

12. B. Martin ("Ephrata and Its Music," 136–42) describes five existing music manuscripts for the *Turtel-Taube,* two evidently prepared in 1747. A later one, in the Cassell Collection, is dated 1754, with the title *Zionitischer Rosen Garten,* but contains only 127 hymns; though faded and its decoration modest, it is a particularly beautiful piece of *Frakturschriften.*

13. Estimates of the number of poems and musical compositions by Beissel vary. Stoudt, *Pennsylvania German Poetry,* xxix–xxx, gives Beissel credit for at least 800, perhaps 1,000, poems, and adds that at Ephrata "there were as many poets as there were English poets in all Colonial America." B. Martin, "Ephrata and Its Music," 192, notes that Peter Miller attributed "fully 1,000 pieces of music" to Beissel, and (pp. 165–67) identifies thirty-two Ephrata Brothers and twenty-six Sisters as authors of one or more hymn-poems.

14. David, "Musical Composition at Ephrata," and Stoudt, *Pennsylvania German Poetry,* lxviii.

15. David, "Hymns and Music," 4–5, 36. A recording of eleven Ephrata chorales by the modern-day Ephrata chorus is available at the Cloister Gift Shop, and director Russell P. Getz's transcripts of ten of these were published by G. Schirmer in 1971.

16. Ernst, *Ephrata,* 145n. *Church Music and Musical Life in Pennsylvania in the Eighteenth Century* is rich with examples; Ephrata's music is treated on pp. 26–84 and 242–53.

17. Seipt's *Schwenkfelder Hymnology* is definitive, with details both on their hymn writers and their illuminated mss. Weiser and Heaney (*Pennsylvania German Fraktur,* xxvii) suppose that their *Fraktur* art was "apparently learned from their Mennonite neighbors."

18. Ernst, *Ephrata,* 285–86.

19. Sachse, *Sectarians,* I, 479–86, reproduces an 1899 exterior photo as well as interior views and ground plan of Bethania, which he calls Ephrata's "most stately building thus far."

20. *Chronicon,* 193. Ernst (*Ephrata,* 280) implicates Beissel but cites no sources.

21. Sachse's account of the fire is in *Sectarians,* II, 259–65.

22. *Chronicon,* 210.

23. A long recital about Jung ("Young") is given in the *Chronicon,* 199–208.

24. Ibid., 197–99; Sachse, *Sectarians,* II, 259–65. The place has various spellings. It is near the Coventry settlement, on which see Falkenstein, *German Baptist Brethren,* 80–84.

25. Jacoby (*Two Mystic Communities,* 49) describes Seymour as "an Englishman, who on leaving the society formed a similar establishment in South Carolina which in 1783 numbered some forty members." On the latter, see *Seventh Day Baptists,* II, 1112–15.

26. On the Gimbsheim (various spellings) migration: *Chronicon,* 218–23; Sachse, *Sectarians,* II, 266–73; Ernst, *Ephrata,* 296–98.

27. *Seventh Day Baptists,* II, 1116–19; Falkenstein, *German Baptist Brethren,* 96–97. Gillin (*The Dunkers,* 144) says that the Bermudian congregation numbered fifty-two by 1770. Their leader Kimmel is the supposed author of *Invendige Glaubens- und Liebes Uebung,* a mystical work published by Ephrata in 1775.

28. Stoudt, *Early Pennsylvania Arts and Crafts,* 280. Shelley, *Fraktur-Writings of the Pennsylvania Germans,* is the most extensive study of the medium as a whole; pp. 101–07 are devoted to "the Ephrata school." See also the works of Borneman, Kauffman, Lichten, and Weiser and Heaney listed in the Bibliography.

29. B. Martin, "Ephrata and Its Music," 165.

30. Lichten, *Folk Art of Rural Pennsylvania,* 206. *Der Christen A B C* manuscript is preserved by the Pennsylvania Historical and Museum Commission.

31. Stoudt, *Pennsylvania Folk-Art,* interprets the background and symbolism of many of the motifs; see also Borneman, *Pennsylvania German Illuminated Manuscripts,* 51–57. In "On the Trail of the 'Hex Signs'," H. F. Alderfer makes a case for tracing the motifs to Byzantine sculptural designs that may have been carried back to Germany from the Near East by medieval migrants and returning Crusaders. For a very different view of motif sources, see Drepperd, "Origins of Pennsylvania Folk Art."

CHAPTER X: REFUGE IN THE FRONTIER CRISIS

1. Part of the letter (dated Skippack, Octo. 19, 1745, and directed to Mennonite churches in Amsterdam and Haarlem) is translated in Smith, *Mennonite Immigration,* 325. Pennypacker ("A Noteworthy Book," 281) says that the Dutch Mennonites took three years to reply, then "threw cold water on the whole enterprise," hence the appeal to Ephrata.

2. On the long evolution of this work, see esp. *The Mennonite Encyclopedia,* III, 527–29, and the *Mennonitisches Lexicon* (Karlsruhe, 1958), III, 49–53. Many of the superb Jan Luyken engravings for the original Van Braght edition are reproduced in Cornelius Krahn's *The Witness of the Martyrs' Mirror for Our Day* (North Newton, Kans., n.d.).

3. The "Memorial" (from a section of the Van Braght work) appeared as an appendix to *Die Ernsthaffte Christenpflicht* (The Earnest Christian's Duty) published by Ephrata in 1745.

4. But Lawrence Wroth's judgment of the work as also "the ugliest book produced in colonial America" is absurd; see *The Colonial Printer* (Portland, Maine: Southworth-Athenaeum, 1938), 211. Especially impressive in the 1748 edition, both in typography and scholarship, are the many marginal notes on each page citing sources.

5. Although described by Sachse with facsimiles, no copy of either booklet is now known to exist.

6. The *Erster Theil der Theosophischen Lectionen Betreffende die*

Schulen des einsamen Lebens (Theosophic Lessons Concerning the Discipline of the Solitary Life) is the most beautiful, classic piece of typography from the Ephrata press. No second part was issued. It contains 350 pp. of *Lectiones,* 44 pp. of theosophical comments on regulating the solitary life, and 146 poems and verses of similar character by Beissel.

7. The German translation of Bunyan's work *(Eines Christen Reise)* was by Christoph Seidel, published in Hamburg 1718. The beautiful 1754 *Paradisisches Wunder-spiel* should not be confused with a different work but similar title issued in 1766. The former was preceded by a manuscript of music for the hymns prepared by Anastasia at Beissel's request, now preserved in the archives of the Moravian church at Lititz. On the 1754 *Wunder-spiel:* B. Martin, "Ephrata and Its Music," 146–47 (she aptly translates the title as "Miracle Play of Paradise"); also *Chronicon,* 167–68, and Sachse, *Sectarians,* II, 150–51. According to Doll and Funke, "Ephrata Bibliography" (no. 382), the work was "partly an adaptation from the Song of Solomon and the Revelation of St. John."

8. *Chronicon,* 149.

9. B. Martin, "Ephrata and Its Music," 230–53, provides her own transcription of the entire "Lobet den Herrn."

10. Ibid., 96–101. The *Neu-vermehrtes Gesäng* especially shows a marked falling off from former Ephrata printing standards, though a sizeable production of 329 pp. The Library of Congress has a modestly illuminated music manuscript for it dated 1772, the work of an unknown scribe.

11. Sauer's letter appeared in *Acta historico-ecclesiastica* 15 (Weimar, 1751), 210–16. Part of it is translated in Reichmann and Doll, *Ephrata As Seen by Contemporaries,* 45–48, from which I quote.

12. Ibid., 49, though the quotation is from a footnote of uncertain authorship.

13. Barton, *Memoirs of the Life of David Rittenhouse,* 112–13.

14. Acrelius (as translated by William Reynolds) is quoted at length by Reichmann and Doll, *Ephrata As Seen by Contemporaries,* 50–77, the source of the quoted material that follows. On editions of the Acrelius history, see Doll and Funke "Ephrata Bibliography," nos. 208–10.

15. The account is reproduced by Reichmann and Doll, *Ephrata As Seen by Contemporaries,* 80–83. See also Altick, "Ephrata Cloisters in 1759."

16. The passage was probably written in the late 1750s. Quoted in Reichmann and Doll, *Ephrata As Seen by Contemporaries,* 84, from *The Works of Voltaire,* trans. W. F. Fleming (New York, 1901), III, 169–70.

17. Ernst, *Ephrata,* 284, 285, 286, but the chronology seems confused.

18. His fellow Solitary referred to Eicher as *der grobe Eleazer* (the uncouth Eleazer), according to Sachse, "Registers of the Ephrata Community," 393.

19. On the drought and recovery: *Chronicon,* 221–23.

20. Ibid., 237–41; also Ernst, *Ephrata,* 303–05.

21. The remainder of this chapter relies heavily on Wust, *Saint-Adventurers,* both as to Sangmeister on the Shenandoah and the frontier camps of the Eckerlings. The earlier work of Richards, *The Pennsylvania-German in the French and Indian War,* is also useful, though it lacks documentation. Part 2 of Sangmeister, *Leben und Wandel,* is a reliable first-hand account of Virginia frontier affairs. Wust notes (p. 44) that Sangmeister's "dissatisfaction with himself and others led to unmotivated attacks against Conrad Beissel whom he made, consciously or not, responsible for his own failures in communal life."

22. Wust (*Saint-Adventurers,* 49) provides a good map of Sandy Hook, and also pictures of remaining ruins there (which on a visit I could not locate).

23. There is some confusion as to the precise location of both the Dunkard Creek and the Cheat River camps. The former was probably on or near what became the Mason-Dixon line, perhaps within present Greene County, Pennsylvania. The latter was evidently within what became West Virginia, perhaps not far from present-day Morgantown.

24. The early history of white penetration of the Monongahela valley is fully detailed by Donehoo (*Indian Villages,* 113–18), though the Eckerlings are not mentioned. See also James Veech, *The Monongahela of Old* (rpt.: Baltimore, 1975), though his brief account of the Eckerlings (pp. 78–79) is not reliable.

25. Washington himself prepared an excellent map of the journey, reproduced by Lloyd Arnold Brown, *Early Maps of the Ohio Valley* (University of Pittsburgh Press, 1959), plate 18. Washington's lively journal of the trip is condensed in *Pen Pictures of Early Western Pennsylvania,* ed. John W. Harpster (University of Pittsburgh Press, 1938), 15–25.

26. The Quaker point of view is presented by Sharpless, *A History of Quaker Government in Pennsylvania,* I, 214–25.

27. Israel's incredibly long letter has yet to be studied or translated. Even Wust gives no account of its contents, though he reproduces the last page of the original preserved at the Historical Society of Pennsylvania.

28. Virginia's official position regarding the Eckerlings and other frontier Dunkers is suggested at various points in the first two volumes of *The Writings of George Washington from the Original Manuscript Sources* (Washington, 1931–1944). See Wust, *Saint-Adventurers,* 33–35. He also notes that the Virginia Council, as early as 1753, granted the Eckerlings 5,000 acres in the Cheat River area.

29. Most accounts of the Eckerling tragedy are shadowy and uncertain, perhaps necessarily so. The accounts of Wust and Richards are useful; see also *Chronicon,* 224–34, and Sachse, *Sectarians,* II, 351–55. Day (*Historical Collections,* 360) perpetuates the spurious local tradition that Israel and Gabriel were massacred by the Indians.

30. Sangmeister, *Leben und Wandel,* pt. 2, 78, 79.

31. Wust, *Saint-Adventurers,* 38, 58. Before the tragedy and when Schilling's term of indenture neared its end, Sangmeister (*Leben und*

Wandel, pt. 2, 46) remarked that "he would gladly have left with me but Gabriel ordered me to talk him out of it."

32. Wust (*Saint-Adventurers,* 37) says flatly that the Eckerlings "did not speak French at all," but this seems unlikely, especially in the case of the learned Israel who had probably studied the French mystics. Wust was perhaps the first to study the relevant French sources.

33. Sangmeister, *Leben und Wandel,* pt. 2, 81, as translated by Wust (*Saint-Adventurers,* 38).

34. Wust, *Saint-Adventurers,* 39.

35. Sessler, *Communal Pietism,* 188–90.

36. But see *Chronicon,* 136–37; Ernst, *Ephrata,* 306–08; and in a broader perspective, Richards, *The Pennsylvania-German in the French and Indian War,* 203–14.

37. Wust, *Saint-Adventurers,* 52–53, describes the abandonment of the Shenandoah settlement.

38. On the Paxton Boys see esp. Sipe, *Indian Wars of Pennsylvania,* 463–69.

CHAPTER XI: END OF THE CHARISMA

1. Rothermund (*Layman's Progress,* 37–56) has a revealing chapter on "The New Denominational Consciousness" of this period.

2. *Chronicon,* 242–62, a long passage signifying the extent to which Adam Martin influenced latter-day Ephrata. See also Brumbaugh, *German Baptist Brethren,* 329–32.

3. Indians ravaged the Stony Creek area in 1763, soon after some Dunker families had settled there (Day, *Historical Collections,* 617). On the early days of the Stony Creek congregation: Durnbaugh, *The Brethren in Colonial America,* 185–86; Mallott, *Studies in Brethren History,* 85–88.

4. Randolph ("German Seventh Day Baptists," 1135–37) records the Antietam pilgrimage in detail.

5. *Chronicon,* 103. Williams ("Monastic Orders," in Klein, *Lancaster County,* I, 434) confirms that the alchemical laboratory "followed the advent of Jacob Martin . . . about 1762," but little is known of it.

6. The story is detailed in the *Chronicon,* 263–68, but more completely in Wust, *Saint-Adventurers,* 82–101. Wust includes his translation of the *Abgeforderte Relation der Erscheinung eines entleibten Geists* (Relation on the Appearance of a Disembodied Spirit), the only known copy of which is at the Historical Society of Pennsylvania.

7. *Chronicon,* 268–77.

8. Wust, *Saint-Adventurers,* 60–65. See also Wayland, *The German Element in the Shenandoah Valley,* 124 ff.; and Smith, Stewart, and Kyger, *The Pennsylvania Germans of the Shenandoah Valley,* 83–100.

9. Sources on the land title affair are given in chap. 12, n.3.

10. On the aging Beissel's alleged drinking problem, Ernst (*Ephrata,* 332, 336–37) cites both Sangmeister and Seidensticker (*Klostergeschichte,* 133–34) who relied on the same source, but the Ernst ac-

count is clearly biased; the known "evidence" is circumstantial and based on gossip.

11. The letter is dated December 11, 1767; the quotation is from the translation of Wust, *Saint-Adventurers,* 67.

12. Stoudt's assessment in Ernst, *Ephrata,* 324n.

13. *Chronicon,* 279, 280.

14. Ernst, *Ephrata,* 334–35, again relying on Sangmeister, *Leben und Wandel,* pt. 3, 51.

15. Identification of Gast with two Brotherhood names, Jethro and Lamech, has produced much confusion. It is only a supposition that the "Lamech" as co-author of the *Chronicon* is the same as Jethro. Max Hark, the translator (1889), confesses not knowing the identity of authors "Lamech and Agrippa," though the latter is unquestionably Peter Miller who conceivably used the biblical name Lamech to indicate reliance on materials other than his own. The community diary attributed to Gast is not extant. Quite conflicting dates of Gast's death, even within the same source, are given by Sachse and Ernst, though the *Chronicon* gives it as October 12, 1749.

16. According to Sangmeister, *Leben und Wandel,* pt. 3, 56. Other confirmation seems to be lacking.

17. The extract was said to have been published in *Die Geistliche Fama,* an Inspirationist periodical of Berleburg, but I have not been able to confirm this.

18. Production of the devotional book by Wudrian (1584–1625) may have been planned several years before, for the title page verso in the copy at the Pennsylvania State Library credits Sauer, who died in 1759, among others, with supporting its production.

19. *Die Beschreibung Des Evangeliums Nicodemi,* a reprint of a 1561 Marburg edition, was "issued" by Michael Müller, Ephrata Householder and former Tulpehocken schoolmaster.

20. It had been published in Amsterdam, having passed through earlier Hebrew, Greek and Latin versions. See Jacoby, *Two Mystic Communities,* 14n.

21. The first 441 poems in the 1766 *Wunder-spiel* are said to constitute the entire corpus of Beissel's own hymn-poetry. The full German title again reflects his "New World" imagery. B. Martin, "Ephrata and Its Music," 101–03; Stoudt, *Pennsylvania Folk-Art,* 91–92; bibliographic details, Doll and Funke "Ephrata Bibliography," no. 408.

22. Names of "deserters" of this period, as well as citations of the civil court cases, seem to be lacking.

23. Randolph ("German Seventh Day Baptists," 1145) claims that Maria, after Beissel's death, "repented her hardness of heart with torrents of bitter tears."

24. *Chronicon,* 280–85. Details about the burial service are minimal. Except for a few notes, the *Chronicon* comes to an end with Beissel's death.

25. Ernst, *Ephrata,* 431.

26. I am indebted to Barbara Deibler, rare books librarian at the Pennsylvania State Library, for an offprint of the very rare broadside of

the Athanasia poem. The imagery and rhythm of the German original, printed at Ephrata, is well-nigh impossible to translate effectively.

CHAPTER XII: THE CLOUDS OF WAR

1. The letter to Franklin (June 17, 1771) is reproduced by Sachse, *A Unique Manuscript,* 1–2. In it Miller apologizes because "I am a Foreigner to the Idiotisms [*sic*] of the Language." He notes there are now twelve Brothers and twenty-six Sisters in the cloister.

2. Edwards, *Baptists in Pennsylvania,* 74–99, 88–99; the first section is reproduced by Reichmann and Doll, *Ephrata As Seen by Contemporaries,* 92–96.

3. Ernst (*Ephrata,* 326–31, 346–47) gives a rather elaborate account of the land-title quarrel but relies overmuch on the Sangmeister gossip. See Sachse, *Sectarians,* II, 414–26; Ellis and Evans, *History of Lancaster County,* 836–43; and *Votes and Proceedings of the House of Representatives of the Province of Pennsylvania* (Philadelphia, 1775), V, 374, 376–77, 385–86.

4. Wust, *Saint-Adventurers,* 119n.

5. On these bequests: Sachse, *Sectarians,* II, 416–18; Ernst, *Ephrata,* 347n.

6. Reichmann and Doll, *Ephrata As Seen by Contemporaries,* 101.

7. Ibid., 102–03. However, Hopkinson also wrote a kindlier poem to Peter Miller, quoted by Zerfass, *Souvenir Book,* 47.

8. Actually, Miller was inducted into the American Society for Promoting Useful Knowledge which merged into the American Philosophical Society a year later. He was elected April 8, 1768, and submitted his paper September 9. It appears in *Transactions of the American Philosophical Society* 1, 2d ed. (1789), 313–14. Minutes of the April meeting are quoted by Randolph in "German Seventh Day Baptists," 1148.

9. *Die Ernsthaffte Christen-Pflicht,* author unknown, and *Christliches Gemüths-Gesprach* by Gerhard Roosen (1612–1711) of Holland.

10. Part 1, in addition to an introduction corresponding to Beissel's *Mystische Abhandlung,* consists of sixty-seven sermons by Beissel. Riley ("Analysis of the Debate") provides translations of two of the most revealing sermons. Part 2, issued in 1773 with the old 1745 title page, is simply a reprint of *Zionitischer Stiffts.*

11. Marshall's letter is reproduced by Reichmann and Doll, *Ephrata As Seen by Contemporaries,* 104–07.

12. Miller's letter was published in *Pennsylvania Magazine of History and Biography* 38 (1914), 227–31. It was written when he was about "to go on a great Jurney to Virginia," presumably to the Shenandoah settlements.

13. Reichmann and Doll, *Ephrata As Seen by Contemporaries,* 189–92. There is reason to believe that Lady Juliana had visited Ephrata. A letter of hers to Miller (September 29, 1774) appears in *Seventh Day Baptists,* II, 1153, and in Sachse, *Sectarians,* II, 408–09.

14. The resolution appears in *The Colonial Records of Pennsylvania,* X, 420. At the same time the Bradfords in Philadelphia were authorized to print 1,000 copies in English, which may reflect the relative proportions of the German and English populations.

15. Worner ("Peter Miller") alleges that there is no basis for the tradition, and attributes the "error" to Sachse. As to Miller translating the Declaration into German, Stoudt (in Ernst, *Ephrata,* 348n) points out that Heinrich Müller, editor of the *Staatsbote,* brought out a German version within a day or two of its adoption.

16. The battle and its effects are described by John F. Reed, *Campaign to Valley Forge* (University of Pennsylvania Press, 1965), 117–40. An additional hundred wounded men were sent to other recovery areas—Lafayette, for example, to the Moravians at Bethlehem.

17. Marshall's entry of December 29, 1777, in Reichmann and Doll, *Ephrata As Seen by Contemporaries,* 116. He was then living in Lancaster (until 1781). Richards, *The Pennsylvania-German in the Revolutionary War,* 356–59, describes the hospital at Ephrata and the spread of disease and death. See also C. H. Martin, "The Military Hospital at the Cloister," and Heiges, "Letters Relating to Colonial Military Hospitals in Lancaster County."

18. Robert Fortenbaugh, *The Nine Capitals of the United States* (York, Pa., 1948), 33–35. Lancaster also became the state capital, 1799–1810.

19. Sachse, *Sectarians,* II, 426; *Seventh Day Baptists,* II, 1159–63. In 1902 an obelisk memorializing the soldiers who died at Ephrata was erected in Zion Hill cemetery.

20. Randolph, "German Seventh Day Baptists," 1163n.

21. Davis included the letter in her *General History;* it is reproduced by Reichmann and Doll, *Ephrata As Seen by Contemporaries,* 115.

22. *Chronicon,* 213–14n. See also Miller's letter to William Barton (April 1788) in Diffenderfer, "The Ephrata Community."

23. The story of Widman has no known contemporary documentation, but see Sachse, *Sectarians,* II, 426–32; Zerfass, *Souvenir Book,* 11, 22–23; and Randolph, "German Seventh Day Baptists," 1163–67, who claims he got the story "from the original manuscript," otherwise unidentified.

24. Entries of August 15 and 21, in Reichmann and Doll, *Ephrata As Seen by Contemporaries,* 116.

25. The entire letter to the Snowbergers, dated May 5, 1782, is quoted by Treher, *Snow Hill Cloister,* 36–38.

26. Based on estimates in a 1784 letter by an unidentified German traveler, translated in Reichmann and Doll, *Ephrata As Seen by Contemporaries,* 119–22.

27. Brooke, *Friend Anthony Benezet,* 76–109, 120–24. The German version of the anti-slavery pamphlet was issued at Ephrata 1763; the tract on the Indians in 1786. Source of the German translations is obscure.

28. Brother Obed's *Schul-Büchlein* of 1786 is, according to its title page, a second edition, but no copy of a first is known. Sachse (*Music*

of the Ephrata Cloister, 95–106) also translates a delightful fable by
Obed against cruelty to animals.

29. Wallace, *Conrad Weiser*, 62.

30. *Das Ganz Neue Testament* was (according to Doll and Funke,
"Ephrata Bibliography," no. 429) "a version according to the Fro-
schauer Bible (Zürich, 1529)."

31. Brumbaugh, *German Baptist Brethren*, 252.

32. On the *Wunderschrift* see chap. 9, n. 4. On the *Geistliche Briefe*
of 1794, Doll and Funke "Ephrata Bibliography," no. 450.

33. Ibid., nos. 436 through 452 (including other ephemera).

34. The *Christliche Bibliothek* (148 pp.) to some degree summarizes
the prevailing views of Ephrata on religious history. Klaus Wust's
translation of the work (1954) has not been published.

35. The Roemeling work is a substantial 465 pages. Tersteegen's
88-page book on spiritual song should be compared with Beissel's writings on music.

36. The *Cazenove Journal 1794* is quoted by Reichmann and Doll,
Ephrata As Seen by Contemporaries, 151. Cazenove was an agent for
the Holland Land Company, 1790–1799.

37. Ibid., 152–55. Rouchefoucauld's *Travels* covered the years 1795–
1797; he came to America to escape the French Revolution.

38. The British officer's account (April 27, 1786) was copied three
years later in Matthew Carey's *American Museum* with a note complaining of its "shamefully misrepresented facts." Miller's comments on
the officer appear in *Hazard's Register* 16 (1835), 253–56. Both items are
found in Reichmann and Doll, *Ephrata As Seen by Contemporaries*,
125–35, 194–95. See also Diffenderfer, "The Ephrata Community."

39. Schöpf's account is translated in Reichmann and Doll, *Ephrata
As Seen by Contemporaries*, 135–38.

40. Even the indefatigible Sachse had to write to Obed Snowberger
at Snow Hill in 1881 that "I have no account of Jabez death or burial."
See Treher, *Snow Hill Cloister*, 90.

41. However, Randolph, ("German Seventh Day Baptists," 1176)
claims that Jacob Kimmel succeeded to Miller's role; probably by then
that was more of a clerical and caretaker assignment.

42. Ebeling's account of Ephrata is translated in Reichmann and
Doll, *Ephrata As Seen by Contemporaries*, 155–56.

CHAPTER XIII: SNOW HILL AFTERGLOW

1. This chapter owes much to Treher, *Snow Hill Cloister;* he was
the first to dig systematically into the records there. Randolph's section
on Snow Hill ("German Seventh Day Baptists," 1133–42) was also
helpful.

2. On Adam Martin: Brumbaugh, *German Baptist Brethren*, 291;
and Sachse, *Sectarians*, II, 361, 364.

3. Cremer ("Seventh Day Baptists of Snow Hill," 10–11) says that
Miller "secured enough adherents to found a congregation and hold

regular meetings," but it was probably then more of a Dunker than a Sabbatarian communion.

4. In spite of Martin, the Stony Creek congregation was more allied to Germantown than Ephrata. See Brumbaugh, *German Baptist Brethren,* 329–32; Durnbaugh, *The Brethren in Colonial America,* 185–86; and H. Austin Cooper, *Two Centuries of Brothersvalley Church of the Brethren* (Westminster, Md., 1962), 184–91.

5. Amish families settled as early as 1762–1763 near where the Stony Creek Dunkers located. One of them founded Johnstown in 1800: Beachy, "The Amish Settlement in Somerset County," *Mennonite Historical Review* 28 (1954), 263–92. Lehman, sometimes identified as a Mennonite, was a native of The Glades, an Amish settlement. Treher, *Snow Hill Cloister,* 107–08, translates Miller's 1788 letter to Lehman, from the Obed Snowberger mss.

6. It was not until September 1823 that the house and 106 acres were formally sold to the congregation for the exclusive use of its "Monastical Branch," then composed of only seven members: Treher, *Snow Hill Cloister,* 50–51. Lehman died in 1823, Andrew Snowberger two years later.

7. Ibid., 44. Randolph ("German Seventh Day Baptists," 1140–41) reviews the orderly daily routine of the commune.

8. Andrew Fahnestock served as *Lehrer* from 1823 to 1840 and at several periods between 1843 and 1855; he died in 1863.

9. Treher, *Snow Hill Cloister,* 58–59.

10. They are listed in ibid. 104–05, with dates of death and age at death when known. Of the twenty-eight whose data are known, nineteen lived beyond the age of seventy, of whom ten passed the age of eighty.

11. Ibid., 65.

12. Snow Hill's principal *Fraktur* artist was David Snowberger; the Cassell Collection at the Historical Society of Pennsylvania possesses an estimated 185 pieces of illuminated music scores by him, mostly from 1817–1820. B. Martin ("Ephrata and Its Music," 152) remarks that the Snow Hill works "lack the delicate fragility" and "exquisite details" of Ephrata's but that they "exhibit a rather stark beauty and distinctiveness of their own."

13. For the Fahnestock comment, see Reichmann and Doll, *Ephrata As Seen by Contemporaries,* 183; the Snowberger comment is recorded in Treher, *Snow Hill Cloister,* 92.

14. Treher, *Snow Hill Cloister,* 91–92; on Brother Obed himself, 87–88.

15. Zerfass, *Souvenir Book,* 30; Durnbaugh, *The Brethren in Colonial America,* 145–48; and Sipe, *Indian Wars of Pennsylvania,* 522–26.

CHAPTER XIV: THE LATER HISTORY OF EPHRATA

1. See Diffenderfer, "The Ephrata Community."

2. Reichmann and Doll, *Ephrata As Seen by Contemporaries,* 161.

3. The best account of Ephrata in the nineteenth century is by Randolph, "German Seventh Day Baptists," 1174–76 and 1182–1204.

4. Hazard's *Register*, V, 331–34; XV, 161–67 (Fahnestock); XVI, 253–56. Strangely, Hazard omitted any mention of Ephrata in his substantial *Annals of Pennsylvania* (Philadelphia, 1850). It should also be noted that Proud's *History of Pennsylvania* (1798) included an erratic account of Ephrata almost three decades before Conyngham and Endress.

5. The full German title of this work, published in four parts or pamphlets, may be loosely translated as the "Life and Conduct of the Blessed and Departed Brother Ezechiel Sangmeister, Formerly an Inhabitant of Ephrata, Written by Himself." Wust's account of it (*Saint-Adventurers*, 66–75) is especially valuable. See also Doll and Funke, "Ephrata Bibliography," no. 198.

6. Wust, *Saint-Adventurers*, 43–44, for Sangmeister's will dated Sept. 16, 1782, pp. 69–70. Sangmeister died Dec. 30, 1784, aged sixty-one.

7. Seidensticker, *Ephrata: Kloster-geschichte,* as translated in Kriebel, "Sangmeister, the Ephrata Chronicler."

8. Reichmann, "Ezechiel Sangmeister's Diary," which also includes a useful review of Sangmeister's life.

9. Wust, *Saint-Adventurers*, 71.

10. The 168 pages of the "Mystical Theology, or True Guidepost to Our Origin and Fatherland" attests to Sangmeister's interest in the ideas of Boehme and the French mystic Mme. Guyon, and to de Benneville's Universalism.

11. Wust, *Saint-Adventurers*, p. 68.

12. According to B. Martin, "Ephrata and Its Music," 41–43.

13. Ibid., 43–45, 327, and notes 106–07. But see also earlier attempts to trace the history of the presses in Potts, "Notes and Queries," and Ziegler, "The Ephrata Printing Press."

14. Act of Feb. 21, 1814. Legal documentation for the later history of the congregation, most of it dealing with internal litigation, is listed in Doll and Funke, "Ephrata Bibliography," nos. 283, 297–320, 323.

15. See Reichmann and Doll, *Ephrata As Seen by Contemporaries,* 184–85, and (the second quotation) Kriebel, "Sangmeister, the Ephrata Chronicler."

16. The Williams watercolor is preserved by the Historical Society of Pennsylvania; a black-and-white reproduction appears as the frontispiece in *Ephrata As Seen by Contemporaries.*

17. Pennell's original was a black-and-white drawing, apparently a wash with pen detailing. It also belongs to the Historical Society of Pennsylvania, but a recent search there failed to locate it. It was reproduced in *Ephrata As Seen by Contemporaries,* opp. p. xvii. It was made specifically for Seidensticker's article, "A Colonial Monastery" (1881–82).

18. Pyle, "A Peculiar People." On the Dunker (as distinct from the Sabbatarian) congregation: [Falkenstein and Reber], *History of the Church of the Brethren of the Eastern District,* 220.

19. Black-and-white reproductions of Sheeler's Ephrata paintings are

on pp. 150–51 of Constance Rourke's *Charles Sheeler* (New York, 1938).

20. "Sister Tabea" appeared in Eggleston's collection of stories, *Duffles* (New York, 1893).

21. Act No. 395, approved June 27, 1939.

22. Biever, "Report of Archaeological Investigations."

23. Fahnestock, "Historical Sketch," in *Ephrata As Seen by Contemporaries,* 185.

CHAPTER XV: POSTLUDE

1. Kanter, *Commitment and Community,* 147–48. This work is an outstanding sociological study of both nineteenth- and twentieth-century communalism as a whole.

2. See, e.g., Kateb, *Utopia and Its Enemies,* and, in a quite different manner, Aldous Huxley's "anti-utopian novel," *Brave New World.*

3. See Gwendolyn Wright, "The Woman's Commonwealth: A Nineteenth-Century Experiment," *Heresies* (New York) no. 11 (1981), 24–27.

4. Zablocki, *The Joyful Community: An Account of the Bruderhof,* includes a section on "The Hippie Response" and an analysis of "the conflict between community and freedom."

5. See Hedgepeth, *The Alternative: Communal Life in New America,* 175–81.

6. For a personalized view of Synanon, Peter Beagle, *The California Feeling* (New York: Doubleday, 1969), 188–93, and for its later excesses, *Reader's Digest,* July 1981, 61–65.

7. See Toennies, *Community and Society.* This theme is summarized by Kanter, *Commitment and Community,* 148–57.

8. Jung, *Aion,* trans. R. F. C. Hull (New York: Pantheon, 1959), 173.

9. Hedgepeth, *The Alternative,* with revealing photography by Dennis Stock, catches the erratic quality of the 1960s communes.

10. Zaretsky and Leone, eds. *Religious Movements in Contemporary America,* contains many perceptive essays on aspects of the new phenomenon.

11. *The Decline of the West,* II, 310–11 and 435.

12. Jung, *Aion,* 176.

13. See, e.g., Kriyananda, *Cooperative Communities,* a primer on communal formation on a Yogananda base.

14. Castaneda, *The Second Ring of Power* (New York: Simon & Schuster, 1977), 140.

15. The German original of *Doktor Faustus* first appeared in Stockholm in 1947. Mann returned to Switzerland in 1952 and died in 1955.

16. *Doctor Faustus,* 66–67. Mann describes Beissel and Ephrata at some length, but without describing the communal system.

17. For the comparable Fahnestock passage: *Ephrata As Seen by*

Contemporaries, 183–84, but there is no evidence that Mann read the Fahnestock "Sketch."

18. "There is so much Nietzsche in the novel that it has been called a Nietzsche novel": Mann, *The Story of a Novel*, trans. Richard and Clara Winston (New York: Knopf, 1961), 33.

19. *Doctor Faustus*, 222–50.

20. *The Story of a Novel*, 63–64.

21. *Doctor Faustus*, 376–77.

22. Ibid., 510.

23. *The Story of a Novel*, 39–40.

24. Karst, "Johann Conrad Beissel in Thomas Manns 'Doktor Faustus'." I am indebted to Christoph Schweitzer of the University of North Carolina for a photocopy of it. See also Briner, "Beissel and Mann," and "Wahrheit und Dichtung"; and Gunilla Bergsten *Thomas Mann's Doctor Faustus* (University of Chicago Press, 1969).

25. From *Deliciae Ephratense, Part 1*, discourse no. 14, as translated in Riley, "Analysis of the Debate," 274–75.

26. The "religious eroticism" in Ephrata poetry has been misunderstood by prudish writers, but Jung (*Aion*, 202 f.) pointed out that "sexual symbolism" occurred also in early Christian and Gnostic writings.

27. Stoudt, *Pennsylvania German Poetry*, lxviii.

Bibliography

Some works, including manuscripts and writings printed at Ephrata, are cited fully in the Notes and thus are not included in the Bibliography. The publisher's name is usually omitted on works published abroad or prior to 1940, as is the city of publication for works published by university presses.

For Ephrata manuscripts and imprints of the Ephrata press I have relied primarily on: (1) the Cassell Collection of the Historical Society of Pennsylvania in Philadelphia; (2) the Rare Books Division of the Pennsylvania State Library in Harrisburg; and (3) the Rare Book Room and the Music Division of the Library of Congress in Washington. Of other depositories having Ephrata items, the most important is the Seventh Day Baptist Historical Society in Plainfield, New Jersey. Several items have also been checked in the Archives of the Moravian Church at Bethlehem and Lititz, Pa., and at the Schwenkfelder Library at Pennsburg, Pa. I suspect there are also important manuscripts and imprints at Snow Hill Cloister near Quincy, Pa., but on two visits there I found them unavailable for perusal.

The principal available Ephrata manuscripts are the *Fraktur* music scores. Most other manuscript sources one would hope to find—personal diaries, correspondence (except for the 1755 Beissel Letter Book and a few items by Peter Miller), and records of the mills and workshops—are apparently no longer extant. Imprints from Ephrata's printing establishment, operative between ca. 1745 and 1800, have been listed in full bibliographic detail by Eugene Doll and Anneliese Funke (see below). Their Ephrata bibliography lists eighty-eight titles produced at the Cloisters, and copies of one or more are held by some fifty depositories. Some, however, are no longer extant, others are mere broadsides. I have consulted most of the important titles.

Acrelius, Israel. *A History of New Sweden; or, the Settlements on the Delaware.* Translated by William M. Reynolds. Philadelphia, 1874. Reprint. New York: Arno Press, 1972.
———. "Visit by the Provost Magister, Israel Acrelius, to the Ephrata Cloister, Aug. 20, 1753." *Memoirs of the Historical Society of Pennsylvania* 11 (1874), 373–401.
Albertson, Ralph. "A Survey of Mutualistic Communities in America." *Iowa Journal of History and Politics* 34 (1936), 375–445.
Alderfer, E. Gordon. "Conrad Beissel and the Ephrata Experiment." *The American-German Review* 21, no. 6 (1955), 23–25.
———. "Johannes Kelpius and the Spiritual Ferment of the Seventeenth Century." *The American-German Review,* 17, no. 6 (1951), 3–6.

————. "Pastorius and the Origins of Pennsylvania German Culture." *The American-German Review* 17, no. 3 (1951), 8–11.

————, ed. *Johannes Kelpius: A Method of Prayer.* New York: Harper, 1951.

Alderfer, H. F. "On the Trail of the 'Hex Signs'." *The American-German Review* 19, no. 6 (1953), 4–8.

Altick, Richard D. "Ephrata Cloisters in 1759." *Pennsylvania History* 6 (1939), 240–45.

"An Account of a Society Called Dunkards, in Pennsylvania." *Royal Magazine; or, Gentleman's Monthly Companion* 1, no. 2 (1759), 61–63. Also in *Dodsley's Annual Register.* 5th ed. London, 1769. Pp. 341–43.

Armstrong, William H. *Organs for America: The Life and Work of David Tannenberg.* University of Pennsylvania Press, 1967.

Aurand, A. Monroe, Jr., *Historical Account of the Ephrata Cloister and the Seventh Day Baptist Society.* Harrisburg, 1940. Pamphlet.

Bainton, Roland. *The Reformation of the Sixteenth Century.* Boston: Beacon Press, 1952.

Barton, William. *Memoirs of the Life of David Rittenhouse.* Philadelphia, 1813.

Bausman, Lottie M. *A Bibliography of Lancaster County, Pennsylvania, 1745–1912.* Pennsylvania Federation of Historical Societies, n.d.

Beidelman, William. *The Story of the Pennsylvania Germans.* Easton, 1898. Reprint. Detroit: Gale Research, 1969.

Bell, Albert D. *The Life and Times of Dr. George de Benneville, 1703–1793.* Boston: Universal Church of America, 1953.

Bender, Harold S. "The Founding of the Mennonite Church in America at Germantown, 1698–1708." *Mennonite Quarterly Review* 7 (1933), 227–50.

————. *Two Centuries of American Mennonite Literature . . . 1727–1928.* Goshen, Ind., 1929.

Bender, Wilbur J. "Pacifism Among the Mennonites, Amish Mennonites, and Schwenkfelders of Pennsylvania to 1783." *Mennonite Quarterly Review* 1, no. 3 (1927), 23–40, and no. 4 (1927), 21–48.

Bernstein, Eduard. *Cromwell and Communism.* 1895. Translated by H. J. Stenning. New York: Schocken Books, 1963.

Bestor, Arthur Eugene, Jr. *Backwoods Utopias: The Sectarian and Owenite Phases of Communitarian Socialism in America, 1663–1829.* University of Pennsylvania Press, 1950.

Biever, Dale E. "A Report of the Archaeological Investigations at the Ephrata Cloister, 1963–1966." In *Four Pennsylvania German Studies,* 1–53. Publications of the Pennsylvania German Society, n.s. 3. Breinigsville, Pa., 1970.

Bittinger, Lucy F. *German Religious Life in Colonial Times.* Philadelphia, 1906.

Blakely, Lloyd G. "Johann Conrad Beissel and Music of the Ephrata Cloister." *Journal of Research in Music Education* 15 (Summer 1967), 120–38.

Boehme, Jacob. *The Confessions of Jacob Boehme.* Compiled and edited by W. Scott Palmer, introduction by Evelyn Underhill. New York: Harper, 1954.

Bolles, Albert S. *Pennsylvania, Province and State: A History, 1609–1790.* 2 vols. Philadelphia, 1899. Reprint. New York: Burt Franklin, 1970.

Bonner, Edwin B. *William Penn's "Holy Experiment" . . . 1681–1701.* Columbia University Press, 1962.

Borneman, Henry S. *Pennsylvania German Illuminated Manuscripts.* Norristown, 1937. Reprint. New York: Dover, 1973.

Bovet, Felix. *The Banished Count; or, the Life of Nicholas Zinzendorf.* London, 1865.

Brandt, Harry A. *Christopher Sower and Son.* Elgin, Ill., 1938.

Briner, Andres. "Conrad Beissel and Thomas Mann." *The American-German Review* 26, no. 2 (1959–60), 24–25, 38.

———. "Wahrheit und Dichtung um J. C. Beissel: Studie um eine Gestalt in Thomas Manns 'Doktor Faustus'." *Schweizerische Musikzeitung* 98, no. 10 (October 1958), 365–69.

Brooke, George S. *Friend Anthony Benezet.* University of Pennsylvania Press, 1937.

Brumbaugh, G. Edwin. *Colonial Architecture of Pennsylvania Germans.* Proceedings of the Pennsylvania German Society 41. Lancaster, 1931.

Brumbaugh, Martin Grove. *A History of the German Baptist Brethren in Europe and America.* Mount Morris, Ill., 1899. Reprint. New York: AMS Press, 1971.

Buber, Martin. *Paths in Utopia.* Translated by R. F. C. Hull. Boston: Beacon, 1949.

Calverton, Victor F. *Where Angels Fear to Tread.* Indianapolis: Bobbs-Merrill, 1941.

Cassel, Daniel K., et al. *History of the Mennonites.* Philadelphia, 1888.

Chronicon Ephratense, enthaltend den Lebens-Lauf des ehrwürdigen Vaters in Christo, Friedsam Gottrecht, weyland Stiffters und Vorstehers des geistlichen Ordens der Einsamen in Ephrata in der Grafschafft Lancaster in Pennsylvania. Zusammen getragen von Br. Lamech u. Agrippa. . . . Ephrata, 1786.

Chronicon Ephratense: A History of the Community of the Seventh Day Baptists at Ephrata. . . . Translated by J. Max Hark. Lancaster, 1889. Reprint. New York: Burt Franklin, 1972.

Church Music and Musical Life in Pennsylvania in the Eighteenth Century. Prepared by the Pennsylvania Society of the Colonial Dames of America. 3 vols. Philadelphia, 1926–27. Reprint. 1947.

Clymer, Reuben Swinburne. *The Rosicrucian Fraternity in America.* Quakertown, Pa.: The Rosicrucian Foundation, 1935.

Comba, Emilio. *History of the Waldenses of Italy.* London, 1888.

Conyngham, Redmond, and Christian Endress. "An Account of the Settlement of the Dunkers at Ephrata" and "A Short History of That Religious Society." *Memoirs of the Pennsylvania Historical Society* 2 (1827), 133–53.

Cremer, C. W. "The Seventh Day Baptists of Snow Hill." *Kittochtinny Historical Society Papers* 6 (1908–10), 10–30.

[Croll, P. C.] "Famous Pennsylvania Germans: John Peter Miller, the Scholarly Mystic of Ephrata." *The Pennsylvania-German* 1, no. 2 (1900), 3–17.

David, Hans Theodore. "Background for Bethlehem: Moravian Music in Pennsylvania." *Magazine of Art* 32 (1939), 222 ff.

———. "Ephrata and Bethlehem in Pennsylvania, a Comparison." *Papers of the American Musicological Society,* 1941, 97–104.

———. "Hymns and Music of the Pennsylvania Seventh Day Baptists." *The American-German Review* 9, no. 5 (1943), 4–6, 36.

———. "Musical Composition at Ephrata." *The American-German Review* 10, no. 5 (1944), 4–5.

———. "Musical Life in the Pennsylvania Settlements of the Unitas Fratrum." *Moravian Historical Society Transactions* 13 (1942), 19–58.

David, Kenneth R. "Anabaptism as a Charismatic Movement." *Mennonite Quarterly Review* 53 (1979), 219–34.

Davis, Mrs. Tamar. *A General History of the Sabbatarian Churches. . . .* Philadelphia, 1851.

Day, Sherman. *Historical Collections of the State of Pennsylvania.* Philadelphia, 1843. Reprint. Port Washington, N.Y.: Ira J. Friedman Inc., 1969.

De Schweinitz, Edmund. *The History of the Church Known as the Unitas Fratrum.* Bethlehem, Pa., 1885.

Diffenderffer, F. R. "The Early Settlement and Population of Lancaster County." *Lancaster County Historical Society Papers* 9 (1905), 151–71.

———. "The Ephrata Community One Hundred and Twenty Years Ago, as Described by an Englishman." *Lancaster County Historical Society Papers* 9 (1905), 127–46.

———. *The German Immigration into Pennsylvania . . . from 1700 to 1775.* Lancaster, 1900. Reprint. Baltimore: Genealogical Publishing Co., 1977.

Doll, Eugene E. *The Ephrata Cloister: An Introduction.* Ephrata Cloister Associates, 1958. Pamphlet.

———. "Historical Guide to the Seventh Day German Baptist Cloister at Ephrata." *Pennsylvania Public Instruction* 9 (1942), 22–26.

———. "Social and Economic Organization in Two Pennsylvania German Religious Communities." *The American Journal of Sociology* 57 (1951), 168–77.

Doll, Eugene E., and Anneliese M. Funke. "The Ephrata Cloisters: An Annotated Bibliography." Philadelphia: Carl Schurz Memorial Foundation, 1944.

Donehoo, George P. *A History of Indian Villages and Place Names in Pennsylvania.* Harrisburg, 1928.

Dreis, Hazel. "Lancaster, Pennsylvania, Bookbindings: An Historical Study." *Papers of the Bibliographical Society of America* 42 (1948), 119–28.

Drepperd, Carl W. "Origins of Pennsylvania Folk Art." *Antiques* 38, no. 2 (1940), 64–68.

Drummond, Robert Rutherford. *Early German Music in Philadelphia.* New York, 1910.

Dubbs, Joseph Henry. *Early German Hymnology of Pennsylvania.* Lancaster, 1882.

———. "Ephrata Hymns and Hymn-Books." *Lancaster County Historical Society Papers* 13 (1909), 21–37.

Durant, Will, and Ariel Durant. *The Age of Louis XIV.* New York: Simon & Schuster, 1963.

Durnbaugh, Donald F. *The Believer's Church: The History and Character of Radical Protestantism.* New York: Macmillan, 1968.

———. "Christopher Sauer, Pennsylvania-German Printer: His Youth in Germany and Later Relationship with Europe." *Pennsylvania Magazine of History and Biography* 82 (1958), 316–40.

———. *European Origins of the Brethren.* Elgin, Ill.: The Brethren Press, 1958.

———. *Every Need Supplied: Mutual Aid and Christian Community . . . 1525–1675.* Philadelphia: Temple University Press, 1974.

———. "Johann Adam Gruber, Pennsylvania-German Prophet and Poet." *Pennsylvania Magazine of History and Biography* 83 (1959), 382–408.

———. "Work and Hope: The Spirituality of the Radical Pietist Communitarians." *Church History* 39, no. 1 (March 1970), 72–90.

———, ed. *The Brethren in Colonial America: A Source Book. . . .* Elgin, Ill.: The Brethren Press, 1967.

Durnbaugh, Donald F., and Lawrence W. Schultz. "A Brethren Bibliography, 1713–1963." *Brethren Life and Thought* 9 (1964), 1–177.

Edwards, Morgan. *Baptists in Pennsylvania, Both British and German. . . .* Vol. 1 of *Materials towards a History of American Baptists.* 12 vols. Philadelphia, 1770.

Egbert, Donald Drew, and Stow Persons, eds. *Socialism and American Life.* 2 vols. Princeton University Press, 1952.

Ellis, Franklin, and Samuel Evans. *History of Lancaster County. . . .* Philadelphia, 1883.

Erbe, Hellmuth. *Bethlehem, Pa.: Eine Kommunistische Herrnhuter Kolonie des 18. Jahrhunderts.* Stuttgart, 1929.

Ernst, James E. *Ephrata, A History.* Edited with Introduction by John Joseph Stoudt. Pennsylvania German Folklore Society Yearbook 25. Allentown, 1963.

Eshleman, H. Frank. "The Birth of Lancaster County." *Lancaster County Historical Society Papers* 12 (1908), 5–39.

———. *Historic Background and Annals of the Swiss and German Pioneer Settlers of Southeastern Pennsylvania.* Lancaster, 1917.

———. ". . . The Political History and Development of Lancaster County's First Twenty Years, 1729–1749. . . ." *Lancaster County Historical Society Papers* 20 (1916), 37–68.

Fahnestock, William M. "Historical Sketch of Ephrata, Together with a

Concise Account of the Seventh Day Baptist Society of Pennsylvania." *Hazard's Register of Pennsylvania* 15 (1835), 161–67.

Falkenstein, George N. *The German Baptist Brethren or Dunkers.* . . . Proceedings of the Pennsylvania German Society 10. Lancaster: 1900.

[Falkenstein, George N., and D. C. Reber.] *History of the Church of the Brethren of the Eastern District of Pennsylvania.* Lancaster, 1915. Reprint. 1977.

Faust, Albert B. *The German Element in the United States.* . . . New York, 1909.

Flory, John S. *Literary Activity of the German Baptist Brethren in the Eighteenth Century.* Elgin, Ill., 1908.

Ford, Edward. *David Rittenhouse, Astronomer-Patriot 1732–1796.* University of Pennsylvania Press, 1946.

Franklin, Benjamin. *The Autobiography of Benjamin Franklin.* Edited by Max Ferrand. University of California Press, 1949.

———. *The Autobiography of Benjamin Franklin.* Edited by Leonard W. Larabee. Yale University Press, 1964.

———. *The Papers of Benjamin Franklin* [1706–1767]. Edited by Leonard W. Larabee and Whitfield J. Bell, Jr. 14 vols. to date. Yale University Press, 1959–.

Fresenius, Johann P., ed. *Bewährte Nachrichten von Herrnhutischen Sachsen.* 3 vols. Frankfurt and Leipzig, 1747–51.

Fretz, J. Winfield. *Christian Mutual Aid: A Handbook of Brotherhood Economics.* Akron, Pa.: Mennonite Central Committee, 1947.

Friedmann, Robert. *Hutterite Studies.* Goshen, Ind.: Mennonite Historical Society, 1961.

———. *Mennonite Piety Through the Centuries: Its Genius and Its Literature.* Goshen, Ind.: Mennonite Historical Society, 1949.

Gibbons, Phebe Earle. *"Pennsylvania Dutch" and Other Essays.* Rev. ed. Philadelphia, 1882. Reprint. New York: AMS Press, 1971.

Gide, Charles. *Communist and Cooperative Colonies.* Translated by Ernest F. Row. London, 1930.

Gilbert, Russell W. *A Picture of the Pennsylvania Germans.* Gettysburg: Pennsylvania Historical Association, 1947.

Gillin, John Lewis. *The Dunkers: A Sociological Interpretation.* New York, 1906. Reprint. New York: AMS Press, 1974.

Gipson, Lawrence H. "The New World Paradise of the Sects," in *The British Empire Before the American Revolution, 1748–1754,* vol. 3, 149–202. Caldwell, Idaho, 1936.

Goertz, Hans-Jürgen. "History and Theology: A Major Problem of Anabaptist Research Today." *Mennonite Quarterly Review,* 53 (1979), 177–88.

———. *Radikale Reformatoren.* Munich, 1978.

Gollin, Gillian Lindt. *Moravians in Two Worlds.* Columbia University Press, 1967.

Graeff, Arthur D. *Conrad Weiser, Pennsylvania Peacemaker.* Pennsylvania German Folklore Society 8. Allentown, 1943.

Hamilton, J. Taylor. *A History of . . . the Moravian Church . . . during the Eighteenth and Nineteenth Centuries.* Bethlehem, Pa., 1900.

Hamilton, Kenneth G., ed. *The Bethlehem Diary*. Vol. 1, *1742–1744*. Bethlehem, Pa.: Archives of the Moravian Church, 1971.

Harder, Leland, and Marvin Harder. *Plockhoy from Zurick-Zee: The Study of a Dutch Reformer in Puritan England and Colonial America*. Mennonite Historical Series 2. Newton, Kans., 1952.

Hausmann, W. A. *German-American Hymnology, 1685–1800*. Philadelphia, 1898.

Hayden, Dolores. *Seven American Utopias: The Architecture of Communitarian Socialism, 1790–1975*. Cambridge, Mass.: MIT Press, 1976.

Hazard, Samuel, ed. *Register of Pennsylvania*. . . . 16 vols. Philadelphia, 1828–36.

Heatwole, Daniel R. *The Ephrata Martyrs' Mirror*. Scottdale, Pa.: Mennonite Publishing House, n.d.

Hedgepeth, William. *The Alternative: Communal Life in the New America*. New York: Macmillan, 1970. Photographs by Dennis Stock.

Heering, G. J. *The Fall of Christianity*. 1928. Translated by J. W. Thompson. New York: Fellowship Publications, 1943.

Heiges, George L. "Letters Relating to Colonial Military Hospitals in Lancaster County." *Lancaster County Historical Society Papers* 52 (1948), 73–96.

Heinicke, Milton H. *History of Ephrata*. Historical Society of the Cocalico Valley, n.d. 3 pamphlets.

Hertz, Daniel Rhine. *History of Ephrata*. . . . Philadelphia, 1894.

Hildeburn, Charles S. *A Century of Printing: The Issues of the Press in Pennsylvania, 1685–1784*. 2 vols. Philadelphia, 1885–86.

Hillquit, Morris. *History of Socialism in the United States*. New York, 1903.

Hinds, William Alfred. *American Communities and Cooperative Colonies*. Rev. ed. Chicago, 1908. Reprint. New York: Corinth Books, 1961.

Hinke, William J., ed. *Life and Letters of the Rev. John Philip Boehm, Founder of the Reformed Church in Pennsylvania, 1683–1749*. Philadelphia, 1916.

Hocker, Edward W. *Germantown, 1683–1933*. Germantown, Philadelphia, 1933.

———. *The Sower Printing House of Colonial Times*. Pennsylvania German Society 53, pt. 2. Norristown, 1948.

Holloway, Mark. *Heavens on Earth: Utopian Communities in America, 1680–1880*. London, 1951. 2d ed. New York: Dover, 1966.

Hollyday, Guy Tilghman. "The Ephrata Codex: Relationships Between Text and Illustration." *Pennsylvania Folk-Life* 20, no. 1 (Autumn 1970), 28–43.

Hollyday, Guy Tilghman, and Christoph E. Schweitzer. "The Present Status of Conrad Beissel/Ephrata Research." *Monatshefte* (University of Wisconsin Press) 68 (Summer 1976), 171–78.

Hostetler, John A. *Amish Society*. Rev. ed. Johns Hopkins University Press, 1968.

———. *Hutterite Society*. Johns Hopkins University Press, 1974.

Hubben, William. "Pilgrims from Krefeld." *The American-German Review* 25, no. 1 (1958–59), 8–11.

Hull, William. *William Penn and the Dutch Quaker Migration to Pennsylvania*. Swarthmore, Pa., 1935.

Infield, Henrik F. *Cooperative Communities at Work*. New York: Dryden, 1945.

————. *Utopia and Experiment: Essays in the Sociology of Cooperation*. New York: Praeger, 1955.

Inge, William Ralph. *Christian Mysticism*. London, 1933.

Jackson, Joseph. *Encyclopedia of Philadelphia*. 4 vols. Harrisburg, 1931–33.

Jacobs, E. F. *Essays in the Conciliar Epoch*. Manchester University Press, 1953.

Jacobs, H. E. *The German Migration to America, 1709–1740*. Pennsylvania German Society 8. Lancaster, 1897.

Jacoby, John E., *Two Mystic Communities in America*. Paris, 1931. Reprint. Westport, Conn.: Hyperion Press, 1975. On Ephrata and Oneida.

James, Henry Ammon. *Communism in America*. New York: Arno Press, 1977.

Jantz, Harold. "Pastorius, Intangible Values." *The American-German Review* 25, no. 1 (1958–59), 4–7.

Jayne, Horace H. F. "Cloisters at Ephrata." *American Magazine of Art* 29 (1936), 594, 620–22.

Jones, Rufus M. *Spiritual Reformers in the Sixteenth and Seventeenth Centuries*. London, 1914.

Kanter, Rosabeth Moss. *Commitment and Community: Communes and Utopias in Sociological Perspective*. Harvard University Press, 1972.

Kaplan, Bert, and Thomas F. A. Plaut. *Personality in a Communal Society: An Analysis of the Mental Health of the Hutterites*. University of Kansas, 1956.

Karst, Theodor. "Johann Conrad Beissel in Thomas Manns 'Doktor Faustus'." *Jahrbuch der Deutschen Schillergesellschaft* 12 (1968), 543–85.

Kateb, George. *Utopia and Its Enemies*. New York: Free Press, 1963.

Kauffman, Henry. *Pennsylvania Dutch American Folk Art*. New York: American Studio Books, 1946. Reprint. New York: Dover, 1973.

Kautsky, Karl. *Communism in Central Europe in the Time of the Reformation*. New York, 1910. Reprint. New York: Russell & Russell, 1959.

Kelley, Joseph J., Jr. *Pennsylvania: The Colonial Years 1681–1776*. New York: Doubleday, 1980.

Keresztesi, Michael, and Gary R. Cocozzoli. *German-American History and Life: A Guide to Information Sources*. Detroit: Gale Research, 1980.

Kieffer, Elizabeth. "An Early Visit to Ephrata." *Der Reggeboge* 2, no. 1 (March 1968), 6f.

Klees, Frederic. *The Pennsylvania Dutch*. New York: Macmillan, 1950.

Klein, H. M. J. *Lancaster County, Pennsylvania: A History*. 3 vols. New York, 1924.

Klein, Walter C. *Johann Conrad Beissel, Mystic and Martinet, 1690–1768.* University of Pennsylvania Press, 1941. Reprint. Philadelphia: Porcupine Press, 1972.

Knauss, James O. *Social Conditions Among the Pennsylvania Germans in the Eighteenth Century.* Lancaster, 1922.

[Koons, Ulysses Sidney.] *A Tale of the Kloster: A Romance of the German Mystics of the Cocalico.* By Brother Jabez. Philadelphia, 1904.

Kraft, John. *Ephrata Cloister: An Eighteenth-Century Religious Commune.* Pennsylvania Historical and Museum Commission, 1980. Pamphlet.

Kriebel, Howard W. "Sangmeister, the Ephrata Chronicler." *Lancaster County Historical Society Papers* 16 (1912), 127–32.

———. *The Schwenkfelders in Pennsylvania.* Pennsylvania German Society 13. Lancaster, 1904.

Kriyananda, Swami. *Cooperative Communities.* Nevada City, Cal.: Ananda Publications, 1968.

Kuhns, Oscar. *The German and Swiss Settlements of Colonial Pennsylvania.* New York, 1914. Reprint. Ann Arbor, Mich.: Gryphon Books, 1971; New York: AMS Press, 1971.

Laidler, Harry W. *Social-Economic Movements: An Historical and Comparative Survey of Socialism, Communism, Co-operation, Utopianism, and Other Systems of Reform and Reconstruction.* New York: Crowell, 1947.

Lasserre, Henri. *The Communities of Tolstoyans.* Rural Cooperative Community Council Pamphlet 2. Toronto, 1944.

Learned, Marion D. *The Life of Francis Daniel Pastorius, the Founder of Germantown. . . .* Philadelphia, 1908.

Ledderhose, Charles T. *Life of Augustus Gottlieb Spangenberg.* London, 1885.

Levering, J. Mortimer. *A History of Bethlehem, Pennsylvania, 1741–1892. . . .* Bethlehem, 1903. Reprint. New York: AMS Press, 1971.

Lichten, Frances. *Folk Art of Rural Pennsylvania.* New York: Scribner's, 1946.

Liefmann, Robert. *Die kommunistischen Gemeinden in Nordamerika.* Jena, 1922.

Littell, Franklin Hamlin. *The Anabaptist View of the Church. . . .* 2d rev. ed. Boston: Starr King Press, 1958.

Loose, Jack W. W. "A Study of Two Distinct Periods of Ephrata Cloister History." *Lancaster County Historical Society Papers* 55 (1951), 145–75.

MacMinn, Edwin A. *A German Hero of the Colonial Times of Pennsylvania; or, The Life and Times of Henry Antes.* Moorestown, N.J., 1886.

Mallott, Floyd. *Studies in Brethren History.* Elgin, Ill., 1954.

Mann, Thomas. *Doctor Faustus. . . .* Translated by H. T. Lowe-Porter. New York: Knopf, 1948. Reprint. New York: Vintage Books, 1971.

Mann, William J. *The Life and Times of Henry Melchior Muhlenberg.* Philadelphia, 1887.

Manuel, Frank E. *Utopias and Utopian Thought*. Boston: Houghton Mifflin, 1966.

Marshall, Christopher. *Extracts from the Diary of Christopher Marshall*. Edited by William Duane. Albany, N.Y., 1877.

———. "Letters from Christopher Marshall to Peter Miller." *Pennsylvania Magazine of History and Biography* 28 (1904), 71–77.

Martensen, Hans L. *Jacob Boehme: Studies in His Life and Teaching*. Notes by Stephen Hobhouse. Rev. ed. New York: Harper, 1953.

Martin, Betty Jean. "The Ephrata Cloister and Its Music, 1732–1785. . . ." Ph.D. diss., University of Maryland, 1974. Facsimile. Ann Arbor, Mich.: University Microfilms, 1977.

Martin, C. H. "The Military Hospital at the Cloister." *Lancaster County Historical Society Papers* 55 (1951), 127–33.

Martin, Willard. "Mystics and Hymnists on the Wissahickon." Ph.D. diss., Pennsylvania State University, 1973.

Mattice, Paul B. "The Palatine Emigration from Schoharie to the Tulpehocken." *Berks County Historical Review* 10 (1944), 17–21.

Maxson, Charles M. *The Great Awakening in the Middle Colonies*. University of Chicago Press, 1920.

The Mennonite Encyclopedia. 4 vols. Scottdale, Pa., 1956–59.

Meynen, Emil. *Bibliography on German Settlements in Colonial North America, Especially on the Pennsylvania Germans . . . 1683–1933*. Leipzig, 1937.

Miller, C. William. *Benjamin Franklin's Philadelphia Printing, 1728–1766: A Descriptive Bibliography*. Philadelphia: American Philosophical Society, 1974.

Miller, Peter. Letter to James Read, Esq., [October 1776]. *Pennsylvania Magazine of History and Biography* 38 (1914), 227–31.

———. Letters to a Gentleman in Philadelphia, 1772 and 1790. *Hazard's Register of Pennsylvania* 16 (1835), 253–56.

——— [Br. Agrippa]. See *Chronicon Ephratense*, German version.

Mittelberger, Gottlieb. *Gottlieb Mittelberger's Journey to Pennsylvania in the Year 1750 and Return to Germany in the Year 1754*. Philadelphia, 1898. Edited and translated by Oscar Handlin and John Clive. Harvard University Press, 1960.

Monn, Emma C. *Historical Sketch of Snow Hill (Nunnery), 1829–1929*. Caslon Press, n.p., 1929.

Muhlenberg, Henry Melchior. *The Journals of Henry Melchior Muhlenberg*. Edited and translated by Theodore G. Tappert and John W. Doberstein. 3 vols. Philadelphia: Muhlenberg Press, 1942–58.

Mumford, Lewis. *The Story of Utopias*. New York, 1922. Reprint. New York: Viking, 1962.

Murtagh, William J. *Moravian Architecture and Town Planning*. University of North Carolina Press, 1967.

Neisser, Georg. *A History of the Beginnings of the Moravian Work in America*. Translated by William N. Schwarze and Samuel H. Gapp. Archives of the Moravian Church 1. Bethlehem, Pa., 1955.

Nordhoff, Charles. *The Communistic Societies of the United States*. New York, 1875. Reprint. New York: Dover, 1966.

Noyes, John Humphrey. *History of American Socialisms.* 1870. Reprint. New York: Hillary House, 1961; and, as *Strange Cults and Utopias of Nineteenth-Century America,* New York: Dover, 1966.

Oda, Wilbur H. "Ephrata German Language Imprints." *The Pennsylvania Dutchman* 4, no. 8 (1952), 12–13, and 4, no. 9 (1953), 10–12.

Packull, Werner O. *Mysticism and the Early South German-Austrian Anabaptist Movement.* Scottdale, Pa.: Herald Press, 1977.

Penn, William. *The Papers of William Penn.* Edited by Edwin B. Bronner, Mary Maples Dunn, and Richard S. Dunn. 2 vols. to date. Philadelphia: Historical Society of Pennsylvania, 1981–.

Pennsylvania Writers' Project. "The Ephrata Cloister." In *Pennsylvania Cavalcade,* 249–58. University of Pennsylvania Press, 1942.

Pennypacker, Samuel W. "The Early Literature of the Pennsylvania Germans." *Pennsylvania German Society Publications* 2 (1892), 33–46.

———. *Historical and Biographical Sketches.* Philadelphia, 1883.

———. "A Noteworthy Book. . . ." [The Ephrata Martyrs' Mirror.] *Pennsylvania Magazine of History and Biography* 2 (1881), 276–89.

———. *Pennsylvania in American History.* Philadelphia, 1910.

———. "The Quarrel Between Christopher Sower . . . and Conrad Beissel. . . ." *Pennsylvania Magazine of History and Biography* 12 (1888), 76–96.

———. *The Settlement of Germantown, Pennsylvania, and the Beginning of German Emigration to North America.* Philadelphia, 1899. Reprint. New York: Benjamin Blom Inc., 1970.

Peters, Victor. *All Things Common: The Hutterian Way of Life.* University of Minnesota Press, 1965. Reprint. New York: Harper Torchbooks, 1971.

Potts, John William. "Notes and Queries." *Pennsylvania Magazine of History and Biography* 4 (1880), 120. The later history of an Ephrata press.

Proud, Robert. *The History of Pennsylvania. . . .* 2 vols. Philadelphia, 1797–98.

Pyle, Howard. "A Peculiar People." *Harper's New Monthly Magazine* 79 (1889), 776–85.

Randolph, Corliss F. "The German Seventh Day Baptists." In *Seventh Day Baptists in Europe and America,* vol. 2, 935–1257. Plainfield, N.J., 1910. Reprint. New York: Arno Press, 1980.

Rattermann, H. A., ed. "Deutsch-Amerikanische Dichter und Dichtungen des 17ten und 18ten Jahrhunderts (Eine Anthologie)." *Deutsch-Amerikanische Geschichtsblätter* 14 (1914), 126–242.

Rau, Albert G. "Development of Music in Bethlehem, Pennsylvania." *Moravian Historical Society Transactions* 13 (1942), 59–64.

Reichmann, Felix. *Christopher Sower Sr., 1694–1758, Printer in Germantown: An Annotated Bibliography.* Philadelphia: Carl Schurz Memorial Foundation, 1943.

———. "Ezechiel Sangmeister's Diary." *Pennsylvania Magazine of History and Biography* 68 (1944), 292–313.

Reichmann, Felix, and Eugene E. Doll. *Ephrata As Seen by Contemporaries.* Pennsylvania German Folklore Society 17. Allentown, 1952.

Renkewitz, Heinz. *Hochmann von Hohenau, 1670–1721, zur Geschichte des Pietismus.* Breslau, 1935.

Richards, Henry M. M. "The Ephrata Cloister and Its Music." *Publications of the Lebanon County Historical Society* 8 (1921–24), 279–99.

———. *The Pennsylvania-German in the French and Indian War.* . . . Pennsylvania German Society 15. Lancaster, 1904–05.

———. *The Pennsylvania-German in the Revolutionary War, 1775–1783.* Pennsylvania German Society 17. Lancaster, 1908. Reprint. Baltimore: Genealogical Publishing Co., 1978.

Richter, Peyton E., ed. *Utopias: Social Ideals and Communal Experiments.* Boston: Holbrook, 1971.

Riley, Jobie E. "An Analysis of the Debate Between Conrad Beissel and Various Eighteenth Century Contemporaries Concerning the Importance of Celibacy." Ph.D. diss., Temple University, 1973.

Robacker, Earl F. *Pennsylvania German Literature: Changing Trends from 1683 to 1942.* University of Pennsylvania Press, 1943.

Rosenberger, Jesse Leonard. *The Pennsylvania Germans.* University of Chicago Press, 1923.

Rosenberry, M. Claude. "The Pennsylvania German in Music." *Proceedings of the Pennsylvania German Society* 41 (1933), 27–44.

Rothermund, Dietmar. "The German Problem of Colonial Pennsylvania." *Pennsylvania Magazine of History and Biography* 84 (1960), 3–21.

———. *The Layman's Progress: Religious and Political Experience in Colonial Pennsylvania, 1740–1770.* University of Pennsylvania Press, 1961.

Rush, Benjamin. *An Account of the Manners of the German Inhabitants of Pennsylvania.* [1789.] Annotated by Theodore E. Schmauk and Isaac D. Rupp. Pennsylvania German Society 19. Lancaster, 1910.

Sachse, Julius Friedrich. *Daniel Falckner's Curieuse Nachricht von Pennsylvania.* Pennsylvania German Society 14. Lancaster, 1905.

———. "The Ephrata Paper Mill." *Lancaster County Historical Society Publications* 1 (1897), 323–38.

———. *The Fatherland, 1450–1700, Showing the Part It Bore in the Discovery, Exploration, and Development of the Western Continent, with Special Reference to . . . Pennsylvania.* Philadelphia, 1897.

———. *The German Pietists of Pennsylvania.* Philadelphia, 1895. Reprint. New York: AMS Press, 1970.

———. *The German Sectarians of Pennsylvania, 1708–1800: A Critical and Legendary History of the Ephrata Cloister and the Dunkers.* 2 vols. Philadelphia, 1899–1900. Reprint. New York: AMS Press, 1971.

———. *Justus Falckner, Mystic and Scholar.* Philadelphia, 1903.

———. *The Music of the Ephrata Cloister; also Conrad Beissel's . . . Preface to the "Turtel Taube" of 1747.* . . . Pennsylvania German Society 12. Lancaster, 1903.

————. "The Registers of the Ephrata Community." *Pennsylvania Magazine of History and Biography* 14 (1890–91), 297–312, 387–402.

————. *A Unique Manuscript by Rev. Peter Miller (Brother Jabez) Prior of the Ephrata Community.* . . . Lancaster, 1912.

————, ed. *The Diarium of Magister Johannes Kelpius.* Pennsylvania German Society 25. Lancaster, 1917.

Sangmeister, Ezechiel. *Das Leben und Wandel des in Gottruhenden und seligen Bruders Ezechiel Sangmeister, weiland ein Einwohner von Ephrata von ihm selbst beschrieben.* Ephrata, 1825–26. 4 pamphlets.

Schmauk, Theodore E. *A History of the Lutheran Church in Pennsylvania, 1638–1820.* Philadelphia, 1903.

Schmoyer, Melville B. "A Record of the Ephrata Cloister Cemeteries." *Allentown Morning Call,* Nov. 12, 1938.

Schöpf, Johann David. *Travels in the Confederation.* [1788.] Translated and edited by Alfred J. Morrison. 2 vols. Philadelphia, 1911.

Schrag, Felix James. *Pietism in Colonial America.* University of Chicago Press, 1948.

Schultz, Lawrence W. *Schwarzenau, 1708–1976 . . . Where the Brethren Began.* Milford, Ind., 1954.

Schultz, Selina G. "The Schwenkfelders in Pennsylvania." *Pennsylvania History* 24 (1957), 293–320.

Seibt, Ferdinand. *Utopica: Modelle Totaler Sozialplannung.* Düsseldorf, 1972.

Seidensticker, Oswald. *Bilder aus der Deutsch-Pennsylvanischen Geschichte.* New York, 1885.

————. "A Colonial Monastery." *The Century Magazine* 1 (1881–82), 208–23.

————. *Ephrata, eine amerikanische Kloster-geschichte.* Cincinnati, 1883.

————. *First Century of German Printing in America, 1728–1830, Preceded by a Notice of the Literary Work of Francis D. Patorius.* Philadelphia, 1893. Supplements issued by A. Stapleton in *The Pennsylvania German* 5 (1904), 81–89; and in pamphlet by Gerhard Friedrich, 1940.

————. "William Penn's Travels in Holland and Germany in 1677." *Pennsylvania Magazine of History and Biography* 2 (1878), 237–82.

Seipt, Allen Anders. *Schwenkfelder Hymnology.* . . . Philadelphia, 1909.

Sessler, John Jacob. *Communal Pietism Among Early American Moravians.* New York, 1933.

Seventh Day Baptists in Europe and America. 2 vols. Plainfield, N.J. 1910. Reprint. New York: Arno Press, 1980.

Sharpless, Isaac. *A History of Quaker Government in Pennsylvania.* 2 vols. Philadelphia, 1899.

Shelley, Donald A. *The Fraktur-Writings or Illuminated Manuscripts of the Pennsylvania Germans.* Pennsylvania German Folklore Society Yearbook 23. Allentown, 1961.

Shoemaker, Alfred L. "The Ephrata Printers." *The Pennsylvania Dutchman* 4, no. 9 (1953), 11–13.

Sipe, C. Hale. *The Indian Wars of Pennsylvania.* 2d ed. Harrisburg, 1931.

Smith, C. Henry. *The Mennonite Immigration to Pennsylvania in the Eighteenth Century.* Norristown, Pa., 1929.

———. *The Story of the Mennonites.* Berne, Ind., 1941.

Smith, Elmer Lewis, John G. Stewart, and M. Ellsworth Kyger. *The Pennsylvania Germans of the Shenandoah Valley.* Pennsylvania German Folklore Society Yearbook 26. Allentown, 1964.

Smithson, R. J. *The Anabaptists.* London, 1935.

Spangenberg, August G. *Life of Nicholas Lewis Count Zinzendorf. . . .* Abridged and translated by Samuel Jackson. London, 1838.

Spengler, Oswald. *The Decline of the West.* Translated by Charles Francis Atkinson. 2 vols. New York: Knopf, 1957.

Stapleton, A. *Memorials of the Huguenots in America, with Special Reference to Their Emigration to Pennsylvania.* 1901. Reprint. Baltimore: Genealogical Publishing Co., 1969.

Steinmetz, Hiram E. "Peter Miller—Michael Witman." *Lancaster County Historical Society Papers* 6 (1901–02), 46–49.

Steirer, William F., Jr. "A New Look at the Ephrata Cloister." *Journal of the Lancaster County Historical Society* 70, no. 2 (1966), 101–16.

Stoeffler, E. Ernest. *Mysticism in the German Devotional Literature of Colonial Pennsylvania.* Pennsylvania German Folklore Society 14. Allentown, 1949.

Stoudt, John Joseph. *Early Pennsylvania Arts and Crafts.* New York: Barnes, 1964.

———. *Pennsylvania Folk-Art: An Interpretation.* Pennsylvania German Folklore Society 13. Allentown, 1948.

———. *Pennsylvania German Poetry, 1685–1830.* Pennsylvania German Folklore Society Yearbook 28. Allentown, 1966.

———. *Sunrise to Eternity: A Study in Jacob Boehme's Life and Thought.* University of Pennsylvania Press, 1957.

Strassburger, Ralph Beaver, and William John Hinke. *Pennsylvania German Pioneers . . . the Original Lists of Arrivals in . . . Philadelphia from 1727 to 1808.* 3 vols. Norristown, Pa., 1934. Reprint. 2 vols. Baltimore: Genealogical Publishing Co., 1966.

Studer, Gerald C. *Christopher Dock, Colonial Schoolmaster.* Scottdale, Pa.: Herald Press, 1967.

Sweet, William Warren. *Religion in Colonial America.* New York: Scribner, 1942.

Thompson, D. W. *The Oldest American Printing Press.* Carlisle, Pa.: Hamilton Library and Historical Association, 1955.

Toennies, Ferdinand. *Community and Society.* Translated by Charles P. Loomis. Michigan State University Press, 1957.

Tolles, Frederick B., and E. Gordon Alderfer, eds. *The Witness of William Penn.* New York: Macmillan, 1957. Reprint. New York: Octagon Books, 1980.

Townsend, George Alfred. *Katy of Catoctin.* New York, 1890. A novel relating to Snow Hill.

Treher, Charles W. *Snow Hill Cloister.* Allentown: Pennsylvania German Society, n.s. 2. Allentown, 1968.

Tyler, Alice Felt. *Freedom's Ferment: Phases of American Social His-*

tory from the Colonial Period to the Outbreak of the Civil War. University of Minnesota Press, 1944. Reprint. New York: Harper Torchbooks, 1962.

Uhlendorf, B. A. "German-American Poetry: A Contribution to Colonial Literature." *Deutsch-Amerikanische Geschichtsblätter*, 1922–23.

Wallace, Paul A. W. *Conrad Weiser, Friend of Colonist and Mohawk.* University of Pennsylvania Press, 1945.

Walton, Joseph S. *Conrad Weiser and the Indian Policy of Colonial Pennsylvania.* Philadelphia, 1900. Reprint. New York: Arno Press, 1971.

Warner, H. J. *The Albigensian Heresy.* New York: Russell & Russell, 1967.

Warrington, James. "A Bibliography of Church Music Books Issued in Pennsylvania, with Annotations." *The Penn Germania,* n.s. 1, nos. 3–8 (March–October, 1912).

Watson, John F. *Annals of Philadelphia and Pennsylvania in the Olden-Time.* 3 vols. Philadelphia, 1898.

Watts, George B. *The Waldenses in the New World.* Duke University Press, 1941.

Wayland, John Walter. *The German Element in the Shenandoah Valley of Virginia.* Charlottesville, Va., 1907.

Webber, Everett. *Escape to Utopia: The Communal Movement in America.* New York: Hastings House, 1959.

Weinlick, John R. *Count Zinzendorf.* Nashville, Tenn.: Abington Press, 1956.

Weiser, C. Z. *The Life of (John) Conrad Weiser. . . .* 2d ed. Reading, Pa. 1899.

Weiser, Frederick S., and Howell J. Heaney. *The Pennsylvania German Fraktur of the Free Library of Philadelphia: An Illustrated Catalog.* 2 vols. Breinigsville, Pa.: Pennsylvania German Society and Free Library of Philadelphia, 1976.

Whitmore, Eleanor H. "Origins of Pennsylvania Folk Art." *Antiques* 38, no. 3 (Sept. 1940), 106–10.

Wilkinson, Norman B., comp. *Bibliography of Pennsylvania History.* Harrisburg: Pennsylvania Historical and Museum Commission, 1957. *Supplement* edited by Carol Wall issued by the Commission, 1976.

Williams, E. Melvin. "The Monastic Orders of Provincial Ephrata." In H. M. J. Klein, *Lancaster County, Pennsylvania: A History,* vol. 1, 384–476. New York, 1924.

Williams, George H. *The Radical Reformation.* Philadelphia: Westminster, 1962.

———, ed. *Spiritual and Anabaptist Writers.* Philadelphia: Westminster, 1957.

Winchester, Elhanan, ed. *Some Remarkable Passages in the Life of Dr. George De Benneville.* Germantown, Philadelphia, 1890.

Wingate, Robert Bray, ed. *Pennsylvania Imprints, 1689–1789.* Harrisburg: Pennsylvania State Library, n.d.

Wood, Jerome H., Jr. *Conestoga Crossroads . . . 1730–1790.* Harrisburg: Pennsylvania Historical and Museum Commission, 1979.

Wood, Ralph, ed. *The Pennsylvania Germans.* Princeton University Press, 1942.

Worner, William F. "Peter Miller Did Not Translate the Declaration of Independence into Seven Languages." *Lancaster County Historical Society Papers* 38 (1934), 98–102.

Wust, Klaus. *The Saint-Adventurers of the Virginia Frontier: Southern Outposts of Ephrata.* Edinburg, Va.: Shenandoah History Publishers, 1977.

Yoder, Don. "The Spiritual Lineage of Shakerism." *Pennsylvania Folklife* 27, no. 3 (Spring 1978), 2–14.

————, ed. *Rhineland Emigrants: Lists of Settlers in Colonial America.* Baltimore: Genealogical Publishing Co., 1981.

Zablocki, Benjamin. *The Joyful Community: An Account of the Bruderhof. . . .* Baltimore: Penguin Books, 1971.

Zaretsky, Irving I., and Mark P. Leone, eds. *Religious Movements in Contemporary America.* Princeton University Press, 1974.

Zerfass, Samuel Grant. *Souvenir Book of the Ephrata Cloister: Complete History from Its Settlement in 1728 to the Present Time.* Lititz, Pa., 1921. Reprint. New York: AMS Press, 1975.

Ziegler, Samuel H. "The Ephrata Printing Press Now in the Printshop of Frank R. King, New Enterprise, Bedford County, Pennsylvania." *Pennsylvania German Folklore Society Proceedings* 5 (1940), 3–12.

Index